Praise for *In Full Color*

"Finally, Rachel Doležal in her own voice and words shares her intriguing account and path of conscious self-definition, embodied in a life of activism. Hers is a meandering journey that evidences a genesis in a very tender age. Her rightful claim to an identity and heritage: Who can challenge its authenticity? The account of a full human, simply being herself, assists us all to see race for what it is, a highly toxic, very destructive and questionable means of defining a common humanity. Rachel forces us all to question what we have come to accept until now without critical engagement. She is undeniably no accidental activist."

—*Bishop Clyde N.S. Ramalaine, author of Preach a Storm, Live a Tornado: A Theology of Preaching and a Khoisan, lifelong activist, and leading mind on building a race-free, just, and equitable society in post-Apartheid SA*

"Rachel Doležal's early life memoir is not simply a narrative of radical activism. It is full of physical textures and sensations—flat-tops, braided hair, oiled moisturized Black skin, Dashikis, and fluidity of sexual orientation—juxtaposed against some horrible domestic brutalities. It serves to critique the cultural straitjacket of traditionalist white 'Protestant work ethic' society. At this moment of alt-right reactionism, it punctures the fake nostalgia for an imagined pre-multiculturalism era of supposed purity and authenticity. Unsurprisingly, her willingness to find a home and cultural vocabulary in the black community makes Ms. Doležal a target for those advocates of continuing conservative orthodoxies and social hierarchies. That in itself should encourage us to be open to her account of her personal and social evolution and pleasures of *différance*."

—*Gavin Lewis, Black British writer and academic*

"The storm of vitriol Rachel received in the national spotlight was as cruel as it was undeserved. Her deep compassion for others shines through every chapter of her life and has clearly motivated her truly outstanding advocacy work."

—*Gerald Hankerson, president of the NAACP Alaska Oregon Washington State*

"US Census Bureau research suggests that millions of Americans change their racial self-identification from one census to the next. Here is the chance to learn about one person's transition, with all the nuance that no media sound bite could ever capture. It's an incredible story, from rural poverty in a white Montana town to historically black Howard University in Washington DC, spanning partnerships with African American activists and confrontations with white supremacists. And it's absolutely necessary to know the whole story in order to understand the extraordinary racial journey that Rachel Doležal has made."

—*Ann Morning, associate professor of sociology at New York University and author of The Nature of Race: How Scientists Think and Teach about Human Difference*

In Full Color

In Full Color

FINDING MY PLACE IN A
BLACK AND WHITE WORLD

Rachel Doležal

with Storms Reback

BenBella Books, Inc.
Dallas, TX

"Mother to Son" from THE COLLECTED POEMS OF LANGSTON HUGHES by Langston Hughes, edited by Arnold Rampersad with David Roessel, Associate Editor, copyright © 1994 by the Estate of Langston Hughes. Used by permission of Alfred A. Knopf, an imprint of the Knopf Doubleday Publishing Group, a division of Penguin Random House LLC. All rights reserved. Additional rights by permission of Harold Ober Associates Incorporated. Any third party use of this material, outside of this publication, is prohibited. Interested parties must apply directly to Penguin Random House LLC for permission.

The events, locations, and conversations in this book while true, are recreated from the author's memory. However, the essence of the story, and the feelings and emotions evoked are intended to be accurate representations. In certain instances, names, persons, organizations, and places have been changed to protect an individual's privacy.

BenBella Books, Inc.
10440 N. Central Expressway, Suite 800
Dallas, TX 75231
www.benbellabooks.com
Send feedback to feedback@benbellabooks.com

Printed in the United States of America
10 9 8 7 6 5 4 3 2 1

Library of Congress Cataloging-in-Publication Data

Names: Doležal, Rachel, 1977– author. | Reback, Storms, author.
Title: In full color : finding my place in a black and white world / Rachel
   Doležal with Storms Reback.
Description: Dallas, TX : BenBella Books, Inc., [2017] | Includes
   bibliographical references and index.
Identifiers: LCCN 2016046569 (print) | LCCN 2016047908 (ebook) | ISBN
   9781944648169 (trade cloth : alk. paper) | ISBN 9781944648176 (electronic)
Subjects: LCSH: Doležal, Rachel, 1977– | Women civil rights workers—United
   States—Biography. | Racially mixed families—United States—Biography. |
   African Americans—Race identity—United States. | Women, White—Race
   identity—United States. | Passing (Identity)—United States. | National
   Association for the Advancement of Colored People—Biography. | Spokane
   (Wash.)—Race relations—Biography. | Racially mixed
   families—Montana—Biography. | Coeur d'Alene (Idaho)—Biography.
Classification: LCC E185.98.D64 D64 A3 2017 (print) | LCC E185.98.D64 (ebook) |
   DDC 306.84/60973—dc23
LC record available at https://lccn.loc.gov/2016046569

Editing by Leah Wilson
Copyediting by James Fraleigh
Proofreading by Jenny Bridges and Cape Cod Compositors, Inc.
Cover design by Sarah Dombrowsky
Doležal cover and author photography by Carl Richardson
Reback author photography by Tammy Brown
Text design and composition by Publishers' Design and Production Services, Inc.
Printed by Lake Book Manufacturing

Distributed by Perseus Distribution
www.perseusdistribution.com

To place orders through Perseus Distribution:
Tel: (800) 343-4499
Fax: (800) 351-5073
E-mail: orderentry@perseusbooks.com

Special discounts for bulk sales (minimum of 25 copies) are available. Please contact Aida Herrera at aida@benbellabooks.com.

For Izaiah, Franklin, Langston, and Esther

Well, son, I'll tell you:
Life for me ain't been no crystal stair.
It's had tacks in it,
And splinters,
And boards torn up,
And places with no carpet on the floor—
Bare.

—LANGSTON HUGHES

Contents

Foreword

I WAS BORN IN 1938 in Birmingham, Alabama, which was one of the most segregated cities in the country at the time. I have vivid memories of the city's strict segregation laws and how they affected me as a child: being barred from "Whites-Only" restaurants, told to sit at the back of the bus, forced to drink from "Colored" water fountains, and obliged to step off the sidewalk to allow white people to pass.

When I was five, my father took me and my three-year-old brother to a theater that was open to Black people for just a single viewing each week—the late show on Thursday evenings—and we had no choice but to sit in the balcony. For every other show, the theater was reserved solely for white people. The show my father took me and my brother to ended so late the buses and trolleys were no longer running, forcing us to walk home. My father chose the most direct route, which happened to go through a white neighborhood. He held our hands as we walked, and when a shadowy figure emerged from beneath a tree, I could feel my father's grip grow tighter. Then came the ominous words:

"What you doing in this neighborhood, *boy*?!"

It was a white police officer. My father told us to look straight ahead and keep moving. We walked past the officer but could hear his steps gaining on us from behind. When the officer caught up to us in the light of a street lamp, he issued another challenge and grabbed my father's left shoulder. My father let go of our hands. The officer raised his billy club to strike him.

Pow!

The sound reverberated down the street. The noise was shocking but not as much as the realization of who had delivered the blow: my father had slapped the policeman so hard I could see the imprint of his hand on the man's face. The policeman fell to his knees. In the blink of an eye, my father pulled out his pocketknife, opened it, and held it to the man's throat. "We're on our way home from a picture show," he calmly explained. "We aren't bothering anyone. I don't want any trouble, but if you harass us anymore, I'll cut your throat."

My father grabbed my brother's hand and mine and swiftly led us away from the officer, who was still down on the ground. I half-expected a shot to ring out, but there was only the echo of our footsteps.

Because of that incident, we had to leave town, and we had to leave quickly. The next night, my father took us to the train station, where we caught the midnight train to Chicago—and safety. By so doing, we became part of the Great Migration, joining millions of other Blacks as they moved from the South to the North in search of better paying jobs (and fewer lynchings) throughout the twentieth century.

The North served as a launch pad to a better life for me. When I was seventeen and living in Detroit, Michigan, I enlisted in the United States Marine Corps and went on to serve in Vietnam. After I returned to the States, I joined the San Diego Police Department, but found my true calling in academia. For nineteen years, I taught in public schools, community colleges, and as a guest lecturer, and that role brought me a great deal of happiness.

While I may have been able to flee the racial discrimination that was so common in Birmingham when I was a child, it continued to haunt me throughout my adult life. I did my best to combat racism with the most positive attitude I could muster given the circumstances. Tasked with this daily chore, I also came to appreciate others—Frederick Douglass, Martin Luther King Jr., Malcolm X, and my father Albert Wilkerson Sr., to name a few—who, by their example and by the power of their convictions, fought racial bias and prejudice.

Rachel Doležal is also such a person.

I first met Rachel while she was serving as the education director of the Human Rights Education Institute (HREI) in Coeur d'Alene, Idaho. Observing her teach children, I saw that she was inclusive and dynamic and a true advocate for every student who attended her programs. One of her duties was to educate people in North Idaho about the Black experience, and in the process she embraced her own African spirit in what was a very toxic part of the country. I saw this special spirit in Rachel in everything she did. It was obvious to me that she was an activist for humanity. I was impressed.

Largely because of Rachel, I became a volunteer at HREI and got to know her and her son Franklin and, later, her son Izaiah. As I grew close to her and she became like a daughter to me, I didn't place a lot of emphasis on her ethnicity and I certainly didn't spend any sleepless nights worrying about what her biological story was. She looked Black and her vibe felt Black, but that's not what drew me to her. It was her work. What she was accomplishing was much more important to me than what color she was. Yes, I saw her as Black, but it wouldn't have mattered to me if she were German or Swedish or Chinese. I simply accepted the way she presented herself to the world as a racial and social justice advocate, and, in addition, admired her amazing artistic talent.

In June 2015, the media "outed" Rachel as a white woman who was passing as Black, using a photograph of me and the fact that she called me Dad as some of their main pieces of evidence. Two reporters, one from the *Spokesman-Review* and one from *People* magazine, approached me and asked if I was Rachel's biological father. I told them no but that I had lots of daughters.

"What do you mean?" they asked.

"There are several people who call me Dad who aren't biologically my children because that's how we do; it's a cultural thing."

They didn't understand. I declined to do any more interviews after that.

That both of Rachel's parents were white was news to me, but I was hardly upset about it. What upset me was that all the work she was doing was suddenly in jeopardy, as her parents, employers, and colleagues all rushed to throw her under the bus. I didn't want any part of that. If this country had more people like Rachel who were concerned with doing good things for people and achieving equity for all, it would be a much better place to live and raise children.

In Full Color is not just an engaging look at one person's journey of self-discovery but also an important tool that should be
studied in classrooms and homes across the United States. It offers
a unique opportunity to reflect on the complex social construct of
race and racism in this country from the perspective of a young
woman who has personally experienced their profound effects
from both sides of the color line. Having been a national delegate
for Barack Obama in Idaho in 2008 and 2012 and having worked
in support of human rights and racial and social justice, I believe
Rachel's book will help cast a light on some of the most pressing
and divisive issues that exist in this country today, namely social
inequality and racial prejudice.

                                        —Albert Wilkerson Jr.

Prologue

PEOPLE ALWAYS ASK ME what it was like living as a Black* woman. As if I no longer live that way. As if my Blackness were just a costume I put on to amuse myself or acquire some sort of benefits. As if what happened on June 10, 2015, altered my identity in any way.

I'll admit to being thrown for a loop when the reporter from a local news channel in Spokane, Washington, who was interviewing me about the hate crimes that had been directed at me and my family, abruptly switched topics and asked, "Are you African American?" On the surface it was a simple question, but in reality it was incredibly complex. Yes, my biological parents were both white, but, after a lifetime spent developing my true identity, I knew that nothing about whiteness described who I was. At the same time, I felt it would have been an oversimplification to have simply said yes. After all, I didn't identify as African American; I identified as Black. I also hadn't been raised by Black parents in a Black community and understood how that might affect the perception of my Blackness. In fact, I grew up in a painfully white world, one I was happy to escape from when I left home for college,

---

* Like numerous linguists and academics, I believe "Black" should always be capitalized when referring to culture or ethnicity. Not everyone agrees. Other than *Ebony* and *Essence*, two magazines that cater to a mostly Black audience, most major publications have refused to make this adjustment. To my mind, "black" describes a color, while "Black," like "Asian" or "Hispanic," denotes a group of people.

I don't capitalize "white" because white Americans don't comprise a single ethnic group and rarely describe themselves this way, preferring labels like "Italian American" or "Scotch Irish."

where my identity as a Black woman began to emerge. Forced into an awkward position by the reporter, I equivocated. When he pressed me, I ended the interview and walked away.

After footage of this small segment of the interview found its way onto the internet and an article appeared in a local paper "outing" me as white, I became one of the hottest trending topics of the day every day for weeks. A handful of people expressed their support of me, but they were drowned out by all the shouting, as nearly everyone else on the planet was calling for my head on a platter. I understood why some people reacted negatively to the fragments of my story they'd seen in the news. As a longtime racial and social justice advocate, I knew there were certain lines that you simply didn't cross if you wanted to be accepted by your community—whether it be white or Black—and crossing the color line was one of them. Because I'd been seen and treated as both white and Black, I was intimately familiar with the misgivings both communities had about people who stepped over this ever-shifting line. I also knew the historic consequences for doing so: shaming, isolation, even death. White people created the color line and the taboo for crossing it as a way to maintain the stranglehold on privilege they've always enjoyed, but due to the painful history surrounding it, many Black people had also grown adamant about enforcing it. If they weren't allowed to cross the color line, at least they could take ownership of their side.

As such, if you dared to cross this boundary, as I have done, and were exposed, you were put in a no-win situation: white folk would see you as a traitor and a liar and never trust you again, and Black folk might see you as an infiltrator and an imposter and never trust you again. As severe as these repercussions were, they didn't dissuade me from making this journey, for not doing so would have meant turning my back on what I see as my true identity and leaving those I loved most in a vulnerable position. If I've hurt anyone in the process, I sincerely apologize. That was never my intention.

To most people, the answer to the reporter's question was binary—yes or no—but race has never been so easily defined. In a letter to Thomas Gray in 1815, Thomas Jefferson struggled to determine "what constituted a mulatto," calling it "a Mathematical problem of the same class with those on the mixtures of different liquors or different metals." In the 1896 case *Plessy v. Ferguson*, the U.S. Supreme Court attempted to clarify the existing racial classifications when it established the "one drop rule"—those with a single Black relative, no matter how distant, were considered Black, even if they appeared white—but this decision only muddled an already complicated issue. If someone who looked white could be considered Black because one of his sixteen great-great-grandparents was Black but a Black person with a white great-great-grandparent was still regarded as Black, what sort of clarity did this provide?

If scrutinizing people's appearances can't provide definitive proof of their racial identity, what does? How do you decide whether certain people are white or Black? What's the determining factor? Is it their DNA? Is it their skin color? Is it how other people perceive them, or is it how they perceive themselves? Is it their heritage? Is it how they were raised, or is it how they currently live? Does how they feel about themselves play a role, and if so, how much? Does one of these questions provide the answer, or do all—or none—apply? And, finally, does the idea of separate human races have any sort of biological justification, or is it merely a creation of racism itself?

Adding further confusion, the definition of Blackness has not only shifted from decade to decade but also differs from person to person. For most, Blackness comprises much more than one's physical appearance. It's the culture you inhabit and the experiences you've lived. It's philosophical, emotional, even spiritual. Was Michael Jackson Black? By the end of his life his skin was nearly white and many of his features had been altered in a way that made him look far less Black than he did as a boy, but nearly everyone would still respond to that question by saying, "Of course." How about O.J. Simpson? With his brown skin and curly hair, he appeared Black, but the way he viewed himself suggested otherwise. When pressured to pull the race card, he reportedly once said, "I'm not Black. I'm O.J.," an opinion seconded by a helicopter pilot for a film crew that filmed Simpson fleeing the police in his white Ford Bronco on June 17, 1994. "If O.J. Simpson were Black, that shit wouldn't have happened," she later told the documentary director Ezra Edelman when describing the LAPD's atypical restraint that day. "He'd be on the ground getting clubbed."

Yes, my parents weren't Black, but that's hardly the only way to define Blackness. The culture you gravitate toward and the worldview you adopt play equally large roles. As soon as I was able to make my exodus from the white world in which I was raised, I made a headlong dash toward the Black one, and in the process I gained enough personal agency to feel confident in defining myself that way.

That I identify as one race while the world insists I'm another underscores the psychological harm the concept of race inflicts. Being denied the right to one's self-determination is a struggle I share with millions of other people. As our culture grows less homogenous, more and more people are finding themselves stuck in a racially ambiguous zone, unable (or not allowed) to identify with the limited available options. One of the few silver linings of the media firestorm that followed my "exposure" is that it sparked an international debate about race and racial identity. I didn't set out to be a spokesperson for people stuck somewhere in the gray zone between Black and white, but after my own life was thrown into disarray because of this issue, I'm happy to share my whole story in the hope that it will bring about some much-needed change.

I became aware long ago that the way I identify is unique and knew I would need to talk about it eventually, but I hoped I could choose the time, the place, and, most importantly, the method. Unfortunately, when the footage of the reporter in Spokane asking me if I was African American went viral, whatever chance I might have had to introduce myself to the world on my own terms, while explaining the nuances of my identity, was taken from me.

Do I regret the way the interview ended (and, as a consequence, the way my story was presented to the world)? Of course. But, as you'll see, the evolution of my identity was far too nuanced—and, frankly, private—to describe to a stranger. How can you explain in a brief conversation on the street a transformation that occurred over the course of a lifetime? You can't. To truly understand someone, you need to hear their whole story.

Chapter One

Delivered by Jesus

W E DON'T GET TO CHOOSE OUR PARENTS.
Mine—Larry and Ruthanne Doležal—met while petitioning the high school principal in Libby, Montana, to set aside a
place on campus for students to pray during their lunch breaks.
Larry had become a fundamentalist Christian after jumping into a
van full of Christ-loving hippies heading west. The van took him
from his childhood home in Montana to a commune in Seattle,
where he walked the streets and tried to convince others to love
the Lord as much as he did. Ruthanne's religious fanaticism was
passed down to her directly from her grandfather, the pastor of
an Assembly of God church in Nampa, Idaho. Ruthanne's brother,
my Uncle Ben, had a "prayer van" with "Supernatural House Calls"
painted on the side, which he and his wife used to cruise around
northwestern Montana while attempting to heal the sick and, in
some cases, raise the dead through spiritual warfare. In short, my
family was overflowing with what people in the mid-seventies
called "Jesus freaks."

After getting married, my parents bought twenty-three acres of
land just west of Troy, Montana, on the side of a mountain, with a
view of the Kootenai River meandering through the valley below.
While they were clearing the land and building the house I grew
up in, they lived in a teepee made from wooden poles Larry had
fashioned from trees he'd felled and canvas Ruthanne had stitched
with an 1870s treadle sewing machine. Whether they were still
living in it (or in a house under construction) at the time of my

birth remains a topic of debate in my family, but, either way, my childhood environment was very nearly the definition of rustic.

As part of their Christian fundamentalism, Larry and Ruthanne were Young Earth Creationists, a group that believes the earth and all living things on it were created by God over a six-day period between six thousand and ten thousand years ago, that dinosaurs were among the creatures on Noah's ark, and that all of us are descended from Adam and Eve. Larry and Ruthanne also believed that since Adam and Eve didn't have an obstetrician or midwife, they didn't need one either. Just as he'd done with my brother Josh, who was born two years before I was, Larry took it upon himself to deliver me, on November 12, 1977, without any medical personnel or assistance on hand; as a result, Ruthanne almost died from excess hemorrhaging. On my birth certificate, Jesus Christ is listed as the attendant to my birth.

I would continually be reminded throughout my childhood just how difficult my delivery had been for my mother. That I'd nearly killed her weighed me down with a sense of guilt I could never fully shed. Compared to mine, Josh's birth had been a piece of cake—or so I was told. It quickly became clear to me that in our family, Josh was the blessed child, while I was the cursed one.

This distinction even made itself known in my name. Many readers of the Bible only see Rachel's virtuous aspects. She was beautiful, beloved by her husband Jacob, and blessed to have two children, Joseph and Benjamin, who were ancestors of the twelve tribes of Israel. But Rachel was also a human illustration of the consequences of sin. Angry at her father Laban for tricking her husband into marrying her sister—like many aspects of the Old Testament, it's complicated—Rachel stole her father's *teraphim* (idols that represented household deities and served as a form of title deed), hid them in saddlebags inside her tent, then took a seat on top of the bags. When Laban came looking for the *teraphim*, Rachel lied and said she couldn't stand up because she was menstruating. Meanwhile, ignorant of the fact that his wife had taken the idols, Jacob issued a curse on whoever was in possession of them. Rachel died in childbirth soon afterward.

Oh, the Bible and its curses! One of the best known occurs in Genesis 9 and involves Noah, his son Ham, and a very drunken night. After Ham visits his father's tent and finds him highly intoxicated and completely naked, Ham tells his brothers Shem and Japheth, who cover their father with a garment while averting their eyes. Noah responded by condemning Ham's son Canaan to a life as "a servant of servants." Most curses in the Bible are generational, which means Noah was censuring all of Ham and Canaan's descendants as well. Although race is never mentioned in the passage, an error in translation—some interpreted "Ham" to mean "dark" or "black"—engendered the idea that Noah had cursed all Black people, and by the eighteenth century this interpretation was being used to justify racism and slavery in the United States. The idea that Black people are victims of the so-called Curse of Ham, that they actually deserve to be treated poorly, remains embedded in our collective psyche to this very day.

That I, too, was somehow cursed was imparted to me before I could even speak. I'd nearly killed Ruthanne as she'd labored to deliver me. That my hair at birth was almost black and my skin was much darker than my parents' and my brother's was a great source of anxiety for Larry and Ruthanne and added to the notion that I was the lesser child in the family. As a child, I cried *all the time*, earning me the nicknames "The Blue Boo Hoo" (during a winter in which I primarily wore a blue coat) and "The Green Grouch" (different winter, different coat). In the rare moments I wasn't crying, I was running, moving, and dancing, which, because I was female and being raised in a stoic Christian household, were equated with sinning. I was told that if I continued to act that way—living by the dictates of my "carnal nature"—I would go to Hell.

Whenever I misbehaved as a child, Larry and Ruthanne reminded me of an incident that occurred when I was eighteen months old. Left unsupervised in the house, I fell down the stairs that led to the unfinished basement and landed on the concrete floor at the bottom, breaking my collarbone and several vertebrae in my neck. Most parents would have rushed me to the nearest hospital with tears in their eyes. How did Larry and Ruthanne respond? They prayed over me and took me to a "natural doctor," who put my arm in a sling and advised me to rest up. No X-rays were taken, no pain medications administered. My neck proceeded to grow straight instead of in a natural curve, as bone spurs fused some of my injured vertebrae together. I've lived with chronic neck pain ever since.

Whenever I complained about the injury when I was growing up, Larry and Ruthanne told me the pain I was experiencing was God's way of punishing "stiff-necked" people, an allusion to the wayward nature of oxen, which were the most important domesticated animals when the Bible was written. Relying on these animals to plow their fields, farmers used "goads," long sticks with pointed ends, to get them to speed up or turn. Despite being repeatedly and painfully stabbed, some oxen refused to obey, and, as a consequence, these obstinate animals were labeled "hard of neck" or "stiff-necked."

To Larry and Ruthanne, my neck pain wasn't a consequence of their negligence (apparently, it was my fault as a one-year-old that I'd fallen down the stairs because they'd instructed me to avoid doing just that) or even an actual physical injury; it was a reminder that I was too obstinate and willful for my own good and a clear indication that I needed to submit to the will of God. That I should feel guilty for acting in a way that felt most natural to me would remain a constant theme throughout my life.

Chapter Two

Escaping to Africa
(in My Head)

A S A LITTLE GIRL, my skin was pale, my hair blonde, and my face full of freckles. While I may have looked like Laura Ingalls Wilder, that's not how I *felt*. I loved drawing pictures of myself when I was young, and whenever it came time to shade in the skin, I usually picked a brown crayon rather than a peach one. Peach simply didn't resonate with me. I felt like brown suited me better and was prettier. I could see that my skin was light, but my perception of myself wasn't limited to what my eyes could take in.

The way I saw myself was instinctual, coming from some place deep inside of me. Living in the mountains of northwest Montana, we were about as far away from Black America as you can get and still be in the United States. The population of the nearest town, Troy, was approximately three thousand, and approximately three thousand of those people were white. We didn't have a television in our house when I was growing up, so I couldn't familiarize myself with Black culture that way. I didn't even know *Good Times*, *Sanford and Son*, or *The Jeffersons* existed until I went to college.

I no longer have all the portraits I made of myself during my childhood, but in one that I've managed to hold onto, I drew myself as a brown-skinned girl with black curly braids. Beyond the color of my skin, what's most notable in retrospect is the cheerful tone of the picture. The sun is shining. Flowers are blooming. Bees are

flitting about. And the little girl standing there beside them—*me*—
is smiling.

This was rarely the case during my childhood. I was a naturally
artistic and imaginative little girl, always painting and drawing,
but Larry and Ruthanne didn't condone creativity or spontaneity
in their household. I was constantly getting punished for expressing myself. "If you're having fun, you're sinning" was the message
my parents drilled into my head at a very young age. Taught that
my natural behavior was somehow wrong, I learned to censor and
repress myself, and cried myself to sleep nearly every single night
during my tween and teen years, with my face jammed into a pil-
low so nobody would hear.

Besides, who had the energy to smile? As soon as we were
physically able to, Josh and I were required to work right alongside
Larry and Ruthanne, who, like many other back-to-the-landers of
that era, practiced a subsistence lifestyle that kept them laboring
from dawn to dusk. In the summer, we cleared brush, pruned our
fruit trees and raspberry canes, excavated dandelion roots from our
yard, and dried mint leaves to be used in tea bags. In the fall, we
harvested vegetables from the garden and fruit from the orchard,
shelled peas, pickled cucumbers and beets, cut corn off the cob
and stored it in the freezer, canned green beans and peaches and
applesauce, made all sorts of jams and preserves, stored root vegetables and apples in the cellar, and shot and butchered enough
elk and deer to fill our freezer. In the winter, we shelled nuts from
our English walnut tree, sewed, knitted, and turned the wool we'd
gotten from Bill and Ruth Wagoner's sheep farm—and sometimes
our dog's fur—into yarn with our foot-pedaled spinning wheel.

It was Ruth Wagoner who taught me how to make cheese.
After apprenticing at her house once a week for a year, I starting
making fresh and aged goat cheeses of every variety. I saved up
my own money so I could buy wax to make cheddar and Gouda. I
also learned to make homemade yogurt, an elaborate process that
takes an entire day. Making bread was an equally labor-intensive
activity. With the goal of producing at least one loaf every other
day, we were always in the process of kneading, proofing, or baking

dough. Just ensuring that we had enough food on the table was incredibly grueling work, and it never ended.

I was so young when I started working in the kitchen I had to stand on a chair just to reach the counter. We didn't have a dishwasher, so Josh and I were tasked with washing and drying all the dishes after every meal. The stakes were high. If we broke any dishes, we'd get a beating. The sort of meticulousness that was expected of us carried over to all the other household chores we were required to do: cleaning the slats of our closets' louvered doors with a washcloth wrapped around a butter knife, dusting the individual leaves of our houseplants, and scrubbing the toilet and tub until they sparkled.

The gardens were my special domain. We had two of them, and they were massive. I spent countless hours there as a child, planting seeds in the spring and weeding and watering them throughout the summer. I actually enjoyed these tasks because, separated from the rest of my family, they allowed me to escape into my own imaginary world. Hidden from view by tall stalks of corn in what we called the "long garden," I'd stir the water from the hose into the earth with a stick and make thin, soupy mud, which I would then rub on my hands, arms, feet, and legs, as if applying a lotion. Covered in this way, I would pretend to be a dark-skinned princess in the Sahara Desert or one of the Bantu women living in the Congo I'd read about in copies of *National Geographic*, which Grandma Doležal gave us a subscription to for Christmas one year. In my fantasy, Larry and Ruthanne had kidnapped me, brought me to the United States, and were now raising me against my will in a foreign land. Back home in Africa, I'd possessed the ability to control the weather, but here in Montana my special power didn't work.

Imagining I was a different person living in a different place was one of the few ways—drawing was another—that I could escape the oppressive environment I was raised in, and I would stay in this fantasy world as long as I possibly could. It was never long enough. When I was finished watering the garden, I would hurriedly rinse the mud off my arms and legs with the same sense of urgency I had when hiding the portraits of the brown-skinned girl I liked to draw, because revealing her—even in my artwork or playtime—could get me punished. Even at this young age, I knew that my instinct that "Black is Beautiful" was not a widely shared sentiment. When it came to talking about skin color—mine or anyone else's—I learned to keep my mouth shut.

I would soon come to accept that I hadn't actually been kidnapped and taken from Africa and that I wouldn't be free of my family anytime soon, but the feeling that I was somehow different from them persisted. I felt Black and saw myself as Black, and only later learned that the idea that Blackness was beautiful went against the grain of everything that was being taught in popular culture at the time, with Black people being portrayed in movies and on television as street hustlers and gangsters, and Africa depicted in the news as a place riddled with debt, disease, and famine. In this one way, the isolation I experienced while living on the side of that mountain in Montana actually benefited me, as it sheltered me from this sort of propaganda. Without television and newspapers to stress the perceived superiority of whiteness over Blackness, I was left to rely on my own feelings.

As a result of constantly having to censor myself when I was growing up, I was a very unhappy child. The only person who seemed to understand what I was going through was my Aunt Becky, who, apparently realizing my preferences, gave me Black Raggedy Ann and Andy dolls for Christmas one year. An excellent seamstress, she made them herself because dolls that looked Black (or, for that matter, any ethnicity beyond white) were in short supply—if they could be found at all.

Given my confusion about my family and my own identity, it was almost a relief when I was told that I would be going to kindergarten at the public elementary school in Troy. Any hope that I'd fit in better there than at home quickly dissipated, when I arrived at school in my homemade clothes, with buttons carved from elk antlers and a sweater made from dog hair. The difference between me and my classmates was reinforced when they pulled out their bags of Doritos and cans of Coke at lunchtime, while I sat alone in a corner with a sandwich made out homemade bread and elk tongue and a thermos full of raw apple juice.

Adding to my dismay, I was met by a sea of white faces. There wasn't a single Black student in my class—or the entire school for that matter—and it didn't take long before I felt just as out of place there as I did at home.

Chapter Three

Oatmeal

THE ORIGINS OF JUST ABOUT EVERYTHING my family ate could be traced to the mountain we lived on. All the vegetables and herbs we consumed came from our gardens, all the fruit from our orchard, all our meat from the woods and meadows that surrounded us. To make bread, we bought wheat in bulk, stored it in a fifty-gallon Rubbermaid garbage can, and used a hand-cranked grinder to make flour. We purchased five-gallon buckets of alfalfa honey from the local beekeeper, Ray Chaffee. For dairy products, we relied on Art Olds, who sold us one-gallon jars of milk with several inches of cream on top. As a result of our parents' desire to live off the land, Josh and I treasured anything that came in a package and was purchased in a grocery store, as they made us feel like we were actual members of the twentieth-century world.

Larry had grown up with a mother who hated cooking, so instead of pancakes and eggs she raised her kids on breakfast cereals and orange juice from concentrate. Whether it was from habit or nostalgia, cereal remained Larry's breakfast of choice well into his adulthood, which delighted me and Josh because it was one of the few store-bought luxuries allowed in our household. It would be difficult to find two kids who got more pleasure from eating Rice Krispies and Cheerios.

So it was with particular sadness that I sat down at the dining room table one morning toward the end of first grade and discovered that my usual bowl of cold cereal had been replaced with a bowl of hot oatmeal. Ruthanne had made the oatmeal using organic whole oats she'd purchased from the local food co-op, the kind that came with the occasional husk still attached to the grains, so it promised to be healthy, but I couldn't stand it. Its consistency reminded me of mucus with fish eyeballs mixed in (raisins had been cooked into it), and there was *way too much* of it. This combination did not bode well for me.

Every meal in our household followed the same script. Before it started, Larry would say grace and read a passage from his Bible with the elk-hide cover that Ruthanne had sewed into the binding, and we weren't allowed to start eating until he was done reading. Josh and I also weren't allowed to serve ourselves; rather, we were given a portion of whatever food was being served and were required to eat it all. Even if there were only a few crumbs left on our plates, Larry would scrape them into one last bite and make us eat it.

The overly generous bowl of oatmeal sitting in the blue stoneware bowl in front of me seemed like a mountain I could not climb. No matter how small of a bite I took, I gagged.

"I can't eat it all, Papa."

"You have to. Now hurry up, or you'll miss the bus," Larry warned me.

This was no idle threat. If I missed the school bus, I would have to walk to school, a two-and-a-half-mile journey Josh once had to make in the snow while carrying his French horn. I was only seven, so that walk would have taken me *hours*. Determined to finish the oatmeal and get to the bus on time, I fit as much of it as I could onto my spoon and downed it in one quick bite, but the slimy gruel made me feel nauseous and I ran to the bathroom and threw up in the toilet.

When I returned to the table, Larry told me I would get three spankings on the bare bottom if I left the table again or didn't finish my oatmeal. In our household this was the standard punishment for even the smallest offenses, from getting bad grades at school to forgetting to do our chores. For larger offenses, the number of spankings could push into the double digits.

The spankings were administered in an almost ritualistic fashion. We had to march into Larry and Ruthanne's bedroom, pull our pants and underwear down, and bend over and touch our toes while Larry smacked us with a wooden paddle that had a picture of a deer with a bear standing behind it and the words, "For the cute little dear with the bear behind." Adding to my terror, an actual bear—albeit one that Larry had killed and a local taxidermist had preserved—stood watch from where it now served as an ornamental blanket on top of the bed, its marble eyes staring right through me, its mouth frozen in an intimidating snarl. If our fingers ever left our toes while we were being spanked, it meant extra lashes.

This was what I had to look forward to if I failed to eat all the oatmeal in my bowl, and yet I still couldn't do it. Picking around the oats, I attempted to eat the raisins first but couldn't stop myself from gagging. When I tried again, I threw up in my bowl.

"That's what you get for being stubborn," Larry said.

Our household's primary disciplinarian, he saw my refusal to finish my breakfast as a defiance of his authority. He made it clear that my having vomited changed nothing; I was still expected to eat everything in my bowl. I felt even more nauseous than I had before, as I stared at the vomit intermixed with the oatmeal. Neither Larry nor Ruthanne was very big. In fact, they were tiny. He was only five foot four, she an even five foot. But when it came to intimidating me, the paddle made up for their lack of size. Motivated by the fear of being beaten, I managed to choke down two small bites of the gruel before I broke down and cried.

"She's going to miss the bus," Larry said to Ruthanne. "Put her bowl in the fridge. She can finish eating it when she gets home. She's not to get dinner or any other food until she's eaten everything in the bowl."

School provided only a short reprieve. When I got home, I found my bowl from the morning sitting on the dining table directly in front of my chair. The oatmeal and vomit had congealed and was cold from being in the fridge all day. Forbidden from getting up from my chair until I'd eaten it all, I sat at the table nudging the gray matter with my spoon until it was nearly time to go to bed. Taking one tiny bite at a time, I chipped away at the disgusting mound of oatmeal and vomit for more than three hours, with tears streaming down my face the entire time. But even after I believed I had finished it, once Larry inspected the bowl, he determined that there was one more bite left, which he scraped together and spoon-fed me.

The horror of that experience carried over to the following morning, when it was announced that in the future we would be having oatmeal for breakfast twice a week to ensure that I overcame my aversion to it. In the Doležal household, discipline and obedience were to be learned no matter what the cost.

Chapter Four

Drowned by Religion

WHEN I WAS NINE, I was baptized in the Kootenai River, committing my life to Jesus. I walked into the ice-cold water in my jeans, and when I emerged with my teeth chattering I was greeted by the sound of tambourines and voices breaking into song. Ruthanne wrapped me in a blanket and tearfully told me how proud she and Larry were of me for renouncing my old life of sin and embracing a new life in the name of Jesus Christ. As dramatic as the experience felt at the time, it didn't change my life all that much, given that Christianity had always been like breathing in our household.

I brought my newly invigorated appreciation of religion with me to school, where, with Bible in hand, I tried to peddle the Gospel to anyone who'd listen. I was on a mission to save souls before the apocalypse and the Second Coming of the Lord, but my pagan classmates were far more interested in playing Dungeons & Dragons and messing around with Ouija boards. They teased me that I would end up marrying a priest and dying a virgin.

As pious as I was, I couldn't come close to replicating Ruthanne's religious devotion, as she became increasingly obsessed with the pro-life movement. She made us watch the anti-abortion film *The Silent Scream* every year following its 1984 release, one of only two exceptions to the household ban on television. (Larry's insistence on watching baseball's World Series each fall was the other.) We had to rent a TV/VCR combo for these viewing parties. The "educational film" was only twenty-nine minutes long, but it contained enough horrific images—babies' arms and legs being torn off, their bodies dumped in garbage bags behind abortion clinics—to give me nightmares for weeks afterward. Three decades have passed, and I still can't get the sound of one of the fetuses in the film apparently screaming in agony—hence the film's title—out of my head.

As far as Ruthanne was concerned, Josh and I were survivors of "a silent holocaust" because we were born after the Supreme Court ruled in favor of a woman's right to have an abortion in the historic 1973 *Roe v. Wade* decision. She also believed that Justice Harry Blackmun, who wrote the majority opinion for that case, was the devil, and that anyone who killed a doctor who performed abortions was a hero for—note the convoluted logic and hypocrisy—saving lives. She even traveled to Washington, DC, one year to take part in the March for Life, the anti-abortion rally that takes place every year on the anniversary of *Roe v. Wade*. It's the only trip I can remember her ever taking by herself.

Josh got caught up in our household's anti-abortion crusade as well. In middle school, he was tasked with debating students who took the pro-choice side of the argument. To help him illustrate his point, Ruthanne and I made stick figures out of paper, which expanded to form a long chain. Josh taped these to the wall in the classroom where the debate was held. Each stick figure represented ten thousand American fatalities suffered in a war. There were three stick figures for the American Revolution, sixty-two for the Civil War, twelve for World War I, forty-one for World War II, and six for the Vietnam War. Then in a moment of triumph toward the end of the debate, Josh marched around the room, unraveling a paper chain of stick figures holding hands that was so long it seemed to have no end. This represented all the "babies" that had been aborted in what Ruthanne referred to as the "War on the Unborn." Game, set, and match, as far as the Doležals were concerned.

As fanatical as this viewpoint seems to me now, it felt perfectly normal when I was growing up because we only socialized with people who shared the same opinions. One of them was Fabian Uzoh. We often saw him at church on Sundays, and from time to time he would come to our house afterward to eat lunch. He was especially fond of the habañero peppers we grew in our garden, which, combined with our homemade meals, reminded him of the food he'd eaten while growing up in Nigeria. Even though I was now ten years old, Fabian was the first Black person I'd ever met, and this, combined with his regal manner, made him seem like a king to me. I found even the most mundane stories he told about life in Africa riveting. He also had the rare ability to make me laugh, something I didn't do very often after learning earlier in life to suppress it.

Fabian had studied forestry at the University of Montana and hoped to get his PhD in the same subject. His goal was to go back to his home country one day and use his knowledge to improve its environment and economy. Sadly, he was never able to return to Nigeria. When his wife Rosie left the church, divorced him, and won custody of their son Emmanuel, Fabian chose to stay in the States so he could remain close to his son. Despite the allegations of domestic violence Rosie made against Fabian, Larry and Ruthanne sided with him. In their eyes, she was a heathen who was being controlled by the "Jezebel spirit." Leaving your husband and falsely accusing him of abuse was the ultimate offense a woman could make against God and the church. In their opinion, she'd committed blasphemy.

Larry and Ruthanne let Fabian sleep on our pullout couch until he got back on his feet, and I would often hear him vent his frustrations about Rosie letting Emmanuel watch TV and eat sausage and candy. I often wondered what was so demonic about junk food. To me, it sounded heavenly, like something only rich people got to eat. Books like *Oliver Twist* and *Charlie and the Chocolate Factory* made me believe that one day I, too, might have access to the glorious world of commercial food. But I was in the minority. Fabian's opinion on this subject was shared by Larry, Ruthanne, and Larry's mother Peggy, aka Grandma Doležal, who'd banished her husband Herman to their cold cement basement because of his refusal to give up junk food and TV. He had his own refrigerator down there, where he kept soda, beer, ice cream, and candy bars, and he spent hours and hours watching TV and chewing Doublemint gum, one half-stick at a time.

Herman, or Grandpa Doležal as he was known to me, wasn't like the rest of us. He'd been in the Navy and had a tattoo on his forearm, visible only when he wore short sleeves in the summer, and his eyes would light up with a bad-boy twinkle whenever someone asked him about his glory days. He hadn't always been saved, either. Larry had led both of his parents to Christ when he was in high school, but instead of joining the Pentecostal church where people spoke in tongues, as Larry had, they'd joined the more practical and sedate Church of God denomination.

There were other differences between Larry and his father. In our house, we adhered to a God-man-woman-child-animal-plant model of value as presented in the Book of Genesis. We were taught that God was the head of the man and the man was the head of the woman. Men were the ultimate authorities, making all the important decisions, while women had very little or no say, no matter what their hearts were telling them. If you were a woman and didn't have a husband, your father was the ultimate authority over you, and if you had a husband, you submitted to him. Women who refused to accept their places in this strict hierarchy were considered godless Jezebels, like Rosie.

Life was much different in Peggy and Herman's house. It was a true matriarchy; Peggy ruled the roost. It was almost weird how browbeaten Herman was. Peggy kept the upstairs dustless, spotless, and, for the most part, Herman-less. During many of our visits, we'd barely see him, and when he did emerge from his subterranean lair, the only topics he seemed free to discuss at leisure without being cut off or reprimanded were weather and sports. As a result, he stuck to those talking points no matter how many times he repeated himself, issuing banalities such as, "It sure is nice out today," or "Looks like we're supposed to get some rain this weekend," over and over again.

More often, he would stay down in the basement watching TV or reading *Sports Illustrated*. Josh liked to sneak into the basement and rifle through Herman's copies of *SI*, and occasionally he'd bring some of them home with him. Magazines had been forbidden in our household when we were little, but as we grew older, Larry and Ruthanne eased up on this restriction a little bit. When

Grandma Doležal gave us the *National Geographic* subscription, they actually let us keep it.

Josh was especially pleased with this gift, as he would tear out and keep any photographs of topless African women he could find. He'd even make me search the magazines for these types of pictures and save them for him, and if I refused, he'd hit me. If he ever got caught hitting me, he'd get spanked, but if I ever got caught hitting him back, I'd also get spanked, so in the end the easiest and safest thing for me to do was help him gather the photos for his soft-porn collection. At the time, I was too young to know what he was using them for, and, besides, I thought the women were beautiful, so I didn't object too vigorously.

Josh was equally enamored with Grandpa Doležal's *Sports Illustrated*s, and after he was done reading the copies he'd absconded with, he'd leave them on the back of his toilet. It was from these magazines that I acquired my first glimpses of Black Americans, and I was enraptured by what I saw. To me, the images of the Black athletes I found on the pages of the magazines were the very height of human beauty. Their complexions, their hair, their features, they were all so captivating to me. Florence Griffith Joyner, aka "Flo Jo," and Jackie Joyner-Kersee became my idols. They were both beautiful and strong. I was also infatuated with the boxer Mike Tyson, the basketball player Earvin "Magic" Johnson, and the baseball player Darryl Strawberry. Three different men involved in three different sports, but they shared common ground. They were at the top of their fields at the time—world champions and All-Stars—and all of them were Black. Though all three soon faded from my consciousness, the idealized image of Blackness I'd developed while studying photographs of them never did.

Chapter Five

Hustling to Make a Dollar

B EING POOR is a condition I've known all too well in my life. Don't be fooled into thinking that when I was a child we grew our own food because we were part of some hipster sustainability movement. We did it because we were nearly destitute. Neither Larry nor Ruthanne had a college degree or, for much of their lives, any sort of dependable job. When I was eight, Larry, in addition to some occasional part-time work surveying land, started working as an EMT with the local ambulance crew, but it was a volunteer position. Three years later, he was elected county commissioner, but the pay was so poor that most of his colleagues were retirees who did it more as a hobby than anything else. Our family's income was so low we regularly qualified for food stamps, although we never actually received them because my parents believed it was shameful to accept handouts from the government. If Larry and Ruthanne hadn't been so adept at following a subsistence lifestyle (and wringing as much labor out of each child as possible), they would have had a hard time keeping us fed and paying the bills.

As I learned about U.S. history in school, I empathized with those whose free labor helped build this country. It never fails to trouble my mind (and hurt my heart) to think that just over a hundred and fifty years ago in the so-called land of the free, people owned other people. The institution of chattel slavery in America was as horrific as it was unconscionable. Millions of Black Africans were kidnapped, packed into the cargo holds of ships, and taken to a foreign land where they were treated as property. All connections to their homelands, including language, customs, hairstyles, religion, culture—even the use of their birth names—were severed. Families were ripped apart. Women were raped. Malnutrition was commonplace. Punishment for even the most trivial offenses was often decided on a whim and included such atrocities as being boiled in oil or drawn and quartered. Meanwhile, those committing these human rights abuses did so with a clear conscience, as they believed they were the "superior race." That dubious distinction allowed them to wantonly abuse Black people, who they often referred to, apparently with no sense of irony, as "uncivilized."

For Black slaves to survive such sustained trauma took an incredible amount of inner fortitude and day-to-day resourcefulness. Learning a different language (while being denied the ability to read) and navigating the ways of a strange new culture were matters of survival. From food and shelter to hair care and clothing, ingenuity was a skill passed from one generation of slaves to the next.

I developed a similar resourcefulness at a very young age. I knew that if I ever wanted to spend any money on myself I'd have to make it on my own, and after being constantly teased at school about my homemade clothes, I became extremely motivated to do so. By the time I was nine years old, I was paying for all my clothes and shoes. I found a variety of ways to earn money. Soon after learning to thread a needle when I was five, I started crafting homemade dolls that I called "Wee Woods Wooleys." Their design was simple, but the actual construction was time-consuming. I cut two circles of scrap cloth, stuffed them with a pinch of sheep's wool, sewed them together to form a head and body, attached a pair of shoes made out of deer hide, applied another pinch of sheep's wool to the top of the head to serve as hair, used recycled beads to make eyes and a mouth, and, as a final touch, added a triangular hat for male dolls or a head scarf for females. A cross between a hobbit, a troll, and a rag doll, these ugly yet cute ornaments proved to be great sellers at the local Christmas arts and crafts fair. I'd attach them to a small tree I'd cut from the mountain behind our house and sell them for two dollars apiece.

After seeing a Smith & Hawken catalogue for the first time and noticing that dried flower wreaths were being sold for more than fifty dollars (and sometimes as much as a hundred!), I started a new business, which I called "Treasures of Field and Forest." I picked as many wildflowers as I could find (and grew others that I couldn't) and pressed them or hung them upside down until they'd dried. I even learned how to dehydrate roses with their blooms intact by baking them in silica sand. I arranged the pressed flowers on greeting cards I'd made and sealed them in place with clear contact paper, and I assembled the flowers I'd hung upside down into wreaths that closely resembled the ones I'd seen in Smith & Hawken. Stuffing the greeting cards into envelopes, I fanned them out on a table, and I displayed the wreaths on a large pegboard panel placed directly behind my card display. Using a small tackle box to store money in, I set up shop at crafts fairs in Troy and nearby Libby.

For my next business venture, I focused on a product for which I knew there was almost limitless demand among my classmates: candy. I found a recipe for hard suckers that only required three basic ingredients (sugar, water, and corn syrup), and I ordered molds, colorings, flavorings, and wrappers via mail order with money I'd saved from previous sales. In my final two years of elementary school, I made a batch (approximately twenty suckers) every single day. I was able to produce more than twenty different flavors, which I sold to my classmates in quick hallway transactions between classes for a quarter apiece. Almost without fail, I'd sell out before lunch. Five dollars a day, twenty-five dollars a week, a hundred dollars a month—not bad for a ten-year-old. But the real payoff came at the end of the year when a local Christmas tree company would order a thousand tree-shaped suckers to give to their customers. The company placed this order three years in a row, and I always looked forward to the nice end-of-the-year bonus. Larry and Ruthanne were just as delighted by my money-making enterprises as I was, as the profits not only allowed me to buy my own clothes and shoes but also chip in for the occasional tank of gas and purchase gifts for them and Josh in my ongoing effort to win their love.

I derived an equally profitable stream of income from the many natural resources we had at our disposal, although this revenue was inconsistent due to seasonal fluctuations. The raspberry canes we had on our property produced a tremendous amount of berries, far more than we could eat ourselves, so I would pick them and store them in our refrigerator in green pint-sized berry baskets salvaged from the grocery store. I painted "Raspberries for Sale" on a piece of plywood, attached it to another piece of plywood with a hinge to make a self-standing sign, and placed it at the end of our driveway. If no buyers came, I would turn the berries into jam, which I could then sell at the next craft fair.

I could make even more money picking and selling huckleberries, which look like, but in my opinion taste better than, blueberries and appear in late July, August, and early September in the mountains of the Northwest. Gathering them was hard work. Larry, Ruthanne, Josh, and I would rise before dawn and take bumpy dirt roads high into the mountains in our blue Ford pickup. Arriving at one of our secret spots, each of us would grab a five-quart and ten-quart bucket and tie them to our waists with strips of cloth. As we headed into the woods, we would beat the empty buckets as if they were drums to scare off any bears. When we came to a patch of huckleberry bushes, we would move methodically from one bush to the next, our hands slowly filling our buckets, our eyes continually searching for more bushes ahead.

As a small child, I dreaded the long days in the mountains, as my back grew sore and I got eaten alive by mosquitoes. I initially struggled to collect a single gallon of berries, but, motivated to improve my standing in my school's social hierarchy by buying myself clothes and footwear that were actually in style, I was soon out-picking Josh and Ruthanne, bringing in as much as four gallons. However, none of us could match Larry's frenetic five-gallon-per-day pace. We didn't quite know how he did it. Before the dust our truck had kicked up on the washboard roads had even settled, he would have wandered out of earshot, and we wouldn't see him until lunchtime. We eagerly anticipated his return because we weren't allowed to take a break until he got back to the truck. After lunch, we'd store the berries we'd picked in a large cooler, head back up the mountain, and continue picking until dark. On good days, I could make more than a hundred dollars, and on exceptional ones as much as two hundred and fifty.

As I grew older, I began to feel a connection to the mountains and the secret spots tucked within them where I found berries and a momentary respite from my life. In these high-altitude locations, where the air was even thinner than what I was used to, my thoughts seemed clearer. While I was picking, I would often imagine I was an indigenous person, gathering food for the winter. My previous fantasy about being a Bantu woman living in the Congo often returned. I imagined I was an only child, and my mother was ill or dead, and I had to dig up enough cassava to feed my entire family. These fantasies came easily, left just as quickly, and helped me get me through grueling thirteen-hour workdays while making my back and neck hurt a little less.

Morels were similar to huckleberries in that they were a natural resource that could be sold for an enormous profit. I earned enough money gathering them to buy myself a $750 Pfaff sewing machine before I'd turned twelve. Josh and Ruthanne never showed much interest in this line of work, so it was usually just Larry and I who hunted for these elusive black and brown mushrooms. They tended to grow in areas that had been burned by forest fires the previous year, but, even armed with this knowledge, I still had a difficult time finding them because they were so well camouflaged amidst the ashes and dirt.

During one excursion high in the mountains, Larry and I came to a spot where the narrow trail crossed a long precarious rock face. On the trail ahead of us, we saw a mountain goat, a creature known for its agility in steep terrain, but even it seemed to be choosing its steps with care.

"If the mountain goats can get around it," Larry said, "we can, too."

Hearing this did not reassure me. I was terrified. The footholds were no more than three or four inches wide, only big enough to place a foot if you set it down parallel to the mountain. The rocks were slick with water. There was a thousand-foot drop below. And I was carrying two five-gallon buckets half full of morels.

"Just lean into the rock wall. You'll be fine." Larry forged ahead, and once he'd gotten past the most dangerous stretch, he stopped and turned around to face me. "You'd better not drop those buckets," he yelled. "I'll see you at the truck. If you're not there by dark, I'm leaving without you."

He continued walking, and soon I couldn't see him anymore. I had no idea how to get back to the truck in any other direction besides the one Larry had just gone. With daylight quickly fading, I had no choice but to move forward. The rock face offered few handholds to grab onto, but with each of my hands clutching the handle of a bucket it didn't matter anyway. I leaned my chest against the rock wall and put one trembling foot in front of the other, tears streaming down my face. As I slid each foot forward, I dragged my body with it, doing my best to ignore the long drop below. In this painstaking fashion, I eventually made it past the treacherous rock face and onto more stable ground.

While Larry may have taken it for granted that I'd make it, I never did. It was at this moment that I first wondered about the place I held in my parents' hearts. Up until this point, I just assumed, as most children do, that my parents loved me without reservation, even if I wasn't their favorite child. I wanted to believe that parental love was like gravity, a natural force that can't be denied or debated. But if Larry was willing to gamble with my life as he'd just done, what did that say about his love for me? What was my life really worth to him? What would Ruthanne have said if she'd known what he'd done? For the entire ride home, I imagined myself slipping on the rocks, falling off the side of the mountain, and landing in a bloody and broken heap, with a trail of morels tracing my long, painful descent to the bottom.

During another trip into the mountains around the same time, Larry shot a six-point bull elk but only succeeded in wounding it. His failure to kill the animal outright was a little surprising, as he was an expert hunter, the type who's willing to smear himself with animal urine and dung to mask his scent, camouflage his face with paint, and tiptoe through the forest for hours on end.

The six-point elk antlers, eight-point deer antlers, and mountain goat head displayed on our living room walls were testaments to his hunting expertise—as was the bear draped across the bed he shared with Ruthanne. He'd killed that bear with the bow he'd come to favor after shooting an animal with a rifle from several hundred yards away stopped feeling sporting. With archery season over and plenty of space left in our freezer for meat, he resorted to using a rifle on this excursion. After all, the Doležals didn't eat store-bought meat. One elk could keep us in food for months, if not a whole year.

Following the blood trail, we tracked the wounded animal until it was so weak it was forced to bed down in the snow. I happened to be in front when the bull suddenly stood up directly in front of me. It was standing broadside to me and I had a clear shot, but, awestruck by its majesty, I couldn't bring myself to pull the trigger. I could hear the animal's labored breathing and could tell that it was scared. I wanted the elk to break free and run away, which after a moment of hesitation it did. As punishment for my failure to shoot, Larry made me track the elk with him through the deep snow for what felt like another ten miles until the sun was going down and we'd come to a place where he was sure the animal would bed down for the night.

Just as he'd predicted, when we returned in the morning, we found the same bull elk we'd tracked the day before, and Larry shot it. The elk was dead, but Larry wasn't finished with the lesson he'd started giving me the day before. Handing me his rifle, he told me to shoot the elk in the head.

That was the last time I ever hunted.

Chapter Six

Chicken Head Baseball
& Huckleberry Stains

M Y CHILDHOOD WAS RIDDLED with corporal punishment. I
got punished so frequently that I began to believe what the
derogatory comments about my difficult birth, my obstinacy, and
my "carnal nature" had always implied: that I was born evil and
was destined to go to Hell. For me, sin lurked around every corner,
and I could never predict its arrival.

I was told one of the most disrespectful things you could do
was laugh at the wrong time. In fifth grade, a classmate made a
funny observation about our teacher in the middle of class, and
I snickered. The appalled expression that came over the teacher's
face when he whipped around and confronted me made me laugh
even harder. He kept telling me to stop, but the more insistent he
grew, the funnier it was to me. He sent me to the principal's office,
where I was given a lecture about why being disruptive in class
was so bad. The way he did it seemed so forced and fake it reignited
my laughing fit. I got sent home from school, and Larry gave me
a whooping three days in a row as punishment.

I suppose my tendency to laugh at all the wrong moments
sprung from some sort of social awkwardness. Because we lived
halfway up a mountain and I was required to do so much work
at home, I simply didn't hang out with other kids my age very
often. There was also an enormous gulf that lay between me and
them, and its name was Christianity. By the time I got to junior

high school, I felt like my classmates were engaging in the devil's work whenever they played with their Ouija boards or snuck beers from their parents' refrigerators, and that's the last thing I needed in my life. Every time I hung out with them, I felt as if my very salvation was at risk.

In seventh grade, the pressure I felt to conform to my classmates' heathen ways became so intense I started researching home-schooling options for myself. Initially, Larry was not in favor of the idea. As a county commissioner, he felt it would reflect badly on him if I wasn't enrolled in the local public school system, but I was determined to see my plan become a reality. After doing some research, I found Christian Liberty Academy Satellite Schools (CLASS), a private school in Indiana that allowed students to register and attend through the mail, but Larry insisted I finish the school year at the local junior high.

Feeling increasingly disconnected from my classmates as well as from Larry and Ruthanne, the only person I could really relate to during this time was Josh, and it was in a very specific, very morbid, way. One of our many chores was looking after the chickens our family raised. It was a year-round job that encompassed their entire life cycle, starting when they were chicks and often ending when we ate them. Every single day, their eggs needed to be collected, their feed scattered, their water topped off.

It's become fashionable for people in cities to raise a backyard flock of chickens, but before they get into it, they're only thinking about the payoff (eating the eggs) and not the often difficult and disgusting work that's required to keep the birds healthy. Cleaning up manure that burns your nostrils with its ammonia-like odor, and having to bury the stiff bodies of dead chicks deep enough in the ground that other animals can't dig them up and eat them, are just a few of the challenging aspects of poultry farming. I can't tell you how many times I got pecked on my hands and arms by an overprotective hen as I was collecting eggs from her nest. All a hen had to do was turn her head toward me, and I'd flinch, a Pavlovian response I'd developed over time. Not unlike humans, chickens also possess an uncanny and lamentable ability to identify and pick on any bird in the flock that stands out in any way, a trait that always bothered me. If one chicken had a slight wound on its head or one of its feathers was sticking out, the other chickens would gang up on it.

When one of our hens got a prolapsed vent, the rest of the chickens wouldn't leave it alone. With reptilian bobs of their heads, they pecked at the increasingly bloody protrusion. The hen was in so much pain I decided that the most merciful option would be for me to end its life. Butchering was typically a man's job, but neither Larry nor Josh was home at the time, so I took it upon myself to do it. I will never forget chasing after that hen, and taking it to the chopping block as its wings flapped wildly. The headless body twitched and writhed long after I'd used an axe to behead it. Following Ruthanne's instructions not to let the hen go to waste, I prepared the body to be stored in the freezer for a future meal. Only after a bowl of chicken soup was set before me that evening did I discover that she'd used the hen to make our dinner. I nearly threw up on the table. I grew up eating chickens we'd raised from birth, but for first time in my life I thought burying this hen in the yard would have been a more humane conclusion to its life than eating it for dinner.

Josh didn't share my sympathy toward the chickens, challenging me to play a game he called "chicken head baseball" whenever it was butchering day. The object was to see who could hit one of the recently removed chicken heads the farthest with a metal baseball bat. As grotesque as it was, this is actually one of the better memories I have of the time I spent growing up with Josh.

The worst involves a night we were left alone at home when I was twelve and he was fourteen. We'd spent the previous day picking huckleberries in the mountains, and our chore that evening was to clean them and store them in Ziploc bags in the freezer. Rolling the berries from one hand to the other, we picked out any stems or leaves, then dropped the berries into a measuring cup and poured them into the bags. Besides school, chores, and baseball, Josh and I didn't have very much in common, so our conversation while cleaning the berries was unremarkable until we got on the subject

of dating. I had a crush on one of Josh's friends, but my brother
informed me that I didn't stand a chance with him because he loved
to suck on boobs and I was severely lacking in that department.

His comment bruised my training-bra ego. "I do so have boobs!"

"Yeah, right. Then let's see 'em."

The idea that I might have to back up my statement with proof
hadn't occurred to me. A lump of anxiety formed in my throat
as I thought about my body being exposed. Josh started chasing
me around the dining room table, and I ran away from him, half
screaming, half laughing. To me it was a game, not unlike chicken
head baseball. I ran clockwise, then counterclockwise, until I grew
exhausted and his catching me came to feel inevitable. In a desperate attempt to keep him at bay, I grabbed a handful of huckleberries from the mound on the table and threw them at him. He
responded by grabbing a handful of his own and throwing them at
me before resuming his pursuit of me. When he finally caught me,
he brought me to the floor with a well-executed tackle and pinned
my arms down with his knees. This was standard brother–sister
stuff. I expected him to tickle me or dangle spit from his lips over
my face. I did not anticipate him pulling up my shirt and bra and
sucking on my nipples.

I fought to get away from him but couldn't. I was in tears. I
was in shock. I was in Hell. Only after the buzzing in my head
subsided enough for me to comprehend what was going on did
I notice the look of disgust on his face. "Like I said, your boobs
aren't big enough to satisfy a man." He took his knees off my arms
and let me go.

I ran to the bathroom and cried. When I returned, I couldn't
look at Josh. I could only stare at the purple stains on the dining room's white walls, where the huckleberries we'd thrown had
splattered. I felt numb, but I knew that if Larry and Ruthanne saw
those stains Josh and I would be severely punished. Expecting them
to return home any minute, we worked together to clean up the
stains, but they wouldn't come off the walls, no matter how hard
we scrubbed. Finally, in an act of desperation, I rifled through one
of the kitchen drawers, found a bottle of Liquid Paper, and used

the miniature brush attached to the underside of the cap to apply several coats over the stains on the wall, finishing just as Larry and Ruthanne pulled into the garage.

The stain left upon my body and mind by the events of that evening has been much harder to remove.

Chapter Seven

Thirteen I

THE YEAR I TURNED THIRTEEN was full of upheaval and major changes in my life. Like many girls, I got my first period, and soon afterward Ruthanne declared that I was too old to be spanked. I wasn't a little girl anymore. I was practically a woman.

She also put an end to the awkward tickling sessions Larry would make me endure from time to time. He liked to poke me in the ribs whenever I walked by him or pat me on the butt with his hand, especially in the evening right before bedtime. I would say, "Stop it, Papa," but he would continue to do it anyway, and eventually he would pin me down on the living room carpet and tickle my armpits and neck with his bearded chin. As I tried to squirm away and he prevented me from doing so, he would inevitably come in contact with my budding breasts, and it didn't feel right to me, a sentiment amplified by the lingering effects of my uncomfortable experience with Josh. According to Ruthanne, I was too "developed" for this sort of horseplay, and while her injunction was a positive development, I still felt disconnected from everyone in my life, including—perhaps especially—her and Larry, who I felt were different from me in ways I was unable to articulate. I felt like no one understood me and I was stuck somewhere I didn't want to be.

Sports provided me with a much-needed diversion. I played volleyball, basketball, and softball, as well as ran track, and I excelled in all of them. My serve in volleyball was nearly unreturnable, and largely because of it I was named the MVP of my team, even though, like Larry and Ruthanne, I wasn't very tall. My lack of height should have worked against me in basketball, but as my team's point guard, I was a great ball handler and was named MVP of that team as well. But my best sport was softball. Larry was a huge baseball fan, Josh played through high school and into college, and I played tee-ball, Little League, and, eventually, fast-pitch softball. I started out at second base, then briefly tried shortstop before landing in the position that suited me best, catcher. I routinely picked off runners who were trying to steal second base, wasn't afraid to dive for foul balls, and was an accomplished hitter and base runner.

When I returned to the local junior high for eighth grade, I was met with an increasing amount of peer pressure, as my classmates had begun dating each other and Larry and Ruthanne didn't allow me to participate. They only approved of "courtship," a period of time during which a man and a woman seek to determine if it's God's will for them to marry each other. Larry and Ruthanne also made me stay home from school on days when sex education was taught because they were convinced that it encouraged fornication, and fornication led to Hell. I was supposed to be a virgin when I got married, so, according to them, I didn't need to know anything about sex until I had a husband. By effectively keeping me cloistered in a nunnery, they succeeded only in making me laughably ignorant. Ruthanne believed using maxi pads during your period was good enough, but the girls I played sports with used tampons, so I wanted to as well. I bought one for a quarter in a public restroom, but unable to figure out how to insert it, I convinced myself I didn't have a vagina.

This incident was quickly overshadowed by an increasing number of uncomfortable social encounters, most of which involved me getting mocked for being such a diehard Christian. I felt like I was caught between two very different worlds, home and school, and while I really didn't belong in either place, I had to choose one. With the threat of eternal damnation weighing heavily on my mind, I resumed trying to sell my homeschooling plan to Larry until he couldn't take it anymore. As my school's first-quarter term was coming to an end, he offered me a deal: If I could finish the entire eighth-grade curriculum offered by CLASS in the three quarters of the school year that remained, he would allow me to choose which educational option (public school or homeschool) I preferred for high school. But, he warned me, once I'd made a decision, that was it. There would be no going back.

I didn't flinch. I took the California Achievement Test for every subject and had CLASS send me the curriculum for the level at which I'd tested. I had to take a biology class meant for high school sophomores as well as twelve other subjects. It was a grueling challenge that required me to read stacks and stacks of thick textbooks and to write perfectly in cursive—penmanship was graded—but I managed to pull it off.

When I started homeschooling, I asked the principal at the junior high in Troy if I could continue to play sports there. When he said no, I had to quit playing basketball and volleyball and running track. Only two outlets for physical activity remained for me. As soon as Harold, the puppy I'd adopted, was big enough, I took him running with me under the power line that ran across the mountain behind our house. I was also able to play fast-pitch softball in the public summer league in Libby, but even this would soon be taken from me.

In my family, I bore the burden of constantly being compared to my great-grandmother, who'd died when I was eight. Her funeral is the only one I've ever been to that made me feel genuinely sad. She was quite a woman, possessing many of the qualities I would come to admire, including independence, creativity, and willpower. These traits were frowned upon in my family because they were considered rebellions against God and I was often told that I possessed all three. According to our family's history, my great-grandmother was, at least partly, Native American, with roots in the Hunkpapa division of the Lakota tribe. She was also known as a woman about town, always wearing hats with veils, dress gloves, costume jewelry, and bright red lipstick, and marrying and divorcing four different men.

To prevent me from ending up like her, I suppose, Larry and Ruthanne forbade me from wearing makeup or cutting my hair when I was a teenager. I also couldn't braid it. They'd reference a verse of Scripture (1 Corinthians 11:15) that describes a woman's long hair being her "glory" and suggests it's sinful for a woman to cut or braid her hair. When I was a little girl, it hadn't mattered so much if I cut my bangs or braided my hair, but now that I was a woman, modesty was essential.

I was expected to maintain a chaste appearance at home. Ruthanne and I were made to wear discreet dresses that covered nearly every inch of our skin besides our hands and faces. Meanwhile, Larry and Josh got to walk around shirtless—sometimes even pantsless—whenever they pleased. Larry treated our home like his own private nudist colony. His penis was the first I ever saw, and, unfortunately, I saw it a lot. That the men in our family got to traipse around naked, while I had to wear outfits that resembled those favored by Mennonite women, taught me at a very young age to feel guilty about my appearance and contributed to me developing all sorts of body image issues down the road. Ruthanne prohibited me from wearing pants because, as she explained to me, "Pants separate a woman's legs, and that tempts men to want to have intercourse with you." I was only to wear skirts or dresses, otherwise I would be disobeying God's desire for women to be modest. Not wanting to defy God or—gulp—get raped, I did as I was told, but this new rule presented some difficulties. To do yard work, for example, I had to wear pants underneath a dress because the wind might lift the dress or a branch might snag it and reveal too much of my body. Larry and Ruthanne didn't always see eye to eye, and my wearing pants was one of the things they viewed differently. Larry would occasionally let me wear pants while I was hiking or doing yard work, but I always felt guilty afterward.

Because of Ruthanne's prohibition against pants, playing softball became problematic for me. The sport required that I wear pants that fell just below the knee and hugged the contours of my body, and in Ruthanne's view my round buttocks and strong thighs might lead any men or boys who saw me to temptation. And who knew what sort of lascivious thoughts the umpire, who stood right behind me when I played catcher, was thinking? I could practically feel him breathing on the back of my neck as I squatted behind home plate. Feeling like a sinner for having such an immodest pastime and fearing the wrath of God, I quit the last sport that had been available to me and the one I'd loved the most.

Now that I was homeschooling and not playing softball anymore, I started spending nearly all my time at home, which, as I would soon come to discover, made me perfectly suited for a job I never asked for nor ever expected to have: full-time stay-at-home nanny.

Chapter Eight

Adopting Ezra

AFTER CHURCH ONE SUNDAY AFTERNOON, Larry and Ruthanne made a shocking announcement. They'd heard a call from God to "save the children from the War on the Unborn" and were going to start adopting babies. Later I overheard them having a conversation that hinted at the real reason for their seemingly altruistic endeavor. On the verge of losing one of their dependents—Josh was about to graduate from high school—they saw adoption as a way to avoid (or, at the very least, limit) paying taxes to a government they blamed for subsidizing abortions.

Their plan was to start adopting children as soon as possible, but they quickly discovered that the wait was much longer and the cost much higher than they'd expected. For white babies, that is. Perhaps no place is our culture's racism more apparent than the adoption of babies whose availability and market value generally reflects their worth in our society's eyes. It can take as long as five years to adopt a white baby and cost as much as fifty thousand dollars, whereas Black babies can be adopted quickly and cheaply. While other factors are involved, including the basic economic principle of supply and demand, it's the role of demand in this scenario that hints at a simple but painful truth: in our culture, white babies are more valued than Black babies.

When Larry and Ruthanne learned how much quicker and cheaper it was to adopt babies with darker skin, they expressed a willingness to take *any* baby as long as it wasn't born with any physical disabilities. After all, physically disabled children would not be able to shoulder the heavy workload required of those who lived under their roof.

After completing the arduous application process, with its tedious paperwork and numerous home visits, we got a call telling us that a pregnant woman in Kansas City, Missouri, was looking to put her baby up for adoption. The one catch was that the woman had some developmental disabilities, so there was a chance her baby could be disabled as well. Larry was so disturbed by the news and the dilemma it presented, he cried. After praying on it, he and Ruthanne decided to move forward and sign the paperwork.

Alexander Joe was born January 13, 1993. Upon getting the news, Larry, Ruthanne, and I piled into our Volvo and drove twenty-four hours straight to Kansas City. Having just acquired my learner's permit, I shared the driving duties with Larry, while Ruthanne served as copilot. With one foot out the door on his way to college, Josh hadn't contributed much to the conversations about adoption and didn't make the trip. In the paperwork we were given at the hospital, the baby's mother, who was white, had written that she had been unable to locate the father but did provide a description of the man: "tall and Black." She was only four foot nine, so how tall her baby would turn out to be was anyone's guess.

I was a big sister all of a sudden, and as such, Larry and Ruthanne included me in the process of picking a new name for the baby—within strict parameters specified by Larry, of course. The first name had to come from the Bible and contain one "z," which Larry thought would look catchy when paired with Doležal, and the middle name had to start with the letter "a," in keeping with our family's custom. (Ruthanne presented the only exception to the latter rule, as she'd combined her first name and middle name to form a single name.) Taking the task seriously, I scoured the Bible in search of names that contained a "z" and made a list of the more memorable ones. There was no shortage of them, so I culled the ones that were too hard to pronounce or had less-than-pleasant meanings. For the middle name, I combed through books full of baby names looking for ones that not only began with "a" but also fit well with the first names I'd written down. Once I'd amassed a long list of suitable names, we voted on them, and that's how Alexander Joe became Ezra Anders. We were now what's come to be known as a transracial family, one where the parents had a different racial classification than the child (or children) they'd adopted.

Ezra's arrival demanded that everyone in our family take on additional work. Unlike most girls my age, my teenage years were only briefly consumed with thoughts about boys. From the time Ezra arrived at our house, I was focused almost solely on doing my part to ensure his health and happiness. My already long list of chores expanded to include making cloth diapers out of bolts of flannel, changing said diapers, rocking Ezra back to sleep in the middle of the night, using a Happy Baby food grinder to make his meals, and, once I'd gotten my driver's license, driving into town to go grocery shopping—in short, many of the things parents are supposed to do.

When Ruthanne developed something like chronic fatigue syndrome, I became the pinch hitter, a second mom who, unlike the first one, was always on call. To get my homework done, I had to wake up before the sun and work nonstop until long after it went down. I could have easily grown resentful, but I didn't. After all, if I was going to be a good Christian woman, someday I would marry and have babies of my own, and Ezra was providing me with excellent practice. Besides, I absolutely adored him.

Because I was taking such an active role in his care, I grew very protective of Ezra. He was a very sweet and very bright boy who smiled easily, and I just wanted to wrap him in my arms and shield him from anything that could potentially hurt him. At first I was mostly concerned about him hitting his head on the underside of a table or chair or putting something harmful in his mouth, but as he grew I came to understand that it was just as important for me to act as a buffer between him and ignorance, particularly when the source of that ignorance was my own family.

As Ezra's first Christmas with us approached, my maternal grandmother, Grandma Schertel, seemed genuinely befuddled when it came to buying him a present—as if the toys he'd want to play with might somehow be different than those desired by white children his age. "I just don't know what to get him," she said, throwing her hands in the air in frustration. "What do Black children like? I know, I could get him a drum!"

From books I'd borrowed from the library, I'd read about racism enough to understand the basic stereotypes and I could almost visualize her thoughts: half-naked Africans dancing around a fire to the sound of beating drums. Apparently, even babies weren't exempt from this sort of profiling.

"Or you could get him some blocks or a picture book," I suggested. "Ezra likes the same things all one-year-olds like."

Grandma Schertel and her husband were extreme in their views, particularly when it came to race and religion. Unlike Larry's parents, who had come to religion late, now belonged to the relatively sedate Church of God, and were fairly tepid in their religious expression, Ruthanne's parents, Rupert and Dorcas Schertel, embraced a radical faith tradition that was almost Taliban-like in its intensity. Grandpa Schertel, who'd emigrated from Germany to the United States when he was nineteen and held very Eurocentric views about race, was particularly austere. He prayed on his knees for an hour every day. His go-to breakfast was shredded carrots and cabbage, served raw. After eating, he would retreat to his immaculately clean garage where he kept his tools, all carefully labeled and organized in rows, and spend the rest of the day in solitude. He rarely showed any emotion, so his reaction when he first found out that Ezra wasn't white was as shocking as it was telling.

The man cried.

That these were tears of sadness, not joy, was clear to me, but no one else seemed to pick up on it or be bothered by it.

"Maybe he's not Black," Ruthanne suggested, pointing to his skin, which was pale, and his hair, which was only slightly curled. "I think he might be Jewish. I've always prayed I'd have a son of Zion."

Grandpa Schertel remained inconsolable. After being introduced to Ezra, he apparently started getting up at five in the morning every day to pray for the strength to accept Ezra as his grandchild.

The Schertels only lived a half-hour drive away, and we always spent Christmas Eve with them at their house, along with Ruthanne's siblings and their spouses and children. Grandpa Schertel would read the Christmas story passage from the Gospel of Luke, and Grandma Schertel would float around the house, tending to grandbabies, making sure everyone ate too much food, and shouting, "Praise Jesus!" or "Hallelujah!" even when it made absolutely no sense in the context of what was going on.

Even though they lived, by Montana standards, just down the road from us, the Schertels almost never came to our house for holiday gatherings—or any other occasion for that matter. We invited them to Christmas dinner every year but grew so used to their inevitable absence that it no longer became noteworthy enough to discuss, and the first Christmas Ezra spent with us was no different.

Grandma and Grandpa Doležal, on the other hand, never missed a single Christmas dinner at our house, and they always arrived first, bringing with them holiday treats like olives, pickles, and sparkling apple cider. Despite Grandma Doležal's apparent disdain for children and the germs they carried and the messes they made—she'd made hers strip down and get hosed off before entering the house every time they played outside—she'd raised two others, besides Larry.

Her son, my Uncle Dan, usually came to our Christmas dinners, but this year he opted to spend the holiday in Idaho with Vern, his longtime partner, and Vern's family. To me, Vern was "Uncle" Vern, but we weren't allowed to refer to him that way in front of Larry and Ruthanne. I can't say that anyone in my extended family had a very healthy reaction to Dan and Vern's homosexuality. Some family members insisted that they were "just roommates," while others openly referred to them as "the sodomites." No wonder Dan always came to our holiday gatherings alone, if he came at all.

Larry's sister JoAnn wasn't held in a much better light. She'd married an abusive man when she was young and religious, then committed one of the worst sins imaginable by divorcing him. Compounding her wickedness, she refused to remarry until she was past her childbearing years and chose a man she'd only known for a couple of years. Rumors circulated within our family that she was now an atheist. It always gave me a nervous thrill to open my eyes while prayers were being said before our holiday meals and catch her looking around the table.

There were certain unwritten rules we had to follow whenever we had guests. Men and boys were rarely allowed in the kitchen. Josh was in charge of chopping wood and inserting leaves into the dining room table. I was responsible for vacuuming, dusting, cleaning the bathrooms, setting out our sturdy and practical dinnerware, helping to cook the meal, and cleaning up afterward. Larry always took it upon himself to say grace and read an entire chapter of Scripture from his Amplified King James Bible, which provides the definitions of certain words as well as commentary, making each chapter twice as long as it normally would be. Only after he was done reading were we permitted to pass the food around the table, and Larry always served himself first.

The passage Larry read this year seemed particularly long, and while he was droning on and on, the food we'd spent all day cooking—elk steaks, roasted potato wedges, green beans, and homemade rolls—was growing cold. At one point, I observed Aunt JoAnn picking at the olive and pickle tray in quiet protest and passing little bites of food to Ezra, who was sitting next to her in his high chair. When it became clear after Larry had finished that Ezra wasn't interested in his food, JoAnn scooped him out of his high chair and put him in his walker, and he happily scooted around the dining room and into the kitchen as the adults started passing the plates of now lukewarm food around the table.

We were having forced conversations about school, the current road conditions, and hunting season, when Ruthanne suddenly cried, "Where's Ezra?!"

Both of us shot up from the table and ran around the corner to the top of the stairs—the same stairs I'd fallen down when I was a one-year-old!—to find Ezra approaching the edge of the top step in his walker. At some point, Larry had gotten up from the table to stoke the woodstove in the basement, our house's sole source of heat, and when he returned to the table, he'd left the door to the stairs open so the rising heat could fill the rest of the house. Ruthanne and I arrived just in time to see Ezra lurch forward over the lip of the top step. She lunged to grab hold of him, but she was too late. He disappeared from sight. I ran after him, but only succeeded in getting a better view of him flipping head over heels down the thinly carpeted steps, his head hitting the stairs one, two, three times, before he came to rest on the thin linoleum now covering the basement's concrete floor. He landed face down, just inches from where I'd fallen as a toddler.

The wheels of his upturned walker continued to spin long after his body had come to rest. I braced myself in preparation of him screaming, but he remained silent and that was much worse. He was so quiet and unresponsive I thought he might be dead. Ruthanne and I bounded down the stairs, taking two and three at a time, and, after reaching him, turned him right side up and worked frantically to unbuckle his seatbelt and remove him from the walker. His body was limp. His eyes had rolled back in their sockets. Ruthanne held him up and lightly slapped his cheeks to no avail.

"Ezra!" I shouted, patting his leg. "Ezra?"

Ruthanne started speaking in tongues. As she held Ezra's body and stared into his eyes, she would occasionally shout, "Praise Jesus!" or "Hallelujah!" or "Life for this baby!" Everything else that came out of her mouth was pure gibberish. I don't remember putting my shoes on or climbing into the car, but soon Larry, Ruthanne, Ezra, and I were whizzing down the highway driving 85 mph on our way to the hospital in Libby. Maybe if I'd been male and only half conscious, I would have received the same treatment after I'd fallen down those stairs fourteen years before.

Unlike his wife, Larry was always eerily calm in a crisis, but I was terrified. Ezra remained unresponsive during the long ride to the hospital, and all I could do was hold his small hand in mine as tears streamed down my cheeks. I was petrified that this wide-eyed baby who I loved so much was never going to walk or talk ever again.

When we arrived at the emergency room, Ezra was whisked through the automatic doors and engulfed in a scrum of doctors and nurses. After an hour or two, we finally got the news:

everything, thank God, was going to be okay. Ezra had a concussion but no broken bones or other significant injuries, a surprisingly fortunate outcome for such a brutal fall. He fully recovered from the head injury, but stopped growing for an entire year following the accident. On his second birthday he was the same size he'd been on his first.

After that night I felt like Ezra and I shared a special, albeit horrifying, bond. We'd both taken nasty falls, we'd both survived, and we'd both learned a painful lesson: in the Doležal family, you couldn't always count on your parents to keep you safe.

Chapter Nine

Separate but Equal

S OON AFTER EZRA'S FIRST BIRTHDAY, an adoption agency in
Chicago called Larry and Ruthanne to inform them that there
was a good chance a baby would be available in June. The mother
and father were both Black, and the mother had hoped to place
her baby with a Black family, but once she discovered that the
only Black families looking to adopt at that time were looking for
a girl, she loosened up her criteria, allowing the Doležals to adopt
Antwon Dante'. In accordance with the guidelines set by Larry, we
renamed him Izaiah Allen. He was born June 11, 1994, and two
weeks later Larry and Ruthanne drove to Chicago to pick him up,
while I stayed home and took care of Ezra.

When Izaiah was six months old, Ezra contracted whooping
cough. Because the disease was so contagious and carried such a
high infant mortality rate, and none of us were immunized thanks
to Larry and Ruthanne's distrust of vaccinations, someone had
to be quarantined with Izaiah. With Ruthanne focused on Ezra's
recovery, the task fell to me. The only time I ventured out of my
bedroom was to use the bathroom and prepare bottles of formula
for Izaiah, and whenever I did, I'd walk on bedsheets to avoid touch-
ing the carpet, which was difficult to sanitize, and always made
sure to thoroughly wash my hands. Izaiah and I lived together in
my room for more than a month, so long I began to lose track of
the days of the week, and it was during this time that I began to
form a deep and lasting bond with him.

When Izaiah was nine months old, we got a call from a couple who'd been doing missionary work in Haiti and had returned to the United States with a baby roughly Izaiah's age. The baby's exact birthdate was a bit of a mystery because he'd been left on the doorstep of a hospital one morning, forcing the doctors to guess his age from studying what remained of his umbilical cord. Did Larry and Ruthanne want him? Certainly! His name was Joshua Alexander, but any possibility of confusing him with my older brother was cleared up after we changed his name to Zachariah Amoz, soon to be shortened to Zach. He arrived with eyes full of wonderment, a persistently runny nose, and lots and lots of energy.

Larry and Ruthanne had planned to stop adopting babies after they'd taken in three. But the very same day that the missionary couple introduced Zach to our family—they were actually sitting on our couch at the time—an adoption agency in St. Louis, Missouri, called to let us know that a female baby was available. Baby Grace had been abandoned at a hospital and placed in temporary care after two prospective families had backed out at the last minute. One of the families thought the hospital bills they were being asked to pay were way too high; the other worried that the baby's dark complexion made her a bad fit for their lighter-skinned Black family. Larry and Ruthanne expressed no such reservations.

Names for women that contain a "z" are scarce in the Bible. Larry wanted to name the baby Ezther, but I lobbied to make the name more palatable to the eyes and ears. Approving my suggestion, he and Ruthanne named her Esther Ahava, which means "beloved star." Larry and Ruthanne often referred to her as the "icing on the cake," the one girl amid three boys and the final piece of the puzzle that, now solved, ensured they wouldn't be paying taxes anytime soon. In eleven hectic months, Larry and Ruthanne had adopted three babies, all born within eight months of each other. Only the parents and siblings of quadruplets can understand the sort of chaos that ensued. Simply changing my adopted siblings' cloth diapers was like working on an assembly line.

With four Black siblings and two white parents, I was now living in a home that was Blacker than it was white. Some of my relatives began referring to Larry and Ruthanne as "colorblind" and "cultural revolutionaries" for adopting four Black babies, but this assessment didn't sit right with me, as I was a firsthand witness to the cultural ignorance and racial bias they continually displayed. Often describing my younger siblings as "a little gang," Larry and Ruthanne treated each of them differently based on the color of their skin. Ezra, whose biological mother was white, had the lightest skin. He passed the "brown paper bag test," a method, popular in the early part of the twentieth century, of determining whether a particular Black person merited inclusion in certain institutions such as a church, fraternity, or university. If your skin was darker than a brown paper bag, you were denied entry. Larry and Ruthanne often referred to him as "the smart one," and it quickly became clear from the preferential treatment they gave him that he was their favorite. They indulged his every whim, and all the attention he received came at the expense of his younger siblings, who were often ignored for long stretches of time.

Zach, who had the darkest skin, was often treated the worst. Larry and Ruthanne made references to him being "blue Black," a variation of an old racial slur. Some people, particularly a certain type of southerner, believed that Black people's ancestry could be determined by looking into their mouths. If their gums were very dark or bluish, it was believed to represent a pure bloodline (100 percent African), proof, in their eyes, that they were dumber, lazier, and more savage than everyone else. This sort of overt racism spawned a myth, accepted as fact in some parts of the Deep South, that you could die if you were bitten by a "blue gum." After bathing Zach one night, Ruthanne commented on the bathtub ring he'd left behind. "This is why [white] people think Black people are dirty," she said. "The residue from their skin looks like dirt."

In the racially determined hierarchy that existed in our household, Esther was just above Zach because her skin was a shade lighter than his. But growing up, she had to endure the double burden of being both Black and female in a household that was white and patriarchal. Izaiah had nearly the same complexion she did, but the fact that he was a boy ensured that he received better treatment than her. Happy-go-lucky as a baby and a toddler, Izaiah grew more serious and cautious as he grew older, trying to avoid making the same sort of mistakes that had gotten Zach and Esther severely punished.

Growing up, my adopted siblings were not only treated differently from each other but were also raised much differently than Josh and I were. Ruthanne would often make them put on their church clothes and sing songs for dinner guests, something that had never been asked of me or Josh. The way they were disciplined was also different. Spooked by the random post-placement visits made by social workers during an adopted baby's first six months in a home, Larry and Ruthanne ditched the wooden paddle they'd used to spank me and Josh in favor of twelve-inch-long glue sticks, which were designed to be used in a hot glue gun but which Larry used like a switch. Whatever redness or welts one of these glue sticks left faded quickly, but, boy, did getting whacked with them sting! Larry and Ruthanne used the glue sticks so often it began to seem more like a way for them to take out their frustrations when dealing with four crying babies than an actual disciplinary tool. The adopted kids' punishment was also doled out in a much more haphazard fashion. While Josh and I only got spanked on our butts, any part of my younger siblings' bodies was fair game. If one of them refused to finish a meal, Larry would "glue stick" that child on the knuckles. As hard as it was to witness, it was even worse when Larry made me (and Josh whenever he was home from college) do it.

I imagine Larry and Ruthanne thought they were treating my adopted siblings fairly, despite treating them differently than they had Josh and me, but in effect, our household was a two-tiered system. When I later read about *Plessy v. Ferguson*, the 1896 U.S. Supreme Court case which gave legal authority to the idea of "separate but equal," I couldn't help thinking about my brothers and sister. In its decision, the court ruled that, as long as services, facilities, housing, medical care, education, employment, and transportation were equal, they could be separated along racial lines. Segregation, the judges determined, didn't violate anyone's constitutional rights. But the facilities and services provided for Blacks were the same as those reserved for whites in name only. In reality, they were almost always inferior.

On May 17, 1954, the Supreme Court ruled that by denying Black children the right to attend schools closest to where they lived and forcing them to go to segregated ones, the Board of Education in Topeka, Kansas, had violated the Equal Protection Clause of the Fourteenth Amendment. The Court's decision in *Brown v. Board of Education* effectively overturned *Plessy v. Ferguson* and brought an end to the Jim Crow era.

In making its historic decision in *Brown v. Board of Education*, the Supreme Court seemed to be particularly moved by the testimony of Drs. Kenneth and Mamie Clark, educational psychologists who'd conducted a series of experiments with Black schoolchildren, ages three to seven, in the 1940s. In the experiments, the Clarks gave each of the children four dolls, identical in every way except for the color of their skin. Two of the dolls were Black, two were white. The Clarks then asked the children a series of questions: Which dolls were "nice"? Which were "bad"? Which were most like them? Which did they like best?

The results were chilling. Most of the children cited a preference for the white dolls, assigning positive characteristics to them, even saying they looked like them. When the Clarks conducted this experiment in Massachusetts, some of the children got so upset they refused to answer the questions, while others cried and ran out of the room. But the response Dr. Kenneth Clark found most disturbing occurred when he asked a Black child in Arkansas which of the dolls most resembled him. The boy smiled, pointed to one of the Black dolls, and said, "That's a nigger. I'm a nigger."* While writing the Supreme Court's opinion in *Brown v. Board of Education*, Chief Justice Earl Warren specifically noted the adverse psychological effects that segregated schools had on Black children, including "a feeling of inferiority as to their status

---

* Due to the long history of hate and oppression associated with this word, I've done my best to limit its usage in this book. Like the NAACP, I believe the word should be permanently removed from our vocabulary. To this end, I have replaced it with "the N-word" wherever possible, but have kept it in places where it was directly quoted to limit awkwardness and underscore the emotional trauma it delivers.

in the community that may affect their hearts and minds in a way unlikely to ever be undone."

When I was a teenager, I was scared that the subtle racism and abuse routinely directed at my younger siblings might affect them in a similar way, but whenever I tried to talk to anyone about it, I was dismissed. How could Larry and Ruthanne possibly be racist? They were devout Christians who were doing God's work! At least that's how Larry and Ruthanne presented themselves in the annual newsletter they sent to the Christian supporters who helped finance the babies' adoptions and ongoing expenses.

The newsletter started its life as a very detailed Christmas card, giving approximately a hundred people an update about what each member of our family was up to, but it quickly turned into a letter of need. For Larry and Ruthanne, adopting babies was an integral part of the mission field to which God was calling them. Of course, missionaries receive donations, and, as Larry and Ruthanne would soon come to find out, missionaries who write newsletters and include photographs of Black children they've adopted get even more donations. They often used pictures of my siblings taken after they'd gotten dirty from playing outside in an attempt, I imagine, to generate more pity (and more money) from donors. As young as I was, I still understood that making money in this way was unacceptable and just plain disturbing, and I didn't want anything to do with it.

After I moved out of the house, Larry and Ruthanne succeeded in pulling in enough money from guilty white do-gooders to pay for moves to Colorado and South Africa, where they lived in a three-story home in a gated community with a pool and Black servants. In describing the adoptions of four Black children as being part of a mission, Larry and Ruthanne created an image of themselves that made them appear holier-than-thou. They deserved medals or a pat on the back.

Given what I'd witnessed inside our house, I knew better.

Chapter Ten

Hair I

A S MUCH TIME AND ENERGY as I devoted to my little brothers
and sister, it rarely felt like work. It was, in fact, true love.
The bond we shared was much deeper than that typically found
between a big sister and her younger siblings. As I was often asked
to assume a maternal role with them, my feelings toward them
became more motherly than sisterly.

There was also something else going on, something that I've
come to realize as an adult but that I wouldn't have been able to
articulate back then, as it was more of a feeling than a thought.
Spending so much time with these four beautiful Black babies—
changing their diapers, feeding them, bathing them, dressing
them, and rocking them to sleep—I found myself drawing closer
to something that felt oddly familiar. With Larry, Ruthanne, and
Josh, I'd always felt distinctly other. We rarely saw eye to eye
about anything. But now, for the first time in my life, I felt like
I was truly part of a family, surrounded by people who loved me
exactly as I was. Growing up in a house where guilt, anxiety, and
occasional moments of terror were the norm, I'd never felt like
I was *home* (and all that word implies: safe, loved, comfortable,
relaxed, happy). But something changed after we adopted these
babies. I suddenly didn't feel so alone.

With love came fear. I grew fiercely protective of my younger
siblings. Having witnessed how they were mistreated within our
household, I began to worry about how they were going to be
treated by the rest of the world.

Despite Larry and Ruthanne's belief that, unless I was studying the Bible, doing chores was a more valuable use of my time, I'd always loved books. I was a voracious reader—imagine how many books you'd consume if you didn't have a television or any electronic devices!—and while reading about Black history I'd started to understand how many land mines there were in America for Black children. Preparing one's kids for negative encounters like the racial profiling they could expect to experience came to be called "The Talk," the painful yet necessary conversation nearly all Black parents give their children to make them mindful of how most white people perceive them and to emphasize the importance of being cautious when confronted by the police. The Talk has become an obligatory responsibility when raising Black children—particularly boys, because it would be difficult to find a Black man who hasn't felt threatened or harassed by the police. As a rule, white parents don't need to have this discussion with their kids, and many haven't even heard of it. I wasn't aware of The Talk at this point in my life, but I instinctually understood the importance of educating my younger siblings about the perils of the world around them—and I had no confidence that Larry and Ruthanne would ever do it.

There were numerous threats to their dignity and self-worth that they needed help avoiding. When our family went to the grocery store or church, strangers often walked up to my siblings and stroked their hair and skin as if they were exhibits in a sideshow. The way these people acted you would have thought it was perfectly normal and acceptable to fondle vulnerable (and confused) children simply to satisfy one's curiosity. Seeing this always turned my stomach. I made it my duty to shield my siblings from such ignorance as best as I could and serve as a bridge between them and the all-white world that surrounded us for miles and miles. I made it clear to them that strangers had no right to touch their bodies or their hair unless they gave them permission. At times, I felt like a ninja, as I whisked them away from hands that threatened to touch them inappropriately and corrected rude comments directed their way.

The slights my younger siblings suffered were often so veiled no one else seemed to pick up on them but me. Grandma Schertel wanting to give Ezra a drum for Christmas. Ruthanne referring to them as a gang. Dinner guests, encouraged by Larry and Ruthanne, asking my siblings to sing for their entertainment. People staring at them whenever we went into town. The sheer absence of Black people, and therefore Black culture, in our small town underscored their otherness. There were no Black doctors, teachers, coaches, or pastors who lived anywhere near us. Even Fabian, now divorced from Rosie, had moved on, settling in Redding, California, to work for the Forest Service.

In 1970, Chester M. Pierce, a professor of education and psychiatry at Harvard University, coined a term to describe instances of racism that were so subtle (but no less offensive) they were easily overlooked or misunderstood: "microaggressions." I wasn't aware of this word when I was growing up, and yet I still had little trouble identifying them when I saw them. And from what I'd read, I knew the treatment my younger siblings could expect to receive as they grew up would only get worse with time. People saying things to them like, "I never think of you as a Black person," or, in a surprised voice, "You're so articulate." Having store managers follow them up and down the aisles to make sure they didn't steal anything. Having white people cross the street to avoid walking past them on the sidewalk. Getting stopped by police officers for no good reason.

Many researchers have argued that microaggressions can actually be more damaging than overt expressions of bigotry because of their frequency and, counterintuitively, their size. Because they're so small—nearly invisible to most white people—they often go ignored or get downplayed. In the white community, that is. In the Black community, these subtle slights are *always* picked up on, and Black people often talk about them with other Black people. This dichotomy often leads to victims of such transgressions feeling isolated, distrustful, hesitant, and abnormal. Studies have shown that long-term exposure to microaggressions affects one's mental health, decreasing happiness, energy, and productivity while increasing frustration and anger.

In 1991, the clinical psychologist and author Na'im Akbar produced a groundbreaking article titled "Mental Disorder Among

African Americans," which claimed that, even in the mental health world, Black Americans were treated unfairly. According to Akbar, the current view of what was considered normal behavior was based on that exhibited by the majority of the population—that is, white people. Akbar argued that many of the mental health disorders Black Americans had been diagnosed with were actually just normal responses to being forced to live in an alien (and often cruel) society. Meanwhile, actual ones, including alien-self disorder (seeing yourself through the lens of the majority, rejecting your true identity, and living in isolation and confusion), anti-self disorder (wanting to be part of the majority so badly you adopt the temperament of that group and promote negative feelings toward your own), and self-destructive disorders (engaging in harmful behavior such as doing drugs or binge eating as a way of escaping oppression), were being overlooked. Studies like Akbar's show how much impact microaggressions can have on the mental health of individuals from minority groups and how often that impact gets overlooked.

Why was I aware of the microaggressions my siblings faced while everyone around me remained ignorant? I believe it was a combination of intuitive awareness, protective instincts that emerged from caring for my siblings, and the knowledge I'd gleaned from reading about Black history. I certainly didn't have a "white" perspective. I was starting to think more from a Black one.

That I was the only one picking up on the microaggressions aimed at my younger siblings flipped something like a light switch inside of me. It was an awareness of just how vulnerable they were and a realization that I was the only one who was willing and somewhat able to protect them. I was aware; therefore, I was responsible. I knew that if I didn't serve as a buffer for them against ignorance, misunderstanding, isolation, and hostility, no one else would. In the process, I became a kind of cultural translator, helping them navigate the white world safely while trying to keep them connected to the Black one.

Because dolls that had white features and books that starred white characters were the norm, I passed my Black Raggedy Ann and Andy dolls down to Esther and painted over the illustrations of the white characters in the Bible Larry and Ruthanne had given to Izaiah to make them look Black. Whenever I went into town, I searched for and collected Black children's books, dolls, and toys. I also became an ardent researcher of African history and Black fashion, culture, dance, music, and food in the United States, making frequent trips to the local library to borrow armfuls of books on these subjects. Larry and Ruthanne grudgingly approved of books that had to do with my younger siblings' heritage. Employing knowledge gleaned from library books, I was able to educate my siblings about Black history in America, including but not limited to the biographies of Harriet Tubman, Nat Turner, Martin Luther King Jr., and Malcolm X. I would soon be going off to college, and my goal before I left was to help my younger brothers and sister gain an appreciation for the wonderful world of Blackness from which they'd come.

A funny thing happened while I was teaching my younger siblings about Black culture and history: I began to feel even more connected to it myself. I began to see the world through Black eyes, and anything that had to do with Blackness or Africa always grabbed my attention. When I'd read about the Rwandan genocide and the plight of the children caught in the crossfire between the Hutu and Tutsi groups, it touched my soul. While I bathed, fed, and dressed my siblings, I couldn't stop thinking about the refugee children, who were being punished just for being born in the wrong place at the wrong time.

Late at night, in between rocking babies to sleep, I worked on a piece of art that allowed me to express my concern for the people of Rwanda. I didn't have canvas or paints, so I took an old white bed sheet and stretched it over a piece of wood. I tacked down the edges and stained the sheet by dunking it in hot tea to give it an earthy hue. With dough made from flour, water, and salt, I sculpted a two-inch relief of two faces and a hand, baked it until it was hard, molded pieces of leather over the faces, and painted them with shoe polish and bear lard. Using a piece of wood I found behind the house, I fashioned a crutch to fit the hand. For the background, I made a mosaic out of eggshells, forming the continent of Africa on one side and a small globe on the other. I titled this mixed-media artwork "In a Broken World" and saved my money to get it framed in a shadowbox relief frame.

When I began reading library books about Black history on my own, I was not only educating myself but unconsciously feeding my soul. I became particularly enamored with the books of James Baldwin, who seemed to perfectly capture what it must have felt like to be Black in America during the 1950s and 60s. While he wrote from a viewpoint that was unapologetically Black, he projected a sense of open-mindedness that resonated with me. I particularly enjoyed *Go Tell It on the Mountain* because it brought all the issues that most concerned me together in one book: corporal punishment, religion, sexuality, and Black culture.

I had a much different opinion of *Uncle Tom's Cabin*. I appreciated the important role the book played in strengthening the abolitionist movement in the Northern states prior to the Civil War and understood how dated books written in a previous era can feel, but the way the characters were written still bothered me. The little white girl, Eva, acts so entitled and condescending toward Tom, the Black slave who saved her from drowning. Everything seems to revolve around this spoiled little girl, and the fact that a grown man must spend his life catering to the needs of someone so young registered as an injustice to me. Why is no attention paid to what Tom wants or what his goals and dreams are? The Black characters Harriet Beecher Stowe describes are basically walking stereotypes, and the ones who get portrayed in the best light are the "good Christian" characters like Tom, who in retrospect I believe suffered from something like the alien-self disorder Na'im Akbar described. Stowe's book may have garnered sympathy for Blacks among nineteenth-century white Northerners, but it simply didn't align with the way I saw Black people. Blackness to me was bold, beautiful, and empowered.

As many hours as I devoted to shaping my younger siblings' minds, I spent just as much time caring for their bodies. Because I was conscious of how they were being viewed and "othered" by the residents of our small white town, I went out of my way to make sure they were well kept and well dressed in an effort to dismantle stereotypes. If one of their noses started to run while I was shopping for groceries, I wiped it immediately. If one of their pants had a hole in the knees, I mended it as soon as I could. I was determined that, on my watch at least, no one would ever find a reason to see them as somehow being beneath them.

Keeping their skin healthy was a challenge. In Montana, the winters were long, cold, and dry, which meant "ashy" skin was even more of a problem than usual. I applied lotion to my siblings' skin at least once a day—several times a day for Zach—and I wouldn't have even considered leaving the house without a bottle on my person. I'm not talking about the watered-down kind so common in white households, either. I made sure Ruthanne ordered thicker, more effective moisturizers made from cocoa butter or shea butter from the local food co-op, because the St. Ives lotion found at the local drugstore was useless.

When it came to taking care of my siblings' hair, I had a steep learning curve. One of the biggest hurdles was the fact that none of the stores in town carried any Black hair products. The biggest shampoo companies design products meant to be used on straight European hair, and most of the information they provide about how to take care of that type of hair is flat-out wrong when applied to Black hair. Most of the shampoos found on grocery store shelves do far more harm to Black hair than good, stripping it of its natural oils and drying it out so badly it causes "breakage."

Unaware of this fact, many white parents who adopt Black or biracial children often cause tremendous damage to their children's hair. Because this is so common, they can expect any Black women they might pass on the street to give their children's hair a long careful look. If it's found to be wanting—chopped off or unkempt—the white parents should also expect to be given a hard side-eye. Such scrutiny is warranted: poorly maintained hair can be a great source of angst for Black children, making them more likely to suffer from low self-esteem and have a much harder time being accepted.

From reading about Black hair in library books, I learned that Black hairstyles are under-braided, not over-braided, so I initially concentrated on giving Esther plaits and cornrows. Unable to find any books that included braiding tutorials, I studied photographs of Black women in *Sports Illustrated* and learned how to style Esther's hair through much practice. As a budding artist, I was used to working with my hands and using photographs in books as inspiration. With regular repetition, I found I could braid hair the same way I saw it done in magazines.

After all, who else was going to do it? There wasn't a Black hairstylist within one hundred and fifty miles of our house—and even if there had been, Larry and Ruthanne weren't about to pay someone else to style their kids' hair. Ruthanne had always cut Larry and Josh's hair herself using scissors, and she did the same for Ezra, whose hair was loosely curled on top and straight in the back and around the sides. But she grew frustrated by my other siblings' "difficult" hair and was relieved that I enjoyed cutting and styling it.

Using clippers to cut Zach and Izaiah's hair, I quickly mastered the flat-top fade, the classic look of the early 1990s with its clean, boxy shape. Izaiah liked getting a bald fade with a part cut into the side, even though Ruthanne thought it looked "silly" and would try to mess it up by rubbing his head whenever she saw him. When I was cutting Zach and Izaiah's hair, Ezra would sometimes sit on the stairs and sulk, complaining that he didn't have a "fancy" cut like his brothers. To appease him, I tried to cut his hair with clippers several times, but it didn't work very well and he and I quickly got discouraged.

I'd gained some confidence working with Zach and Izaiah's hair, but Esther's hair was much more challenging. Some friends of Larry and Ruthanne's in Libby had adopted a Black baby a couple of years before Esther was born and, knowing how interested I was in Black culture, they'd asked me if I'd like to style her hair. I was happy to do it, so I'd already had a bit of practice by the time Esther's hair was long enough to braid. As soon as Esther had an inch of hair to work with when she was ten or eleven months old, I started moisturizing and styling it with the Luster's Pink Hair Lotion I'd ordered in the mail, but she was very tender-headed, so the days I washed her hair and detangled it were her least favorite.

Thanks to my prior experience, I was also aware of the effects of "shrinkage," the natural tendency for virgin Black hair to coil and appear much shorter than it actually is, especially in humid weather. Black hair that's six inches long can appear as short as two inches in length when it's coiled. Shrinkage isn't bad per se—it's actually a sign of healthy hair—but it's often perceived as such by a white culture that associates long hair with femininity and beauty. Nearly all the classically beautiful women portrayed in Western children's lore—in Walt Disney movies, that would be Cinderella, Snow White, Princess Jasmine, and Belle—have long, flowing hair. Tiana, the first Black princess portrayed in a Disney film, released four years after Larry and Ruthanne adopted Esther, hardly ever wore her hair out, and she definitely wasn't wearing an Angela Davis Black Power afro at any point in the movie.

To help Esther avoid shrinkage, I braided her hair in a variety of styles. The first time I styled her hair, I had her sit in a chair while I stood above her, but the angle wasn't right, so I moved her to the floor as I sat on the couch with her head between my legs. I moved her head from one knee to the other while I worked, but she would still fall asleep from time to time. When she woke after I'd finished, she ran to look at herself in the mirror, smiling from ear to ear and swinging her new braids back and forth while I told her how pretty she was. Sometimes I strung beads in various patterns in her braids. Other times I used ribbons that matched her dress. I learned how to do two-strand twists and part her hair in a variety of geometric patterns. Her favorite hairstyle was cornrows with beads, which pleased me because underhand braids such as these held better and looked neater than the overhand French braids Ruthanne had let me wear as a child. Styling Black hair is a labor-intensive process, but braiding Esther's hair was always a great source of joy for me.

At the time, I was so focused on taking care of Esther I didn't realize the extent to which I was also performing an act of rebellion against Larry and Ruthanne and their decree against braiding my own hair once I turned twelve, thanks to the passage from the Bible (1 Peter 3:3) discouraging personal adornment. Ruthanne was particularly opposed to Esther's hair being braided in "elaborate" and "worldly" ways that were "too fancy" and "vain"—until she realized how fortunate she was to be getting help from me and saw how much time these braids saved us when detangling Esther's hair. Esther had a habit of rubbing the back of her head on her mattress when she slept, so if her hair wasn't braided, it would always tangle in the back.

To help Esther see how beautiful her natural hair was—and give her something to read beyond the Bible and Grandma Schertel's books about Br'er Rabbit—I made her a homemade book titled *Ebony Tresses*. Ruthanne had convinced me that while I was a good artist, I wasn't much of a writer, so I asked her to help me turn some of my thoughts into poetry. "My hair is powerful, coiled, and comely," we wrote in the book. "Glistening with oils and sculpted with care." The book included full-color illustrations I drew of Esther wearing her favorite natural hairstyles and a paper doll that looked like her and had six hairstyle options, allowing her to change the doll's hair whenever she pleased.

Styling my siblings' hair undoubtedly deepened my connection to them. The many hours I spent cutting and braiding their hair not only strengthened our bond but also awakened a part of me I'd never been allowed to express. In the process of doing something I enjoyed (styling Black hair) for those I loved (my brothers and sister), I felt like I was free, free from the confinement and oppression of the household I grew up in and free to be myself, if only in those moments.

Chapter Eleven

Million Man March

WHILE SERVING AS COUNTY COMMISSIONER, Larry traveled to Washington, DC, to attend the National Prayer Breakfast, an annual event that celebrates the importance of prayer and faith in our lives, and there he met Merle Morgan. When Merle told him he was looking for help with the fine-art greeting card company he ran with his wife, Edita von Uslar-Gleichen, Larry mentioned that I was a budding artist and might be available to work as an assistant. The two of them worked out a deal, the exact details of which I was never privy to, that involved me working for the Morgans and staying with them at their home in Arlington, Virginia, for two months when I was seventeen.

I was excited to learn about the business side of art publishing from someone who'd managed to create a successful career for herself doing it. Turning watercolors she'd made of well-known Washington monuments and buildings into calendars, posters, and greeting cards, Edita had become especially popular with politicians on Capitol Hill.

The focus of my artwork at the time was mixed-media collage. Living in an area where good paints were impossible to buy, I relied on a variety of other materials: thread, recycled paper, animal skins, whatever I could find. I entered my best pieces in competitions at the county fair. Grand champions earned five dollars, blue ribbons two dollars, and reds a dollar, but even though I won plenty of ribbons, this income stream never added up to very much.

I was looking forward to seeing how Edita made a living as an artist, but when I arrived in DC, I discovered that my role wouldn't be limited to the art publishing business but also included being a nanny and a cook. Some days I delivered greeting cards to the offices of senators and members of Congress but I was just as likely to be asked to entertain the Morgans' four little kids. Living in a community full of rich white people for the first time in my life, I felt like a second-class citizen. I was the help. Despite the hard work and long hours—I once had to work twenty-three hours in a row!—I loved being in DC and longed to see and do as much as I possibly could while I was there. Unfortunately, the only time I managed to get out of the Morgans' house was to deliver greeting cards with Merle or help Edita with the shopping.

While I'd been educating my younger siblings about Black history and culture, the name of one university kept popping up in my research. When you consider the many fine historically Black colleges and universities (HBCUs) in the United States, Howard University always comes at or near the top of the list. Its alumni directory reads like a Who's Who of the world's best and brightest in law (Vernon Jordan, Thurgood Marshall), literature (Ta-Nehisi Coates, Zora Neale Hurston, Toni Morrison), politics (Stokely Carmichael, David Dinkins, Andrew Young), music (Sean Combs, Roberta Flack, Crystal Waters), and acting (Anthony Anderson, Ossie Davis, Taraji P. Henson).

In a speech given to Howard's graduating class on May 7, 2016, President Barack Obama called the university "a centerpiece of African American intellectual life and a central part of our larger American story." He continued, "This institution has been the home of many firsts: The first Black Nobel Peace Prize winner. The first Black Supreme Court justice. But its mission has been to ensure those firsts were not the last. Countless scholars, professionals, artists, and leaders from every field received their training here. The generations of men and women who walked through this yard helped reform our government, cure disease, grow a Black middle class, advance civil rights, shape our culture."

For anyone as interested in the Black experience as I'd become, how could I possibly take a trip to Washington, DC, without visiting the campus of Howard University? But when I expressed my desire to spend an afternoon there, the Morgans noticeably cringed. "Oh, we can't let you go there," Merle said. "It's in a very dangerous area." He described it as being in an "inner city" neighborhood, code language that meant "Black, poor, and violent."

Coming from northwest Montana, I wasn't intimidated by the idea of venturing into so-called bad neighborhoods. Where I grew up, you took your life in your own hands every time you wandered off the beaten path in the fall. Hunters would drink beer and drive their trucks into the mountains to "road hunt," looking for something—*anything*—to shoot. When Merle told me that he couldn't let me venture into a bad neighborhood all by myself, what he was really saying was that I was a white girl and therefore shouldn't visit parts of town that were predominately Black. That he may have been more concerned about my gender than the color of my skin didn't take the sting out of his comment. His attitude was in keeping with the times. A verdict had recently been announced in the O. J. Simpson murder trial, and the racial tension it had dredged up still lingered. For its entire ten months, the trial shined a spotlight on the country's racial dysfunction. The case was so divisive, President Bill Clinton was briefed on what sort of security measures would be put in place should the verdict incite riots.

Amidst this racially charged climate, Louis Farrakhan, the leader of the Nation of Islam, urged Black men from all over the country to come to DC and gather on the National Mall on October 16, 1995, for what would become known as the Million Man March. The event's keynote speaker, Farrakhan spoke for two hours to one of the largest gatherings of Black people in American history. Some of Black America's most influential figures, including Maya Angelou, Rosa Parks, Martin Luther King III, Cornel West, Jesse Jackson, Stevie Wonder, and Marion Barry, also spoke that day.

In the many speeches that were given over the course of the ten-hour-long event, several themes emerged, namely atonement, reconciliation, and responsibility. The audience responded by exhibiting an unprecedented display of unity and love. Men from every part of the country and all walks of life could be seen hugging, laughing, and crying. Toward the end of the day, Minister

Farrakhan asked members of the audience to pledge to take responsibility for their own actions and an active role in improving the
Black community. In the immediate aftermath of the March, nearly
two million Black men registered to vote and the NAACP enjoyed
a surge in membership.

The March received attention from news outlets around the
world, and in words and images they relayed the almost church-
like atmosphere that prevailed during the gathering. There was
no smoking or drinking. Not a single fight took place. No one
got arrested. Everyone cleaned up after themselves. Many of the
attendees fasted. Others spent much of their time praying.

When reflecting on that historic day, many of those who
attended the event describe having gotten goosebumps. Sadly, I
never got to experience that feeling myself. During dinner with
the Morgans the night before the March, I voiced my intention of
going downtown the next day to join the event, even if that meant
observing from the fringes. As upset as I'd been about not getting
to see Howard University, I'd been given a second chance to be
involved with a uniquely Black experience and I felt compelled
to participate and support it somehow. I was hungry to be part of
something that was bold and beautiful, something revolutionary,
something historic. Simply hearing Maya Angelou or Rosa Parks
speak would have been a dream fulfilled!

My enthusiasm had little effect on the Morgans. Edita just
sighed and shrugged her shoulders, as if to say she wanted no
part in the discussion. Merle did most of the talking, telling me
he simply couldn't allow me to go because he and his wife were
responsible for my safety and they were scared of the trouble such
a gathering might cause.

Sequestered in this way, I escaped into the pages of any books
I could get my hands on. Having gained an appreciation for books
about Black history and culture while reading to my siblings, I
now gravitated toward them on my own.

Reading *The Autobiography of Miss Jane Pittman* provided me
with some much-needed solace. Because the narrator is a 110-year-
old Black woman, I would never know what it was like to walk
in her shoes, but I could still relate to aspects of her struggle. I

certainly wasn't enslaved, as Miss Pittman had been as a little girl, but it wouldn't have been too much of a stretch to call me an indentured servant to the Morgans (and to Larry and Ruthanne before them). I was dependent upon them for the food I ate and the bed I slept in, and if I quit working before I'd fulfilled my obligation to them, I'd have no way of getting home. Larry wasn't buying my return plane ticket until Merle had paid him for my services, and Merle wasn't paying Larry until I'd done my time.

Miss Pittman's plight and her perseverance resonated with me. I knew what it was like to be a child and have to work as hard as an adult, and how it felt to be used and abused. I also understood the pain that comes from being treated like less than a full human being—mostly on the basis of my gender rather than my perceived race—and the fortitude required to fight this sort of injustice. At the end of the book, when Miss Pittman joined the civil rights movement and dedicated herself to fighting for social justice, I knew that's what I wanted to do with my own life someday.

A more academic but no less influential book I read while living with the Morgans was *Beyond Charity: The Call to Christian Community Development*, which I'd found in the Christian bookstore in Libby before I'd left. It appealed to me because it addressed the two most important aspects of my life: religion and race. The book argued that the current approach taken by those considered to be good Christians (mostly white) when addressing the plight of disadvantaged communities (mostly Black) had failed. It took the wraps off the sort of cheap Christian charity I was all too familiar with, and showed how flawed and outdated the model of the "white savior" rescuing the "noble Black savage" was. It also encouraged its readers to go beyond giving sympathy (and, yes, charity), asking them to do the kind of meaningful, hands-on work that might lead to some actual change.

Beyond Charity was written by Dr. John Perkins, an older Black man who'd been raised by sharecroppers in New Hebron, Mississippi, where poverty and racial injustice were the predominant features of nearly every Black person's life. After a police officer shot and killed his older brother Clyde, seventeen-year-old Perkins fled to California, vowing never to return to Mississippi.

But in 1960, soon after his son Spencer convinced him to start going to church, he converted to Christianity and returned to his home state, where, along with his wife Vera Mae, he founded a Christian community-development ministry.

After nearly three decades of ministry work that saw the creation of several health centers, thrift stores, and churches, as well as numerous programs (including adult education and leadership development) and at least one daycare center and cooperative farm, Perkins formed the Christian Community Development Association, a network of Christians from across America committed to following the example of reconciliation provided by Jesus Christ. By moving to and living in some of the poorest neighborhoods in the country, they hoped to break down any barriers that might have existed between themselves and their neighbors.

Perkins was also active in the civil rights movement. On February 7, 1970, he was arrested while taking part in a protest march in Mendenhall, Mississippi, and taken to the Rankin County jail, where the white sheriff beat him so badly a mop had to be used to clean his blood off the floor. When his family visited him at the jail, his fourteen-year-old daughter Joanie took one look at her bloodied and beaten father and shouted, "I hate white people. I will never like them!" before running out of the room.

The experience left an equally big impression on his sixteen-year-old son Spencer, who would go on to devote his life to reconciling the racial divide in the United States. He believed that the solution to the country's race problem would not come through the law but through religion, and to that end he encouraged churches to become more inclusive, embracing people of all races. Spencer didn't just talk the talk; for more than a decade he lived in an intentional Christian community called Antioch, where white and Black families lived side by side, pooled their wages into a single bank account, and shared all their meals.

Living one house over from Spencer at Antioch was Chris Rice, a white man and the son of Christian missionaries. Together, the two men directed Reconcilers Fellowship in Jackson, Mississippi, served as coeditors of *Reconcilers* magazine, and traveled the nation preaching about reconciliation. They also coauthored *More*

Than Equals: Racial Healing for the Sake of the Gospel, another influential book I read during my time with the Morgans.

Reading *More Than Equals* was a thrilling experience for me. It laid out a clear vision of the practical yet powerful work that could be done to heal the racial divide. The authors proposed that, in absence of making reparations, white people should move back to the cities they'd fled decades earlier during the "white flight" era. As Black people in the South moved to northern cities during the Great Migration of the first half of the twentieth century, white people responded by embarking on a migration of their own, fleeing inner cities in favor of the suburbs. Their ample resources and the cities' attention to public services left with them. Rice and Perkins suggested that the white people who returned could share their financial resources with the surrounding community and create a world where Blacks and whites could live together in peace and harmony, enjoying an equal amount of privilege. While living on the East Coast, it wasn't hard for me to see that, while the civil rights movement might have accomplished the goal of giving Black Americans equal access to jobs and schools, it didn't guarantee equitable treatment for them. Anytime I left the house, I could see the difference between equality and equity and what sort of impact that had on people's lives, and it inspired me to want to help the Black community realize economic and social justice.

My admiration for this book helped me in another unexpected way. When I'd finally finished all the course work necessary to graduate from high school and it was time for me to figure out where I wanted to go to college, my decision was easy. Even though I applied to thirteen different schools, all neatly listed on an Excel spreadsheet I'd made, one stood out from all the rest. Belhaven College in Jackson, Mississippi, had friendly and personable instructors and a stellar art department. It was also a Christian school, so Larry and Ruthanne could have no complaints about my decision. But, most importantly for me, Dr. John Perkins and his son Spencer both lived in Jackson.

Chapter Twelve

Belhaven College

DIAPERS HAD BEEN HANGING from our clothesline in Montana for more than two years, but by the time I left for college in Mississippi in 1996, all my younger siblings were potty-trained—as well as walking, talking, and using utensils to feed themselves. I'd even taught Ruthanne how to braid Esther's hair and, just as importantly, helped her to see that braids were beautiful—at the very least because of their practicality. Packing up and leaving the only home I'd ever known was difficult, but not for the reasons you might think. After I'd helped raise four children from infancy, moving to Mississippi felt more like a midlife transition than a coming-of-age one and I knew that I was far too young to be feeling that way.

Before leaving Montana, I called Spencer Perkins. He'd been the first Black student ever to attend Belhaven, but it wasn't his thoughts about campus life that drew me to him. After reading *More Than Equals*, I felt such a powerful connection to him and his philosophy on racial reconciliation I asked him if he'd mentor me while I was living in Jackson.

"Why don't you come to church when you get here," he said, "and afterward we'll go to the house and talk and go from there."

After services at the Voice of Cavalry Fellowship, the church Spencer's father John founded in 1972, I went with Spencer, his wife Nancy, and their three kids to the large lot on Robinson Road where Antioch was located. The three spacious Antebellum houses on the property had been divvied up to accommodate several different families, but I spent most of my time with the Perkinses. We hit it off so well that I was soon living something of a double life. During the week, I shared a dorm room on campus with a petite ballet dancer who had blonde hair and blue eyes, and I spent an inordinate amount of time in the library; on the weekends I went to church in all-Black West Jackson and hung out with Spencer and his family.

The first time I visited Antioch, Spencer and I talked at length about one of his favorite activities (in addition to barbecuing and shooting hoops), fishing. When I asked him where I could find a shovel and set about digging worms for him, I couldn't have made him any happier if I'd handed him a million dollars.

Whenever I think about fishing, I'm always reminded of a passage from one of Grandpa Perkins' speeches in which he gave the old proverb "If you give a man a fish . . ." a decidedly new twist. "If you teach a man to fish," he said, "he may *never eat* because all that really matters is—*who owns the pond.*" As someone who'd lived through the Jim Crow era, he'd seen plenty of capable Black people denied jobs and opportunities even though they'd been "taught how to fish."

After my first visit, eating lunch at Antioch after church on Sunday became a weekly ritual. One afternoon while chatting with Spencer in the family room of his house, he asked me what sort of artwork I did. Unfortunately, I didn't have any pictures with me to show him. "I bet your art doesn't look like that," he said, pointing to a large framed print on the wall. It was a beautiful but tragic painting of a Black mother with a baby strapped to her back, picking cotton in a field.

"Actually, that's *exactly* the kind of art I do," I told him.

When he finally saw some of my pieces, his initial skepticism turned into unmitigated support. Spencer was always smiling and laughing, but he grew very serious when talking about my artwork. "You need to focus on your art," he often told me. "It's a gift."

My comfort level wasn't nearly as high on campus—at least initially. I arrived there looking like I'd just stepped off the set of *Little House on the Prairie* or escaped from a religious cult. Wearing a homemade ankle-length dress and no makeup, I walked into the cafeteria the first day of classes and was greeted by a picture as strange to my eyes as the sight of me must have been to everyone else: the cafeteria was completely segregated, with all the tables occupied by white students except for one on the far side of the room. At the start of my freshman year only 5 percent of Belhaven's student body was Black, and most of them could be found hanging out at the "Black table" at some point during the day.

As I walked through the cavernous room buzzing with chatter, my heart nearly skipped a beat. Everyone looked so *normal* compared to me. I could see it on their faces whenever they glanced my way: Who the heck is *this*? Searching for a reassuring face and not finding one, I carried my tray through the gauntlet of white faces until I arrived at the Black table in the corner. That I shouldn't sit there because I was born to white parents and all the table's occupants were Black didn't occur to me. A true fish out of water, more than two thousand miles from where I'd been born, I'd gravitated to where I felt most comfortable, and, after the initial awkwardness wore off, that's how the people sitting there made me feel.

Looking back on this moment, I wonder if the students at that table were so nice because they felt sorry for me. I was dressed like a peasant, after all, and I obviously had no friends. Regardless of their motivations, they were incredibly kind to me, almost sympathetic. When they started talking about the Black Student Association (BSA) meeting scheduled for that afternoon and I asked where and when it was, they let me know the location and the time and only shrugged and smiled when I expressed a desire to join them.

It was the first BSA meeting of the year, which meant dues needed to be paid and all the leadership positions filled. Excited to join my first student organization, I secured my membership with a five-dollar bill and watched as members were voted into office. We elected a president, vice president, treasurer, and secretary that afternoon, but it quickly became clear that no one wanted to be the historian.

There was a long, awkward moment of silence. Finally, I raised my hand and started walking toward the front of the room just as I'd seen the previous candidates do, and as I did, I was greeted with barely muffled snickering.

Even the newly elected president, Winston Trotter, couldn't stop himself from laughing. "Hold up," he said. "Why are you here, and why do you want to be the historian?"

Being raised with no sense of humor whatsoever, I delivered an overly earnest speech explaining how passionate I was about Black culture, how I'd always felt a connection with Blackness, and how deeply I cared about my siblings' future. My enthusiasm caught everyone in the room a little off guard.

"But what exactly do you know about Black history?" someone asked.

The rambling dissertation that followed encompassed all the Black historical figures I admired most and was so long-winded Winston had to cut me off. "We need to wrap this meeting up, so let's just go ahead and vote."

Running unopposed, I won in a landslide.

As the BSA's historian, my main responsibility was documenting all the club's activities, but I took the role much more seriously than that. I wanted to educate people about why BSAs were so important to have on campuses. I also took it upon myself to inspire my fellow members by continually reminding them about pivotal moments in Black history. To this end, I revised the historian's duties to include preparing a brief Black history lesson for each meeting and giving a historical presentation during mandatory chapel every Tuesday of Black History Month. Rewarding my commitment and knowledge, my fellow BSA members reelected me to the position all four years I was in college.

My affiliation with the BSA made it impossible to ignore the many issues confronting Belhaven's Black students, and, as time passed, I grew more determined to do something about them. I helped create the first African American history course ever taught there, and it remains a part of the curriculum to this day. I worked with the college's president to increase the recruitment and retention of Black students, and by the time I graduated, the Black population on campus had increased to nearly 15 percent. And I helped organize a conference to discuss "racial reconciliation"—the restoration of peace between Black and white communities I'd read about in *Beyond Charity* and *More Than Equals*–that paired Belhaven, which was historically white, with nearby Tougaloo College, which was historically Black.

While I was at Belhaven, I also developed a radar for anything that seemed inequitable to or dismissive of the college's Black students and committed myself to changing it. For instance, I was just about to settle into a three-day weekend in the middle of January my freshman year, when I looked at my Biology syllabus and saw that class was scheduled for Monday. What was going on? Surely a college wouldn't schedule classes on Martin Luther King Jr. Day, would it? Wasn't it a federal holiday? It had to be a mistake, right?

I brought all my questions with me to the office of Dr. Roger Parrott, Belhaven's president, first thing Monday morning. Dr. Parrott informed me that Belhaven had never given its students and staff that day off. I was surprised to hear this, but anyone who knew Mississippi better than I did wouldn't have been. While the federal government made MLK Day a national holiday in 1983, it wasn't recognized on the state level by all fifty states until 2000. One of the states that initially dragged its feet was Mississippi. When it finally did come on board, it managed to rob the day of much of its power by giving equal billing to the leader of the Confederate Army during the Civil War, making the third Monday in January a holiday with a name as awkward to say as it is to celebrate: "Martin Luther King's and Robert E. Lee's Birthdays." While post offices and banks had no choice, schools and businesses were given some latitude when it came to observing the holiday.

Fortunately, Dr. Parrott was new to the college, shockingly young, and very broad-minded, and he let me know that he was open to the idea of recognizing MLK Day on campus if a consensus among the student body could be obtained. That's all I needed to hear. I wrote a petition and shamelessly pushed it in front of everyone I could find, and within a month I'd acquired enough signatures to make the holiday an official celebration on campus the following year. And not just as a vacation day. In keeping with the King Holiday and Service Act, which President Clinton made a law on August 23, 1994, I worked with the administration to organize a day of service. During the first year the holiday was observed at Belhaven, more than two hundred and fifty (mostly white) students worked on Habitat for Humanity homes in West Jackson, which, in a city that remained nearly as segregated as it was in the 1960s, was known as "the Black side of town."

My growing connection to Black culture was also apparent in my artwork, which, like the pieces I'd shown Spencer, focused on Black faces and figures and was unashamedly pro-Black. The images almost exclusively depicted aspects of the Black experience I felt were beautiful and empowering. Tired of seeing white people taking center stage all the time, I wanted to use my art skills to offer a more equitable and compassionate treatment of Black culture. Two such pieces—one done on elk hide ("Irma Leah"), the other on deer hide ("Tatters of Time")—helped me pay for my first year of college after I won the national Tandy Leather Art Scholarship. Another landed me an exhibition in New York City after Fabian Uzoh gave a woman from the United Nations a very compelling description of the piece about the Rwandan genocide I'd made in high school. She called me to say that she wanted to display it in the lobby of the UN headquarters, saying it perfectly captured the type of empathy they wanted to promote about the Rwandan refugee situation. As a financially strapped college student, I couldn't afford to fly there for the reception, but apparently the staff was so moved by the piece that they renewed the usual three-month loan period four times. When the piece was returned to me after a year away, I donated it to Tougaloo College, where it remains today.

My predilection for painting Black figures didn't sit well with some of the white students in my art classes, who often made fun of me for it. If I wanted to focus on human rights and injustice, a few of them told me, I should paint Irish people. I got so sick of being pressured in this way I actually tried painting white people a couple times, but it never looked or felt right to me. I had difficulty seeing highlights and reflections on pale skin. Even when the models in my figure drawing class were white, they came out looking Black on my sketch pad. In the end, I embraced the talents I had and stopped trying to please other people or help them understand me.

Some of my professors noted that, unlike most freshmen majoring in art, my body of work already had a clear focus. That didn't do me much good as I looked for a place in North Jackson (read: the white part of town) to display my artwork during my second semester at Belhaven. When none of the art galleries there took an interest in my work, I visited the Smith Robertson Museum and Cultural Center in West Jackson. Originally the site of Jackson's first public school for Black children—the novelist Richard Wright graduated from there in 1925—Smith Robertson was enjoying a second life as a museum that celebrated the art and experiences of Black Mississippians.

Turry Flucker, the museum's curator, gave me a tour of the building. When I mentioned that I was looking for a place to display my artwork and had brought some slides with me, he was kind enough to ask the receptionist to set up a projector on the table in his office. Soon after we sat down, he broke step with the formality he'd previously displayed. "I understand you want to show your art here," he said, "but we're a Black museum and you're white. What could you possibly show me that I would be interested in?"

His words stung, but I got it. All he could see was the color of my skin. I dropped my slides into the projector carousel. "Let me show you."

The first slide showed one of my signature pieces, "AFRIKA," and after seeing it, Turry leaned back in his chair and said, "Wow." When I got to the end of my ten-slide presentation, he surprised me with his enthusiasm. "So," he said, "we're going to need at least fifteen mid- to large-sized pieces for the show."

Two months later, a mixed-media exhibit by Rachel Doležal made its debut at the Smith Robertson Museum and Cultural Center. At the opening reception, the educator and artist Jolivette Anderson read her poem "Pieces of You, Pieces of Me," which was inspired by "AFRIKA" and made me cry. I didn't sell any paintings at that show, but it was a rewarding experience nevertheless. The audience was roughly half white and half Black and everyone was a bit out of their comfort zone, but they were all together under a single roof with a single purpose and that's one of the first steps on the road to healing race relations.

As I got more involved with the BSA, campus activism, and my artwork, the more Afrocentric my appearance became. I started wearing my hair in *Poetic Justice* box braids and sporting dashikis and African-patterned dresses. I thought the patterns and embroidery of these clothes were beautiful, and in the Mississippi heat, the fabric did a good job of keeping you cool without being immodest. Wearing this style of clothing made me feel more confident and more beautiful.

As a result, most people didn't know what to make of me. "So, what are you?" I was asked all too often. My responses tended to be awkward, tortuous, strained. Because I didn't fit neatly into a box and didn't know how to articulate who I was or how I felt in a way that made sense to people, I'd end up bouncing from one story to the next until I'd told them nearly *everything* about my life. I'd usually start off by saying that Larry and Ruthanne were white before describing how I was instinctively drawn to Black aesthetics, culture, and history, and then I would mention my siblings and the racial justice work I was currently doing.

These long, rambling answers satisfied very few people—and seemed to bore the pants off most. You know how when most people ask how you are, they don't really want to know the answer? They just want you to say, "Fine." That's how these encounters felt. People just wanted me to say I was Black or white. They didn't want to hear, in all its boring complexity, about the journey to self-identification I was on. I could see it in the way they shifted their weight from one foot to the other and stopped making eye contact with me while I was talking. They were tired of listening. They were done having this conversation, and before long I was, too.

I stopped volunteering information about my identity to people unless I knew them really well. It became much easier for me to let them make assumptions about me. I noticed how much more relaxed and comfortable Black people who assumed I was Black were around me. The minute I corrected them, the comfort level we'd enjoyed just a moment before disappeared, so I stopped doing it and started letting them identify me however they wanted to. If they identified me as a light-skinned Black woman or a mixed-race woman, which they frequently did, I didn't mind.

My laissez-faire attitude toward my racial identification was much more difficult to maintain when it came to filling out applications and medical forms. Prior to my departure from Montana, I generally felt obligated to choose WHITE, CAUCASIAN, or EUROPEAN AMERICAN when I was asked to check a box identifying my race. If the form allowed me to choose more than one category, I would also check NATIVE AMERICAN because of what I'd been told about my great-grandmother's ancestry.

When I was living in Mississippi, I felt like I should continue checking WHITE on such forms. According to other people's perception of racial categories, that was the truth—even though I'd begun to feel like that description was increasingly misrepresentative of who I was and how I was being treated by others. I would sometimes check OTHER when that was an available option, as a way of clarifying the difference between me and the distinctive breed of white people who lived in the Deep South. If providing an answer was optional, I would avoid making a selection altogether. The more I learned about race in college—that it has no genetic underpinnings, but is a social construct—the less obligated I felt to check WHITE. Some of my biracial friends would play around with these forms, alternately checking WHITE, BLACK, or OTHER, just to see how it would affect the way people responded to them. I thought it was a clever idea and a useful sociological experiment, particularly as I grew more ethnically indeterminate in my appearance.

The increasingly Afrocentric look I sported invited all sorts of criticism. Some said that my identification with Black culture was "just a phase," while others, mostly white students, told me I shouldn't dress the way I did because they felt it was disingenuous or just looked silly. While walking through the cafeteria one day, proudly wearing a dashiki and a headwrap, I passed a table full of white girls and heard one of them say, "Who does she think she is, wearing all that stupid African shit? She's not Black!"

As I continued to make my way toward the Black table, my friend Nikki, who was a member of the BSA and a star of the women's basketball team, wheeled around and confronted the girl. "You're sitting there talking about Rachel's outfit while you're probably getting a yeast infection from wearing those skintight jeans," she said loud enough for everyone within twenty feet to hear. "Besides, Rachel's a lot Blacker than I am, so deal with it!"

A smile took over my face. This was the first time anyone had recognized and defended how I felt. Hearing Nikki say that made me feel good, whole, *understood*, like I'd finally found my place in the world.

Chapter Thirteen

Hair II

THE VOICE OF CAVALRY FELLOWSHIP, which Spencer had introduced me to and which I regularly attended, had a Black pastor and a white pastor. The congregation was mixed as well, with
approximately two to three Black people for every white person.
Paying as much attention to racial reconciliation as it did the basic
tenets of Christianity, the church served as a bridge from where
I came from, fanatically studying the Bible, to where I wanted to
go, promoting racial and social justice.

Unlike the sleek modern megachurches of today, VOC was
housed in a plain-looking building in West Jackson. What it lacked
in glitz and glamor it more than made up for in heart and soul. It
may not have had any big-screen TVs or a deluxe PA system, but
it did have a dedicated flock and an exuberant gospel choir. The
congregation would encourage anyone in the choir who came up
to the microphone, shouting, "All right now!" or "Sing it!"

Members of the congregation were also encouraged to clap—
whether they possessed a sense of a rhythm or not. This often led
to some humorous moments because, as I soon discovered, Black
people and white people in the South tend to clap a little differently. Whereas Black people are inclined to clap on the second
and fourth beats of every note, producing a sound that aligns
with the music, white people have a habit of clapping on one
and three, which sounds at best sluggish and at worst jarring.
Some musicians, including Justin Bieber, Neil Young, and Bruce
Springsteen, have gotten so thrown off by people in the audience

clapping on one and three during their concerts they've had to stop mid-song to educate them. While playing "Come by Me" for a clapping-challenged audience in England several years back, the famed singer and pianist Harry Connick Jr. found what has to be the best solution to this problem when he added an extra bar to each note during his piano solo, forcing the audience's clapping to land on the right beats. During services at VOC, I found myself instinctively clapping on two and four. Not everyone was so fortunate, but the clapping always sorted itself out, with no one ever feeling isolated or ashamed.

Some members of the congregation, myself included, felt like there was more energy waiting to be released beyond singing and clapping, so we decided to form a praise dance team. Dancing wasn't a part of my life when I was growing up. Simply walking in a "provocative manner" was forbidden, so dancing with swaying hips and gyrating thighs was out of the question. The closest I ever saw someone in my family get to dancing occurred while I was accompanying Larry on a drive into town. When a song he liked came on the oldies station, he started lurching his neck forward and backward in a robot-like fashion not unlike the dancers in The Bangles' "Walk Like an Egyptian" video.

I soon saw the energy I devoted to the VOC dance team pay off, when we began to receive invitations to perform at venues besides the church, including Belhaven's chapel. The "Reconciliation Dance" was a crowd favorite and one that often moved people to tears. One of the other members of the dance team, LaShawnda Wilson, wore a white leotard and white skirt and I wore a black leotard and black skirt, and at the end of the dance we wrapped our arms together and combined our hands in a single fist as a symbol of Black and white uniting in love.

Donna Pollard, a thirty-two-year-old Black woman who'd worked at VOC for five years, was the dance troupe's organizer and choreographer. I became her assistant, often helping her make the costumes for our performances, and as I did I began to spend more and more time in West Jackson. That I felt so at home there, coupled with an awkward living situation on campus—my roommate started skipping classes and sleeping for days on end after she injured her hip and saw her dream of dancing professionally come to a crashing halt—encouraged me to move to West Jackson after my freshman year. That summer, I shared a bed with a VOC intern at Antioch in a room cooled only by an incredibly noisy fan. Before the start of my second year at Belhaven, Donna and her husband Sam offered to rent me a spare bedroom in their home, not too far from Antioch. Sam even found me an orange 1977 Toyota Corolla that only cost five hundred dollars. With its seats ripped to shreds by mice, it was a real "hoopty," but I sewed some new seat covers for it and it never failed to get me to and from campus. Better still, it was all mine.

Many American towns are divided in two by railroad tracks—there's usually a "right side" and a "wrong side"—and Jackson was no different. The railroad tracks separated rich from poor and white from Black, helping to enforce the unofficial segregation that still lingered there. I chose to live on the poor Black side of that line. I was breaking the color barrier by living in a Black neighborhood, but I didn't move there because I was a white missionary. I wasn't trying to be a "white ally" or a "white savior." I wasn't trying to make some sort of contrived social statement. Quite the opposite. My decision to live there felt natural and organic. I was simply moving to where I felt most comfortable, a place where I could be myself.

Rich white people considered the neighborhood in which Antioch and the Pollards' house was located to be "the bad part of town," but I never saw it that way. To me, it always felt like home. I was rarely able to walk more than a block or two without bumping into someone I knew. By the time I moved off campus I knew more people in West Jackson than I did at Belhaven. As a consequence, I felt safer there than I did in the white part of town, where I was unknown and few people cared about me.

The needs of the community I'd moved to quickly became my own. One of the biggest concerns was that too many young kids were hanging out on the street unsupervised. Typically they were being raised by single mothers who had to work all day and couldn't afford to pay for after-school care. This phenomenon was especially prevalent and troubling near West Capitol Street, which tended to attract people who were a little shady or down on their luck. Drug dealers, pimps, prostitutes, and homeless people frequented the area at all hours. That nearly all of them were Black gave West Capitol a reputation for being a place where white people would be wise not to go.

Young children who lived in this neighborhood faced a variety of perils, ranging from not being able to get their homework done to being placed in life-threatening situations. When I heard that Capitol Street Ministries provided a food pantry and some other basic services, I decided to start an after-school program in conjunction with it. The service I offered was perfectly matched with a need, and within just a few weeks I was looking after twenty-five elementary-school-age kids. I helped them with their homework. I organized games for them to play. I handed out snacks. I taught them art. I even redid a few two-strand twists or braids that had gotten messed up during the school day. I was a nanny, babysitter, and big sister once again.

The volunteer work I did in West Jackson, when combined with the racial justice work I was doing on campus, my Afrocentric appearance, and my growing appreciation of Black historical figures such as Malcolm X and Assata Shakur, led even more people, both Black and white, to assume that I was a mixed-race or light-skinned Black woman, that I was an albino, or that as a child I'd been adopted and raised by a Black family. They stopped identifying and relating to me as a white person, and because I was untroubled by the idea, was in fact *pleased* by it, I didn't bother to correct them.

Being seen as Black also made social interactions in the community I lived in much easier. Black people related to me in a more relaxed way. Instead of putting up a wall and thinking of me as an outsider, they treated me as a member of the community, part of the family. I would laugh at jokes told at the expense of white people and lodge some pretty fierce critiques about white culture myself. I didn't act scared, stiff, or too privileged to relate, all telltale signs of being a white outsider. I blended in, not by wearing a disguise or being deceitful, but simply by being myself. It felt less like I was adopting a new identity and more like I was unveiling one that had been there all along. Finally able to embrace my true self, I allowed the little girl I'd colored with a brown crayon so long ago to emerge.

As happy as I was to be seen as Black, it was still confusing, awkward, painful, and isolating for me at times—because who was I going to talk to about what felt like a major life transition? One of the few people I felt comfortable discussing my rapidly changing identity with was Donna. As I tried to reconcile how I felt, how I was born, and how I was being viewed by others, I had numerous conversations with her about race and identity. We would stay up late and talk, conversations that often ended in tears. It was Donna who I chose to be with the night of my twenty-first birthday. Determined to get drunk, I brought home a bottle of Manischewitz, which I was familiar with from celebrating Passover every year, thanks to Ruthanne's Zionist obsession, and Donna sat with me while I sipped from it. We talked deep into the night, but I only got about a third of the way through the bottle before I felt sick and went to bed.

A deeply religious woman, Donna would mention certain passages from the Bible as a way of suggesting that my feelings about my racial identity might just be a phase, but she also seemed to understand when I told her that I didn't feel white and that I felt a stronger connection to Black people than I did to white people. She often told me that when it came to hairstyles and clothing, "to copy is to compliment," an assessment I took as permission to embrace the exterior expressions of my feelings. I could live with this appraisal of my journey, but I also feared it, as I realized that very few people in the world knew me as well as Donna did and that my evolving appearance could be seen by others as cultural appropriation.

Cultural appropriation is a tricky subject. It's often viewed as one of the great sins of our times—an indefensible act of racism—as it typically involves people from a majority ethnic group borrowing cultural elements from a minority ethnic group and exploiting those elements for fun or profit. The NFL's Washington Redskins using a profile of a Native American as a team mascot is a good example, and it shouldn't be hard to understand why. Using an image of an ethnic group in the same way other teams use animals or icons turns those people into stereotypes, reeks of neocolonialism, robs that group of their intellectual property rights, and promotes racist behavior. Turning people who have suffered for generations into a brand isn't showing reverence for their culture; it's giving it the finger. As obvious as this example is, there are countless others that are less so (but no less annoying and offensive), including white musicians stealing blues riffs from Black guitar players or rapping about the trials of life on the streets.

While living in West Jackson, I dedicated no small amount of thought and reflection to understanding cultural appropriation and examining my life to ensure that I was making authentic choices, not offensive or insincere ones. When it comes to cultural appropriation, it's important to know which acts cross the line and which don't. As with many nuanced subjects built on the foundation of past wrongs, not everything that's called appropriation is false or inauthentic. Thanks to air travel, the internet, and global trade, the world has grown smaller. As it's done so, diversity has increased, and so have cultural exchanges. Without such borrowing, Americans wouldn't know the joys of eating sushi, doing yoga, or wearing a pashmina. Examining one's intent and getting permission and guidance from the cultural source is the best way to judge the appropriateness of the action. Mocking another culture is obviously wrong, but how can applauding it be viewed as anything but positive? Historically, one of the most common ways racists mocked Black culture was by wearing blackface (or attending performances by those who did), but anyone who knew me then, particularly Donna, could tell you that's not what I was doing.

When Donna and I weren't talking into the wee hours, we were educating each other on practical matters. I shared my recipes for pot roast and homemade rolls with her, and she taught some of her unique methods of hair styling to me. From the moment I'd stepped off the plane and into Jackson's airport at the start of freshman year, I'd fallen in love with all the creative braiding patterns I saw. Within a month of being in Mississippi, I'd seen nearly every version of updos, braids, twists, locs, and weaves.

One night I mentioned how beautiful I thought braids were, and Donna asked me if I'd like her to braid my hair. Up to this point, I'd been hesitant to wear my hair in more than two braids, thanks to that passage in 1 Peter 3:3 that discourages adornment of any kind and Larry and Ruthanne's insistence that it was a "falsity." Equally important was my desire before I started wearing such a culturally specific style to get permission from the Black women who knew me best.

Well, here it was.

In the entire VOC community, no one had a better reputation for doing hair than Donna. She could lay edges, braid any pattern you suggested, and apply a relaxer without burning your scalp or causing breakage to your hair. Not letting her braid my hair would have been like passing up an opportunity to discuss politics with Barack Obama.

Donna was the first person to braid my hair, and it was a seminal moment in the evolution of my identity. White girls in Mississippi simply didn't do that. At first, she just braided the back of my blonde hair in jumbo box braids, but soon I was rocking a full head of individual box braids and getting creative with them, wrapping them in scarves or wearing them in updos. Before long, I was braiding my own hair and just having Donna help me with any hair in the back I couldn't reach.

There was a beauty store in West Jackson dedicated to Black hair care products, and in it I found everything I needed to keep my braids looking good. Goldstar Beauty Supply was like Wonderland to me. Bobbles, beads, ribbons, clips, moisturizers, detangling products, gels, relaxers, waxes, hair mayonnaise, wigs, braid hair, wefted hair, weaving caps, weaving needles, weaving thread, and lighters for burning the ends of braids—Goldstar had it all.

I wore braids most of the time I was at Belhaven. To me, they were beautiful, and I felt beautiful wearing them. I also wanted to show the young Black girls I worked with at Capitol Street Ministries and those I saw at church every Sunday that all textures of hair, like all shades of Black, were beautiful. When it comes to braiding, there is no "good hair" or "bad hair," only good braiders and bad braiders. Braids are the great equalizer, leveling the playing field between women born with fine, wavy hair and those with thick, kinky hair.

One day after church, I saw Donna's five-year-old daughter Jessica running her hands through a white college intern's hair. I could see it on Jessica's face: she wasn't merely paying the intern a compliment; she was enchanted, as if her small Black fingers had found the pinnacle of beauty. Then she touched the stiff crochet braids in her own hair, and the look of rapture vanished and she hung her head.

There's a long history of European colonial powers forcing native people they've driven from lands they've conquered to cut off their hair. For some Native Americans, identity is so entwined with their hair they describe it as being a manifestation of their thoughts and an extension of themselves. They believe it should only be cut under very specific circumstances, typically mourning the loss of a loved one. This didn't stop the teachers at the boarding schools the Bureau of Indian Affairs established in the 1800s from chopping off Native American children's hair as soon as they set foot on campus. Likewise, white Christian missionaries in the colonial era often made African women cut off their braids.

This same sort of callousness has frequently been directed at Black women. In her 2006 book *From the Kitchen to the Parlor: Language and Becoming in African American Women's Hair Care*, anthropologist Lanita Jacobs-Huey hinted at the significance of Black women's hair when she described it as "a window into African American women's ethnic and gender identities." What often appears in this window doesn't bode well for the mental health of Black women. In a culture where white has long been exalted as right, naturally kinky-curly hair has been associated with unattractiveness and intractability. After being conditioned to believe this lie during the Plantation and Jim Crow eras, many Black women came to view straight hair (and everything else that was white) as being more beautiful and more closely linked to success than coiled hair. In the early part of the twentieth century, Madam C. J. Walker, a Black entrepreneur and the daughter of two former slaves, recognized the pressure Black women felt to adhere to white standards of beauty in order to survive economically and socially as an opportunity to create a commercial empire. Her "Walker System" for straightening hair was so popular she went on to become the first female—and first Black—self-made millionaire in the United States.

Walker wasn't the only entrepreneur to get rich by addressing Black women's desire—and to some extent, social need—to straighten their hair. In 1909, Garrett Morgan, the inventor of the gas mask and the three-position traffic light, set about finding a way to prevent a sewing machine's needle from burning the fabric it was working on. A chemical solution he created solved the problem. He also noticed that it made the fibers of the pony-fur cloth he used to clean his hands stand straight up. When he applied the liquid to his neighbor's curly-haired dog, it made the dog's hair so straight its owner no longer recognized it—or so the story goes. After Morgan applied the solution to his own hair and got the same result, the G. A. Morgan Hair Refining Company—and the highly lucrative (and highly damaging) lye relaxer industry—was born.

It's now estimated that more than 65 percent of all the Black women in the United States chemically straighten their hair. In her 1996 book *Skin Trade*, Ann DuCille, an English professor at Wesleyan University, suggests a reason: "Unless I have missed a few pageants along the way, the body types, the apparel, and the hairstyles of the Black women crowned Miss America or of the colored women crowned Miss America have differed little from those of the white contestants . . . We have yet to see Miss America or Black Miss Universe with an Afro or cornrows or dreadlocks."

Fortunately, over the course of the past several decades, a movement has (re)emerged that's helped Black women embrace their natural hair. Some consider it the second wave of the Natural Hair Movement from the sixties, while others refer to the trend as the Texture Movement. We're now seeing Black celebrities such as Esperanza Spalding, Solange Knowles, Janelle Monáe, Lupita Nyong'o, Viola Davis, and Tracee Ellis Ross "slaying" with their textured hair and #BlackGirlMagic. Inspired by these women, many young Black girls are starting to wear their hair naturally, sending a message to the world about how they want to be viewed and how they view themselves. Sadly, the establishment's response hasn't always been favorable.

This issue gained national attention in September 2013, when administrators at Deborah Brown Community School in Tulsa, Oklahoma, informed the parents of seven-year-old Tiana Parker that their daughter's locs violated the school's dress-code policy, which reads, "Hairstyles such as dreadlocks, afros, and other faddish styles are unacceptable." The idea of having to cut off all her hair upset Tiana so much she opted to switch schools instead. Two months later, administrators at Faith Christian Academy in Orlando, Florida, gave twelve-year-old Vanessa VanDyke a week to cut or straighten her big and bold natural hairstyle, calling it a "distraction." In 2016, Pretoria High School for Girls in South Africa banned afros and called natural Black hair styles "untidy." What sort of message do these incidents send to little Black girls?

That Donna's five-year-old daughter Jessica was so entranced with the white college intern's hair and so disappointed in her own underscored the otherness of Black hair in the same way that having strangers in Montana paw at my siblings' hair did.*

"I wish I had your hair," she said to the intern.

When the intern, clueless about what was happening to Jessica's self-esteem, thanked her and got up to leave, it sickened me. I walked over and said, "Jessica, your hair is so beautiful. I wish I had *your* hair."

Her smile returned, and she ran off to play with the other kids.

Whenever I wore braids, Jessica and the other little girls at church would smile at me and say, "You have hair just like me!" as they swung their braids back and forth. At a certain point, I began to feel that if I *didn't* wear my hair in braids I was reinforcing European beauty standards among the young girls in the community I lived in, and that was not something I wanted to support.

---

* Those looking for a positive example of a Black child responding to his own hair need look no further than President Obama in 2009 bowing down to let a five-year-old Black boy named Jacob Philadelphia touch his hair after the boy wondered if his hair was just like the president's.

Something else happened when I wore braids. People started responding to me differently. Because I truly owned the look, my hair seemed to reinforce the belief that I was a biracial or light-skinned Black woman. Because I felt Black, I liked being seen as Black, not as a white girl with braids like Bo Derek in the movie *10*. When other people assumed I was Black, it invited me to interact with them as a Black woman, which always felt perfectly natural to me.

This made for some interesting social interactions. White people often approached me and said that my hair looked like rope or yarn. They asked if I could wash it, if it hurt, if it was "real." It was annoying and frustrating, and encouraged me to avoid interacting with them as much as I possibly could.

My hair never discomfited Black people. Quite the opposite. They seemed much more relaxed in my presence when I wore braids. Many described my hair as being "so Rachel." Even when I hadn't been in the sun for a while and my skin was extra pale, they still didn't see me as white. People often told me, "You're a pretty biracial," or "You're the prettiest albino I've ever seen." Others insisted they had a family member—if not two or three—who was even lighter than I was. I lost track of how many people said something to me that affirmed that my look perfectly matched how I felt inside, and every time, I felt even more at home, as if my light skin was no longer a barrier to being seen as who I really was.

Chapter Fourteen

Adopting a New Dad I

WHILE I WAS AT BELHAVEN, I returned to Montana to see my siblings as often as I could. My visits grew increasingly awkward as time passed. People in town would stare at my braids and my dashikis as though they belonged to an alien. They didn't know what to make of me and appeared utterly perplexed whenever they saw me. As alienating as their reactions were, they were more charitable than the ones I received from Larry and Ruthanne, who were clearly embarrassed by my new look.

I was equally embarrassed by them, as the news from home was never very good. Larry had been indicted for felony theft after allegedly filing false claims for meal and mileage expenses while working as a county commissioner. After adopting the babies, he and Ruthanne had switched churches from Troy Christian Fellowship to the Yaak Community Church, which was about an hour's drive north of our house, and every Sunday Larry would "check the county roads" on his way to church. Inspecting roads and the work done by road crews was part of his job description, but, as some pointed out, those roads certainly didn't need to be inspected *every* Sunday. Nevertheless, he still billed Lincoln County for the mileage he accrued driving to and from church week after week and got reimbursed for it. The charges were eventually dropped, but the damage was done. In 1998, he lost his bid for reelection.

On another occasion, I learned that Larry had taken my dog Harold up the mountain and shot him. Harold was less than eight years old, not terribly old by dog standards, but Larry said that

Harold was hit by a car on the road below our house and his leg was broken. Larry didn't believe in spending money on animals when they got hurt or sick. For years, Harold had loyally and enthusiastically chased deer away from our gardens and barked whenever a bear raided our apple tree. Once he could no longer perform those tasks and lost his utilitarian value, Larry put a bullet in his head.

Because of such callousness, I began to grow even more distant from Larry and Ruthanne, and as I did, I found solace in all the love I received from the West Jackson community, where I lived, worshiped, and socialized. In many Black communities such as this one, it's not unusual for people to refer to each other using familial titles, even though they don't have an actual biological connection. While living with Donna and Sam Pollard, it wasn't long before I was calling her "Mom," him "Dad," and their children my brothers and sisters. I did the same with the Perkinses. I truly felt like I was part of their family, and as a way of expressing this love I called Spencer "Dad," his older sister "Aunt Joanie," her husband "Uncle Ron," Spencer's father "Grandpa Perkins," and Spencer's mother "Grandma Perkins."* Because this is a common practice in the Black community, particularly amongst regular churchgoers, the gesture was received kindly.

It also seemed perfectly natural. More than anyone I'd ever known, Spencer felt like a father to me, a notion strengthened by the fact that my biological one did not. I went to church with him and Nancy so often that some people in the community assumed I was their daughter, and the fact that Nancy was white only reinforced the idea. However, just to be clear, Spencer never would have identified me as Black. More likely, he would have called me "a different kind of white person" who was unlike most of the other white people he knew, even those at VOC.

Of all Spencer's admirable qualities, his commitment to Antioch was one of his greatest, as the community was a living embodiment of his belief that Black people and white people not only

---

* I did not, however, call Spencer's wife Nancy "Mom." That she was white may explain why neither one of us was comfortable adopting that level of familiarity with each other.

could live together in harmony but that they *should*. Ask anyone who's ever lived in a cooperative living situation what it was like, and you'll get responses that run the gamut from "Unbelievable! It was Heaven!" to "Unbelievable! It was Hell!" During the seventeen years Spencer and Chris Rice lived together at Antioch, their relationship knew incredible highs and lows and everything in between. The two men had very different styles, so challenging situations were bound to arise. After spending so much time in such close proximity, they eventually began to resent each other, both of them clinging to a list of grievances about the other and refusing to let go. By the time I'd arrived in Mississippi, they could barely stand to eat their meals at the same table, and like an old married couple who's fallen out of love, they were prepared to go their separate ways.

In the fall of 1997, when I was a sophomore at Belhaven, Chris and his wife Donna wrote a letter that revealed the extent of their dismay and shared it at one of the community's meetings. It was time for them to leave Antioch, they informed the rest of the group. Many of the residents commiserated with them, but Spencer bristled at what he felt was an act of betrayal. In a desperate attempt to heal their relationship and avoid a nasty split, they had John Alexander, founder of the evangelical magazine *The Other Side* and pastor of the Church of the Sojourners in San Francisco, come to Mississippi to counsel them. Alexander reminded them that Jesus was at the center of their community, not either one of them.

Alexander's advice had a deep impact on Spencer. Previously, the whole premise for his racial reconciliation movement required white people to remain white and Black people to remain Black, and for the two sides to harmonize. Now suddenly he'd experienced a shift of insight in which he encouraged others to cultivate what he called "a culture of Grace." He no longer advocated changing the attitudes of the members of each racial group one person at a time but asked us instead to change our perceptions about the groups themselves.

On October 18, 1997, Spencer found the grace to retract the scorn he'd previously directed at Chris. "I want Chris and Donna to be happy," he said, "even if it means them leaving."

That was all it took to convince Chris to stay.

The grace and forgiveness the two men shared with each other had a ripple effect on their ministry. Two months later, they convened twenty-five Black Christian leaders and twenty-five white Christian leaders for a dialogue on racial reconciliation. The ensuing conversation was so honest and powerful it brought Aunt Joanie to tears and convinced her to start forgiving white people, something she'd vowed never to do after her father had been beaten in jail by a white sheriff in 1970.

The following month, Spencer and Chris hosted a conference on racial reconciliation at Belhaven and I participated by displaying some of my artwork. The first night of the conference, I was supposed to go out to dinner with Adrian "Buddy" Lee. This was the first real date I'd ever been on in my entire life. In the two and a half years I'd been at Belhaven, I'd somehow managed to turn down every single guy who'd asked me out. I didn't reject them because I wasn't curious about or interested in romance and sex. I did it because I was scared that I would be punished with eternal damnation. Larry and Ruthanne had taught me that sex was for procreation, not enjoyment, that it should be saved for marriage, and that once I was married I must "lie completely still" as my husband completed the task. Following these rules, I came to fear not only sex but intimacy and relationships as well.

This isn't to say that guys weren't interested in me. In fact, my lack of interest seemed to make me more attractive to them. One guy in particular took all my polite rejections as invitations. A star player on the basketball team, Clarence was used to getting what he wanted. During my freshman year, he would call me from time to time and say he was going to break into my dorm room and have his way with me. As aggressive as his advances were, I didn't report them. The deck was already stacked against the Black students on our predominantly white campus, and I didn't want to make life any harder for Clarence.

I was also confused because when he said, "You know you want it," it was kind of true. I did want it—but at the same time I didn't. I had a burning desire to lose my "V-card" and plenty of sex drive, but I couldn't allow this to happen because of the high-minded notions that had been drilled into my head. Just masturbating was sinful, so going any further than that was unimaginable to me. The solution to my quandary was bad for the basketball team and worse for Clarence's future: poor grades forced him to drop out of school.

Somehow Buddy Lee managed to put an end to my no-dating policy. When he asked me out after we'd been "just good friends" for two and a half years, I accepted. I got all dressed up and was excited about the prospect of dating him. He was biracial—his mother was Italian and his father was Black—and cute and charismatic. However, he was also a bit of a player, so I wanted to see what Spencer thought of him before I went out with him.

When I introduced Buddy to Spencer at the conference, Spencer took Buddy's hand in his and said with genuine conviction, "Wow, it's a real pleasure to meet you. You must be an amazing person if Rachel has decided to go out with you."

Buddy must have walked away from that conversation feeling pretty good about himself, but I understood the true meaning behind Spencer's words. He didn't have to spell it out for me. This was Spencer's way of telling me that Buddy had better be an extraordinary individual or I shouldn't go out with him. Was Buddy amazing? No, he was not. He was a smooth-talking ladies' man who was on a very different path than me when it came to romance (he was far from a virgin) and religion (he wasn't a committed Christian). I deserved better. When Spencer offered advice, I took it. Buddy Lee and I got some ice cream after the conference, but that was the last date I ever had with him.

On the final day of the conference Spencer suffered a diabetic seizure and passed out. Rejuvenated by his reconciliation with Chris, he insisted he was healthy enough to deliver the event's closing address, a speech entitled "Playing the Grace Card." In it, he addressed the rift he'd had with Chris and the understanding they'd come to, and he used it as an example of what needed to be done on a much larger scale to achieve racial reconciliation in the United States.

"At our relationship's weakest moment, Chris and I saw, as clearly as we had ever seen anything, that only by giving each other grace could we find healing and restoration," he told the audience. "We could either hold on to our grievances, demanding that all our hurts be redressed, or we could follow God's example, give each other grace, and trust God for the lack. We chose grace."

That night, Spencer was even more honest and blunt than usual in his discussion of the racial problem, including himself in the list of "African Americans who are growing tired of the tiptoeing that takes place in so many racial reconciliation gatherings." "For us," he continued, "it is time to move into deeper waters."

He went on to describe the "safe, time-tested method for emotionally dealing with whites" that many Black people rely on. "There is an automatic mental procedure that takes place for many Blacks upon first meeting a white. First a decision must be made as to whether or not we will give him or her the time of day. If so, then, immediately the 'Is he for real or phony?' antennas are raised, the 'white superiority' sensors powered up, and the 'racism' detector activated—all in an effort to analyze quickly any 'vibes' and interpret any data, verbal or nonverbal, from the subject. All this is necessary to determine whether the white person deserves special consideration as an 'individual,' that is, a 'good white person,' or as a 'typical' white person who should be quickly relegated to the simple category 'white folks,' as in, 'You know how white folks is.'"

He acknowledged that this sort of judgement, although understandably caused by pain, was unfair, and advocated letting go of the pejorative "white folks" label, viewing each white person as an individual, and responding with "Christ-like compassion and kindness" to people instead of judging their worthiness first.

"Although we must continue to speak on behalf of those who are oppressed and warn oppressors," he said toward the end of his speech that evening, "my willingness to forgive them is not dependent on how they respond. Being able to extend grace and to forgive people sets us free. We no longer need to spend precious emotional energy thinking about the day oppressors will get what they deserve. What I am learning about grace lifts a weight from my shoulders, which is nothing short of invigorating."

His renewed enthusiasm and fresh vision would be tragically short-lived. Three days after the conference, on January 28, 1998, he told Nancy he was feeling light-headed and asked for a glass of juice. She went to get one for him, and when she returned she found him dead of heart failure. He was only forty-four years old.

Spencer's passing had a wide ripple effect. He was the glue that held our community together, and without him things began to fall apart. VOC members became more withdrawn, relying on their most intimate circles for support. Nancy and her children moved to Pennsylvania to be closer to her family. Antioch disbanded.

It had an equally profound impact on me. Before he'd died, I'd drawn a portrait of him, which he'd loved, and I was honored when his family chose to display it on an easel beside the closed casket at his funeral. In the drawing Spencer was full of life, grinning from ear to ear. I was pleased to remember him like this, but my heart was shattered. For me, Spencer had not only been a sounding board but also a compass that helped me find my way as I was sorting out my feelings about my cloistered childhood and my passion for civil rights. He'd always treated me like a daughter and made it clear from his words and actions that he genuinely cared about me. Although he was a Christian, the love he gave people wasn't just a list of rules and tactics for dodging Hell. It was kind; it was real.

Spencer wasn't just a father figure to me. He was also a mentor, lending me insight and clarity whenever I was confused about something. Determined to make him proud, I somehow managed to graduate *magna cum laude*, despite feeling almost completely adrift during my final year and a half at Belhaven. For months after his death I would visit his grave just to sit there and have a one-sided conversation with him. He'd been everything I'd hoped a father could be, and without him a huge void appeared in my life. What filled it would send my life in an entirely new direction.

Chapter Fifteen

Kevin & Howard

WHEN I FINALLY STARTED dating someone in college, I went with a safe choice. Lawrence "Law" Quinn was a highly analytical Black man, belonged to a Pentecostal Holiness church, and, like me, was still a virgin. Everyone in the BSA thought we made a great couple, as we were perfectly matched in our naïveté and creativity. Like me, he was an art major, and he often kept me company in the art studio. "You don't think like a white girl," he told me while I was sitting on his lap in the studio one day. "You respond to things in the same way that a lot of my biracial friends did growing up. You have a biracial mentality." That he seemed to truly understand me made me feel good, but when he grew too clingy it started to get on my nerves and I broke up with him.

The time I'd devoted to Law I now put toward my new job. Five nights a week from 10 PM to 3 AM, I loaded trucks at the local United Parcel Service distribution center. As the lone female on the night shift, I was frequently subjected to whistles and catcalls. One of my coworkers Kevin Moore declined to join in, and I soon found out why—he was interested in me. We started dating, but I broke up with him after only a couple of weeks because he kept trying to violate my Christian boundaries, which forbade premarital sex.

Kevin had seemed like a good match for me. He was quiet, especially when compared to some of our rowdy coworkers, and he was religious, or at least that's what he told me. He'd been raised in the Church of God in Christ, a Pentecostal church where some of the members were known to speak in tongues just like Ruthanne did, and he claimed he'd been born again just two weeks before he'd met me.

I'd soon wonder if he'd made his new conversion up as a way of convincing me to date him. As it turned out, there was a lot I didn't know about Kevin, and very little of it was good. Before finding religion, he was known on the streets as "Profane," thanks to his foul mouth and shady activities. This was all news to me, delivered by Kevin's best friend, who also told me that Kevin wanted me back and that I'd better be careful because I would be in grave danger if I didn't agree to see him again.

On paper, it seems obvious that I should have refused to go out with Kevin again. But with Spencer's death and Antioch disbanding, I no longer had an adequate support system in place. I'd never been taught how to turn people down gently. And there was also some shame involved. I didn't want anyone to know that I'd allowed Kevin to do things to me sexually that I barely knew the terms for at the time. In the end, I thought I could fix him, and if I did that, I might be able to keep my place in Heaven and salvage my own dignity as well. I decided to give our relationship one more shot.

Over the course of the next four months, Kevin managed to detach himself from many of his former associates and focused on work and community college. He and I also engaged in just about every sex act you could possibly think of except male-on-female oral sex and the one I believed would send us both to Hell—vaginal sex. Somehow I managed to preserve my sacred virginity while satisfying his sexual appetite. None of it was very enjoyable for me.

My commitment to abstinence only seemed to make Kevin want me more. He must have asked me to marry him twenty-one times before we flew to Montana during Christmas break so he could ask for Larry's permission in person. At this point in my life I was still (for the most part) following the rules Larry and Ruthanne had imposed on me, and one of them was that if a man wanted to marry a woman he needed to ask the woman's father for permission first. By giving his consent, the father was transferring his authority over his daughter to the man who would be her husband. While Larry and Kevin went on a hike together,

I stayed behind and secretly hoped that Larry would tell Kevin that he wasn't worthy of me, just as Spencer had implied that Buddy Lee didn't deserve me. This would have provided me with an excellent excuse to end our relationship. But it didn't happen. Kevin seemed just as surprised as I was when Larry gave him his blessing. When Kevin asked me to marry him moments later, he didn't even have a ring. Larry's approval came with a dig directed at me. "She's the stubbornest woman I know," he told Kevin. "Good luck breaking her." The plan was for us to get married in June when I graduated from Belhaven so that my family could be there for the wedding and my graduation, but you know what they say about best-laid plans.

When I started dating Kevin, I was living in a duplex in West Jackson with Kim Stevenson, a Black woman in her late twenties. Kim and I both attended services at Voice of Calvary Fellowship, and we were both in committed relationships—she was dating a tall white guy from church named Will. Beyond that, Kim and I were an unlikely duo, opposite in nearly every way. I was artistic; she was practical. I was relaxed; she was particular, almost to the point of being obsessive-compulsive. I was from a lower-class family that lived on the side of a mountain; she was from a middle-class family that lived in the suburbs. When we went to church, I felt most comfortable hanging out with the Black parishioners; she preferred the company of the white folks. I also had a natural sense of rhythm, whereas Kim did not. I tried to teach her. We stood in our living room and practiced rocking back and forth while clapping at the same time. First we worked on the rocking part. Then we worked on the clapping. It took several weeks, but she was eventually able to do both at the same time. That I had rhythm while she did not, that she was uptight while I was chill, and that she dated white guys while I had dated two Black guys made us the butt of a running joke. People often said that I was a Black girl in a white body and Kim was a white girl in a Black body.

Our love lives were also quite different. She and Will liked to go on very romantic dates. They would pack a basket with sandwiches and strawberries and have a picnic somewhere. Kevin and I were a bit more prosaic in our dating habits. With our work schedules, going on an actual date, like to dinner or a movie, was a luxury we simply didn't have. We were forced to content ourselves with brief physical encounters in places that were never completely private: his car or mine, the art studio I had on campus, the living room in his mom's house where he still lived, or the common area in the duplex I shared with Kim.

It was in the last location on March 27, 2000, that we engaged in roughly two hurried minutes of sex on the orange couch Kim had purchased from a nearby thrift store. Twenty-two years of suppressing all my lustful urges and sexual curiosities were erased in less time than it takes to listen to a song on the radio.

Terrified that we might have punched our ticket to Hell, I knew there was only one solution to the crisis we'd put ourselves in: a quickie marriage. We rushed to the courthouse, got the paperwork completed, and were married on March 31. I wore a black dress out of shame, and Kevin and I exchanged cross necklaces to symbolize our commitment to God. Only the pastor and his wife, Kevin's mother, and a couple of my college friends attended. Kevin and I spent one night at a three-star hotel—our honeymoon!—and both of us were back at work the following day. When we called Larry and Ruthanne the day after the ceremony to tell them we'd gotten married early, Larry thought it was an April Fool's joke.

None of the signs pointed toward Kevin and I having a long and happy marriage. Like the sex that had precipitated it, our marriage was unplanned, unwise, and unsatisfying. If Spencer had still been alive, I have no doubt I never would have married Kevin Moore.

Soon after Kevin and I were married, I got hit by an extremely painful kidney stone. Doubled over in agony, I had to crawl across the floor to get to the phone. Kemba, one of my friends from Belhaven, got to me before the ambulance did and drove me to the hospital. By the time we got there, I was so incapacitated she had to fill out the paperwork for me. As she handed in the forms, the receptionist started arguing with her about what she'd written down. The receptionist's confusion was understandable. On my Montana driver's license, I looked white and my name was Rachel Doležal. On my UPS employee ID, I looked Black and my name was Rachel Doležal. And on the intake form, Kemba had put down my married name, Rachel Moore—and who knows how I appeared to this woman? Given the discrepancies, the receptionist couldn't figure out which race I belonged to or what my real name was.

When Kevin arrived, he became part of the ongoing dispute about my identity. The receptionist didn't seem to believe he was my husband. Meanwhile, I was writhing in agony, couldn't put two words together, and started vomiting over the side of the gurney. By the time a resolution had been reached and a doctor had taken a look at me, I'd already passed the kidney stone on my own.

One of the first things I did after receiving my diploma was ask Larry and Ruthanne when they planned on paying back the money they'd borrowed from me before I'd left for college. My great-grandmother, the one who was reputed to be Hunkpapa Lakota and who'd died when I was eight, had managed to squirrel away quite a bit of money over the course of her four marriages. When she'd died, she'd left each of her children $56,000, each of her grandchildren $28,000, and each of her great-grandchildren, including me and Josh, $14,000. Larry had told me that he and Ruthanne could save a bunch of money if they paid off their mortgage by the end of the year and the remaining balance on the loan was almost the same as the amount I'd inherited. He assured me that I would get more financial aid if I didn't have any assets and promised that he and Ruthanne would pay me back as soon as I was done with college. Now that day had arrived.

If I live a thousand years, I'll never forget Larry's response when I asked him about the money. "We already paid you back," he told me. "It cost more than that to raise you."

It felt like I'd been punched in the stomach. I'd upheld my end of the unwritten agreement that bound us together. I'd tended the garden, picked apples, canned food, hunted elk, butchered chickens, collected eggs, and scrubbed the bathroom floor, and in return I'd been rewarded with what? A roof over my head and three meals a day. I'd worked just as hard to make my own money and had always been allowed to keep it. When I loaned Larry and Ruthanne my inheritance, I expected the same treatment.

Yet Larry had the gall to insist it had been otherwise: *We already paid you back.*

If I ever wanted anything that wasn't considered absolutely necessary during my childhood, I'd had to pay for it myself. Harvesting and bagging an entire field of potatoes might have earned me a fountain soda or a candy bar. I even helped pay for some of my younger siblings' adoption expenses. I'd worked non-stop, forgoing any sense of a normal childhood, much less any free-spirited teenage years.

And yet: *It cost more than that to raise you.*

Being betrayed by one's parents always comes as a shock. All I ever wanted was for them to love me, and I remained hopelessly optimistic long after it had become clear that that was not the case. After deluding myself into thinking that Larry and Ruthanne loved me and Josh equally—or even loved me at all—I now knew the truth. Any trust I had in them dissolved. From that day forward, I stopped calling him "Papa" and her "Mama," and started referring to them only by their given names. I now viewed them not as my parents but merely as two people who'd helped raise me. The distance that lay between us came with a silver lining: now that I was free of their judgment and control, I could relax and be my true self. But the newfound sense of freedom I enjoyed didn't last very long.

Kevin knew that I'd always dreamed of moving to DC and going to Howard University, but when I told him I wanted to apply to grad school there, Kevin said he didn't want to go, complaining that I would be taking him away from his mom and everything he knew—he'd never left the state of Mississippi. Eventually, he relented.

Unlike the hospital in Mississippi where I passed the kidney stone (and other primarily white institutions that require detailed information about race and ethnicity), Howard didn't have a box on the application for its graduate Master of Fine Arts program asking me to identify my race. The university's mission was clearly explained by the motto listed on its website at the time: "We exist to promote Black values." I, of course, was completely on board with that. I wanted to go to Howard so badly it was the only grad school I applied to, so you can imagine my excitement when I got in. I was even more thrilled when the chair of the art department, Winston Kennedy, upon seeing my academic records from

Belhaven and my growing portfolio of artwork, offered me a full scholarship and a teaching assistant (TA) position.

With no money to fly there, I hadn't visited Howard before I applied. Why bother? I didn't need to inspect the dorm rooms or walk through The Yard to confirm what I already knew: this was my dream school, the Black Harvard, the Mecca. Having never set foot on campus before, the day I arrived at Howard was especially thrilling for me. Here, Blackness came in every shape, size, and hue, and I immediately felt at home.

I'll never forget my first visit to the Gallery of Art. Established in 1928, the gallery contained a permanent collection that featured the works of some of my favorite Black artists such as Henry Ossawa Tanner, Robert Scott Duncanson, and Edmonia Lewis. In awe of the content of their work and the mastery of their technique, I admired them more than Michelangelo, Vincent van Gogh, or Pablo Picasso and was eager to have my artwork critiqued by those who revered them as much as I did. I was just as excited to be in a place that's considered by many to be the epicenter of Black education, philosophy, and culture. Even though Howard was one of the leading HBCUs in the country and its student body was almost entirely Black, I wasn't trying to be some sort of racial pioneer by going there.* It was simply the best fit for me, as my art focused on the Black experience and racial and social justice.

People at Howard had all sorts of ideas about my ethnicity. In an interesting evolution, some HBCUs now have more white students than Black ones—Bluefield State College in Bluefield, West Virginia, for example, is 90 percent white—but Howard has remained steadfastly Black, and because of that, many people assumed I was, too.

---

* Earning that distinction would have been impossible anyway. Howard's founder, General Oliver Howard, was actually a white man, its first graduating class was entirely white, and the university has never rejected applicants based on the color of their skin. If you're looking for a true pioneer, try the "grandfather of the restorative justice movement," Howard Zehr, who in 1966 became the first white student to graduate from Morehouse College.

Others, however, upon first seeing me, assumed I was white—and with good reason. Even though I was fulfilling a dream by attending Howard, my evolution toward Blackness actually took a step back during this time because Kevin disapproved of the fact that I didn't mind—even preferred—being seen as Black or biracial. He didn't understand why I had such an affinity for Blackness and why I felt more comfortable in the Black community than the white one. He also made it clear that he preferred my hair to be straight—and bleached blonde—and forbade me from wearing braids or Black hairstyles. It saddened me and made my efforts to blend in and socialize with my peers on campus more difficult, but I acquiesced. I was still operating under the belief that God's law required me to submit to male authority, and if I didn't, I wouldn't go to Heaven. Now that I was married I needed to yield to my husband's will, even if that meant burying my own thoughts, feelings, and identity.

Kevin's worldview sprang from a poverty-stricken childhood in all-Black West Jackson, Mississippi. He'd grown up in a cockroach-infested home, where the kitchen sink was propped up on bricks, the bathroom sink was permanently clogged, and the shower had to be turned on and off with pliers. As a consequence, he'd come to equate poverty with Blackness and to idolize the rich white people he saw on television. He wasn't the only Black child to think this way.

The "White is Right" narrative is so ingrained in our culture most white people don't even notice it. That most of the actors on the television shows we watch are white (a situation that was even more skewed during the 1980s and 90s), most of the people sporting Rolexes and driving Mercedes-Benzes in the advertisements we're bombarded with are white, and most of the faces on the covers of the magazines we read are white casts whiteness as the norm, if not the pinnacle of beauty and success.

Inroads are starting to be made. TV shows with Black leading characters or predominantly Black casts, such as *Black-ish*, *Scandal*, *Queen Sugar*, and *Empire*, have become more common and offer more nuanced approaches to discussing Black culture while addressing contemporary hot-button issues Black families face on a daily basis. But when Kevin was growing up, there weren't any shows on television like them. From watching the shows that were popular at the time, he saw two very different worlds—the poor Black one he came from and the rich white one he saw on the screen—and if he had to pick one, who would choose poverty?

The world outside his home only confirmed this polarity. His dad owned a small company that built pools for rich white folks, and whenever Kevin tagged along with his father and saw the expensive homes in North Jackson with their manicured lawns and luxury pools, it only reinforced the idea that whiteness equals success. Growing up with hard-packed dirt for a front yard and a house with extreme plumbing issues, Kevin came to see the Black world as something to flee from and the white one as something to run toward. In short, he viewed whiteness as being superior to Blackness. Mental health professionals call this "psychological misorientation," and those who suffer from it often get called "Oreos"—Black on the outside and white on the inside.

Equating whiteness with success and beauty, Kevin would have liked nothing more than to live in a white suburban neighborhood and drive a Toyota Camry, a car popular with Jackson's white population. He also said Black girls were "nasty" and "had attitudes," and although he'd dated a few of them, he preferred dating white girls. Before me, he'd dated one named Misty, who he referred to as "Spray Bottle." (Misty, mist, spray, spray bottle—get it?)

With my light skin and college education, I appeared to be the perfect woman for Kevin, but, as it turned out, I was a little too Black for his tastes. Not only did he discourage me from wearing my hair in braids or other Black hairstyles, he also dissuaded me from sitting in the sun, preferring my skin to be as pale as it could possibly be. He frequently urged me to speak and act "whiter" and often complained about my figure. "You know a white woman ain't got no business having a big butt like that," he'd say to me. Nicole Kidman was his standard of beauty, and he encouraged me to do everything I could to look more like her. It saddened me that he didn't find beauty and pride in Black culture and consciousness, but I was his wife and I'd been raised to believe that I had no choice but to submit to his authority, so that's what I did.

Being forced to look white while wanting to be seen and social-ize as Black was very confusing for me. I found myself ping-pong-ing back and forth across the color line based on the perceptions of others while also having to act the part of a proper and submissive wife. Lost in this confusion was any sense of personal agency I might have possessed. Instead of making me feel like I was a part of something, my appearance made me feel misunderstood, alien, other. Learning that a Black man could be, culturally and philo-sophically, as white as any white man was a painful lesson for me. The momentary freedom I'd enjoyed after distancing myself from Larry and Ruthanne was now gone. As far as the evolution of my racial identity was concerned, marrying Kevin had catapulted me all the way back to square one.

One Sunday at church we heard a sermon in which birth control pills were referred to as "early term abortions." Kevin immediately insisted I go off the pill, and before I'd completed my first semester of graduate school I got pregnant. I was very excited, even though I knew it was going to make many aspects of my life much harder. I was prepared for my sleep to be disrupted and for standing for long periods of time to be more difficult. I didn't anticipate interac-tions with one of my professors, Al Smith, becoming so awkward. Before I got pregnant, Al was always very friendly to me; after, I felt he became inappropriately so.

To distance myself from him, I started working at home more often, but running into him on campus was inevitable. As I was walking down the hallway one day, he called to me from his office, "How's our baby doing?" I stopped and glared at him. "It's not 'our' baby. It's my and my husband's baby." I went out of my way to avoid him after that, but when Winston Kennedy vacated his position as chair of the Art Department during the summer after my first year and Al was named to replace him, that strategy became much more difficult.

That summer I worked for Howard's Young Artist Academy, a recruitment effort designed to bolster the university's art program. It attracted talented high school juniors, who lived on campus the summer before their senior years, studied drawing, painting, and design, and built up their portfolios so they'd be more likely to

earn an art scholarship for college. I'd just finished teaching some
of these kids the basics of matting and framing in August 2001,
when I ducked into Al's office to double-check that my paperwork
was in order for the upcoming semester. I shouldn't have been concerned at all. I had a 4.0 GPA and had won nearly all the awards
at the juried graduate student art show at the end of my first year.
But I wanted to make sure all the i's had been dotted and all the
t's crossed.

They weren't.

I discovered that my scholarship and teaching position had
been rescinded. Al told me that because my due date was fast
approaching—I was seven months pregnant at the time—I "needed
to spend time with the baby" and "didn't need to be going to school
with a new baby."* I was stunned. I'd been told that my scholarship could only be taken away if I got poor grades, and I'd worked
hard to ensure that never happened. My small family depended on
my support. Money was always tight while we were living in DC.
To make ends meet, I worked a variety of jobs. In addition to my
TA position, which was our main source of income, I also braided
hair, sold art, and catered meals during the holidays. It still wasn't
enough. I had to take out student loans, which we used to live off
of and pay for Kevin's tuition at Northern Virginia Community
College, where he was studying to be a physical therapist assistant.
Without my TA job and scholarship, I would never be able to pay
tuition, our bills would go unpaid, and I'd be forced to drop out
of school.

In a bid to get my scholarship back and keep my family afloat,
I sought the counsel of an attorney, who told me the university
claimed that I'd neglected to fill out the proper paperwork to renew
my scholarship and TA position for another year. That I had to fill
out any paperwork—or that such paperwork even existed—was news
to me. I hadn't filled out any forms prior to enrolling for my first
semester, nor, I believed, had any of the other graduate students
who'd received similar deals.

---

* As stated in the complaint I eventually filed against Smith and his employer,
  Howard University.

Given some of the recent awkward encounters I'd endured on campus with Al Smith, I felt like I'd been discriminated against on the basis of my gender, more specifically my pregnancy, but my attorney advised me to broaden the scope of the lawsuit I was considering to include race because he thought it would be more effective. He also advised me to sue for the loss of a potential post-graduate instructor position, should the suit delay or prevent my graduating from the university. I loved Howard and hated that I'd been forced into the position of having to play the race card and sue the university of my dreams, but I put my family first. In the end I agreed to do it because we were in such dire straits financially and, with me in the third trimester of my pregnancy, we needed all the help we could get.

Just a few days before classes started, my attorney sent the university a letter stating that it couldn't prevent me from registering for classes while the lawsuit was being litigated, so I was able to continue my studies. The big question at that point was, who was going to pay for those studies? After a lot of back and forth that included mediation meetings and depositions before my complaint was officially filed in August 2002, I ultimately lost the lawsuit after the judge ruled she could find no evidence that I'd been discriminated against.* But when the university never billed me for tuition for my final year of grad school and granted me another TA position at the start of my last semester, to me it felt like a victory (and an admission on the part of the university that it wasn't blameless in the matter and hoped it would go away quietly). While I was never able to prove to the court that Howard University had forced me to work in a "hostile work environment," I know what I felt, and that was that I'd been discriminated against for reasons other than my ability and performance. I knew going in that the lawsuit was going to be difficult to win. Workplace discrimination is often subtle and nearly impossible to prove. If

---

* My lawyer filed an appeal in February 2004, in hopes of at least recouping his legal expenses from the original case; unfortunately, the appellate court affirmed the lower court's decision and dismissed the case in June 2005.

I'd carried a voice recorder on my person at all times and been able to record some of the comments directed at me, things might have turned out differently.

The lawsuit added another layer of distance between me and some of my colleagues. My second year at Howard was filled with awkward and tense moments, but my reinstatement allowed me to stay on track academically. To earn my degree, I needed to complete sixty hours of coursework, and nearly all the hours I devoted to painting, sculpting, and teaching during my final semester were spent sitting down. During the first trimester of my pregnancy, the baby had started to separate from the womb, so, technically, I was supposed to be on bed rest. I tried to stay off my feet as much as possible but couldn't afford to take any time off—not with my scholarship hanging in the balance.

Franklin was born during the first semester of my second and final year at Howard. He was two weeks overdue, and my labor lasted from Wednesday night to Sunday morning—ninety-four hours! I was unconscious for four hours after Franklin was born, knocked out by sheer exhaustion, and by the time I came around he was in the neonatal intensive care unit. With the long labor and the visit to the NICU, Franklin's birth cost more than $24,000, and my student health insurance only covered $1,000 of it. I wouldn't finish paying off the debt until he was six years old.

Raising a baby while finishing grad school was challenging but, given my proclivity for industriousness, I never let it overwhelm me. By being organized and working hard, I kept up with my schoolwork and soon reached the final step I needed to take before graduating: defending my thesis before a committee. After filing the lawsuit, I'd switched my major from painting to sculpture, and for my thesis I incorporated both art forms as well as drawing and collage. All the pieces I made for my thesis questioned the notion of light being good and dark being bad, particularly when it came to the color of one's skin. While I was at Belhaven, I'd noticed that the portraits I'd made of Black women and children were more popular with collectors than those I'd done of Black men, and I wondered, as an artist, how I could create more empathy with the Black male figure. To challenge myself and, hopefully, break down stereotypes and prejudice, I used my thesis to depict the inner journey of the Black man and humanize him in a way that would connect with every demographic, white and Black, male and female, young and old.

The pieces I created were well received by the thesis committee. When I graduated *summa cum laude*, the idea that I might actually be able to make a living selling my artwork began to seem possible. I'd already begun to be commissioned to create art for various patrons. One of them was Robert, a general in the U.S. Army who I'd met at church. He asked me to make him a drawing illustrating the history of his Black fraternity. Despite the $8.99 Kmart wedding ring I wore on my finger, I began to suspect that Robert was interested in me romantically. My suspicions were confirmed when I dropped off his drawing at the Pentagon and he snuck a kiss in the parking lot.

When I told Kevin what had happened, he was irate. He talked about murdering Robert and said that we needed to move or else he was going to end up in prison for killing the man. Kevin had been saying for a while that he wanted us to move "away from Black culture" and that he didn't want Black guys hitting on me, so when Robert kissed me, it gave Kevin the perfect excuse to insist that we pull up stakes and relocate. In the summer of 2003, he found a job working as a physical therapist assistant at the hospital in Bonners Ferry, Idaho, a lily-white town on the banks of the Kootenai River less than an hour's drive from where I'd grown up. I had no choice but to go. As much as my identity had evolved over the course of the past six years living in the racial diversity of the South, I suddenly found myself right back where I'd started.

Chapter Sixteen

Emancipation

IN THE ISOLATION OF RURAL IDAHO, the tension between me and Kevin escalated. Early in our relationship, I believed that I could inspire him to embrace Black culture and fall in love with African history and Afrocentric aesthetics, and that in the process he'd come to understand me better and love himself more. But after moving to Idaho any hope I'd once possessed disappeared.

Our relationship had always been a one-sided affair, with Kevin's values taking precedence over mine. I was expected to be a submissive wife, while he ruled with an iron fist. I wasn't allowed to have anything that belonged entirely to me. I didn't have my own cell phone. I didn't even have my own email account. He insisted that I share my password with him, and whenever I protested he'd use what happened with Robert, the general who'd kissed me, to justify his need to monitor my correspondence.

Kevin also wouldn't let me go out on my own. The only times I left the house were Friday afternoons, when he'd accompany me to the grocery store after he got home from work, and Sunday mornings, when we went to church. "You're a silly little girl," he often told me. "Some guy is going to hit on you and you aren't going to know what to do." As stifling as this treatment was, I didn't feel like I had a choice but to bend to his will. After all, he was my husband. Married life in Bonners Ferry soon became every bit as confining and oppressive as my childhood in Troy.

Kevin's insistence that I never leave the house alone extended to work. He refused to let me get a job. His mandate was reinforced by my upbringing. Larry and Ruthanne had taught me that mothers who worked were abandoning their children at godless daycares. Careers were for men, and women were expected to set everything aside for their husbands and children. Kevin let me do art as a hobby, but because everything I created focused on the Black experience it was always misunderstood by people who still thought of me as white, including my husband. In Idaho, my creativity shriveled to a husk, and I struggled to produce any work. I'd barely made any new pieces since completing the MFA program at Howard. A year after graduating *summa cum laude*, I was now a barely coping stay-at-home mom searching for inspiration in the sticks of Idaho, my career path having come to a sudden dead end.

Franklin, now a toddler at two, helped me keep my head above water. He was the center of my world, the main source of joy in my life, my reason for waking up in the morning. Like me, he was expected to submit unquestioningly to Kevin's authority, and having to observe that dynamic was difficult for me.

Franklin didn't like to eat meat when he was little. His favorite breakfast was "hot leaves"—greens such as rainbow Swiss chard that he'd helped me pick from the garden and that I cooked the way he liked it best, boiled and flavored with just a pinch of salt. One morning I placed a piece of bacon on his highchair's tray, but he was only interested in tearing it into little pieces. "Stop playing with your food, boy!" Kevin yelled before shoving an entire piece of bacon into Franklin's mouth while Franklin protested by pounding his chubby fists on the tray. On another occasion Kevin forced a bite of sausage into Franklin's mouth, and when Franklin refused to swallow, Kevin grabbed a rolling pin and waved it in the air like a club. Terrified, Franklin started crying, and the sausage fell out of his mouth. Hoping to defuse the situation before it got any worse, I removed Franklin from his high chair and told Kevin that Franklin needed to go potty.

These sorts of violent outbursts were common in our household. When Kevin and I argued, he often threatened to paralyze me from the neck down if I ever betrayed him. I took this warning seriously because as a physical therapist assistant he'd worked with numerous quadriplegics and knew exactly which vertebrae they'd injured. Adding to my fear, Kevin kept two loaded guns in our bedroom closet, where he could easily get to them if need be. I was so scared whenever he came home my body stiffened, my teeth clenched, and I could barely eat. Anorexia led to bulimia, and I grew precariously thin. I went from wearing a size six or eight to a size zero and experienced an equally extreme nosedive in my health.

Into this toxic environment stepped Josh. I hadn't seen him since he'd visited me in DC right after Kevin and I'd gotten married. During that visit he'd apologized for molesting me when we were younger, and I'd forgiven him just as I'd been taught to do in church. Although I was still wary of him, we'd kept in touch, emailing each other every so often. When he mentioned he was going to be driving with his girlfriend Brennan from the University of Nebraska, where he was studying to get his PhD in American literature, to the Pacific Northwest, I invited them to stay with us at our place in Bonners Ferry.

I was in the kitchen making dinner when Josh's white Buick pulled into the driveway and he and Brennan stepped out of the car. While I'd been cooking, cleaning, and taking care of Franklin, Kevin, as was his habit, was using the computer in the basement. I called down to him, letting him know that our guests had arrived. He came upstairs to say hello, but it was up to me to show them to their rooms and explain the sleeping arrangements to them.

Our house had three bedrooms—one for me and Kevin, one for Franklin, and one for guests—but when I'd told Kevin that Josh was bringing along a girlfriend, he'd insisted they sleep in separate rooms. "This is a Christian household," he'd said to me. "We don't allow fornication." To appease him, I moved Franklin's toddler bed into our bedroom and set up an air mattress in Franklin's room for Brennan to sleep on, while Josh slept in the guest room. It felt strange imposing Christian morality on Josh, as he'd strayed far away from the faith we'd been raised in, bouncing between agnosticism and atheism, screwing women he wasn't married to, drinking, and smoking, but I had little choice. I apologized and shrugged to let him and Brennan know that it was Kevin's decision and I couldn't do anything about it.

The conversation at dinner that night was forced and awkward. Josh and Kevin had only hung out twice before, and during the first occasion in DC, Josh had made his objections to my life choices known, telling me he didn't think marrying a Black man was a good idea. "Marriage is hard enough," he'd said. "Race will just complicate an already difficult situation."

I didn't consider my marriage to Kevin to be an "interracial marriage," but Josh did. He believed that race would be the undoing of my relationship with my husband. But I knew that Kevin's Blackness wasn't the cause of our disconnect; if anything, it was his *disdain* for Blackness that created so much distance between us.

Besides a relationship with me, Kevin and Josh didn't have much in common. As a consequence, they didn't have anything to talk about. During dinner that evening, I did my best to keep the conversation going, but quickly exhausted the main topics of interest in the small world I inhabited: the food we were eating, the house we lived in, and Franklin's growth and development. Josh filled in the gaps with animated discourses about life in grad school, poems he'd recently written, and his eagerness to show off the area he'd grown up in to Brennan.

The next morning, as Kevin was leaving the house to go to work, he bumped into Josh and Brennan on the deck. They were smoking, which Kevin considered sinful, so I braced myself for an explosion, but he only asked them what their plans for the day were.

"I was thinking we might all go up to Yaak Falls for a swim," said Josh.

"That would be really fun," I said. "I'd love to go. I'll get Franklin's life jacket."

Kevin shot me a look of disbelief before leveling his gaze at Josh. "She doesn't go anywhere without me. That goes for my son, too." He turned back to me. "You're not to leave this house until I get home."

I nodded and handed Kevin the lunch I'd made him.

As Kevin walked to his car, Josh looked at me incredulously. "Seriously?"

"It's fine," I said. "I'm sure you and Brennan will have a great time."

Josh shook his head. "How do you live like this? You're too special for this."

"No, I'm not," I muttered.

My heart nearly skipped a beat from the impact of my own words. At that moment, I could see just how removed I'd become from my goals, my ambitions, myself. I'd lost all hope and desire and traded in all my dreams of changing the world, and for what? To be a stay-at-home mom? A submissive wife? All the energy I'd devoted to conforming to what Larry and Ruthanne wanted (religious obedience) and what Kevin wanted (a white wife) had left me feeling dead inside. I'd cut off oxygen to the parts of my life that didn't fit with Kevin's narrow worldview, and while doing that may have saved my marriage, it was killing me. I was doing little more than existing. That I felt so lifeless scared me, but with this fear came hope, for that was the moment I began to wake up and feel like I might be able to start living again.

Josh was so disturbed by the state of my marriage he addressed the issue in several emails after he and Brennan left. In one, he wrote that he had "never witnessed a civil conversation between [me] and Kevin, even about groceries," and was concerned that I wasn't happy. In another, he wrote, "Thankfully, there hasn't been any physical violence, or you would have no choice but to consider divorce." If he only knew.

Kevin was home from work the day Josh sent the latter email, and he intercepted it before I had a chance to read and delete it, as had become my habit. Livid, he yelled for me to come downstairs. I picked up Franklin and carried him on my hip as I walked down to the basement. The room pulsed with Kevin's rage. He said he never wanted to see Josh's face again and if he did he would kill him for planting ideas about divorce in my head. When I tried to calm him, he lunged at me, and as he did I wrapped Franklin in my arms and turned to shield his body with mine. Kevin grabbed the back of my hair and threw me across the room. My side and back slammed into the wooden cupboards that ran along the floor, as my body curled into a ball to protect Franklin from the impact.

As I checked to make sure Franklin was all right, Josh's words broke through the fog in my head: *You'd have no choice but to consider divorce.* Up to this point I'd accepted the abuse I'd received at Kevin's hands to be an atonement for my sins and endured it out of guilt and stubbornness, but now that he'd involved Franklin I could no longer stand by and take it. I had to find a way out. I memorized our bank account numbers, packed a suitcase, hid the guns, and devised a plan. I would rent a U-Haul truck and take off with Franklin and all my artwork—essentially, all that was precious to me. I was terrified about the prospect of leaving, but staying was even more frightening. I tried to take off in the car on two separate occasions, but both times Kevin heard me sneak out and got to me before I could get Franklin in his car seat and drive away.

The tension in our house was like an obnoxious guest who'd long overstayed his welcome but is related to you so you can't kick him out. It lingered into the fall. One Tuesday morning in September I was washing dishes in the kitchen and Kevin got upset about something as he was walking out the door to go to work. We got into an argument. He swung at me, but I managed to avoid the blow. Franklin, who'd been playing on the kitchen floor, stepped between us. "Stop it, Daddy!" he yelled. "Don't hurt Mommy!" Kevin kicked him out of the way, and Franklin went flying across the linoleum and split his forehead open on a cupboard door. As routine as this sort of abuse had become, Franklin had never been hurt before.

A grim line had been crossed.

As scared as I was about going to Hell for failing to be a submissive wife, I was willing to do it to protect my child. While Kevin was at work, I snuck into town and reported the incident at the Child Protective Services office, showing them the injury on Franklin's forehead. After explaining what had happened that morning and how it was part of a pattern of violence and abuse, the social worker I talked to told me I had one month to get Franklin out of the house or else he'd be removed and put into foster care.

I'd wanted to leave Kevin for some time but had lacked the courage and self-esteem to actually do it. My love for Franklin made up for those deficiencies. Now that he'd been hurt I had no choice. I went straight home and forged an escape plan, while being careful to cover my tracks. Whenever I called the victim advocate CPS had assigned me, I remembered to delete the call log on our land line. Any time I used the internet, I erased the search history afterward. And any time I wrote an email, I'd tell the receiver not to email me back, and then I'd delete the copy of the message I'd sent.

I needed to go somewhere I'd be safe, but when I appealed to Josh he relied on an Iraq War reference to say no, telling me he wasn't "going to be George Bush" and intervene in such a volatile situation. Larry and Ruthanne were now living in South Africa, but even if they'd been in the country I wouldn't have bothered to call them. Which left "Uncle" Vern. The week before I left Kevin, I'd called Uncle Dan, told him about the escalating abuse, and asked if Franklin and I could stay with him. As a gay man, he was an outsider like me, so I thought he might sympathize with my situation, and he did. He offered me his place as a safe house while I figured out my next move. He warned me that he was about to fly out of the country to visit Larry and Ruthanne but assured me that Vern would take care of us while he was gone.

On October 24, 2004, three days after Franklin turned three, I executed my escape plan. I told Paul and Tami, friends from church, that my marriage to Kevin had hit a rough patch and I needed to leave with Franklin so I could think and pray. I asked them to come to our house after church, and when they arrived I called Kevin upstairs and read him a statement I'd written. After explaining why I needed some time away from him, I picked up my suitcase and with Franklin on my hip headed toward the door.

"You aren't taking my son anywhere," he said, grabbing Franklin's arm in a grip so tight it made Franklin cry. "I don't care what you do, but he stays with me."

"Then let Paul and Tami take him," I said before doing the hardest thing I've ever had to do in my entire life—leaving my child behind as I walked out the door.

I called the police from a pay phone at a gas station, but the officers who arrived at our house told me they couldn't take a child from one parent and give him to the other parent without a court order. Concerned about Franklin's safety, I called Paul and Tami every thirty minutes. Finally, after three and a half miserable hours, they picked up their landline and let me know Franklin was with them. My heart lifted. I filed for an emergency protection order, and as soon as it was granted, I gave a copy of it to Paul and Tami to protect them from Kevin's wrath and took Franklin straight to "Uncle" Vern's place.

When we arrived, Vern was feeding the pheasants, peacocks, emus, and other exotic birds he raised. Besides being a bird lover, he was also an expert landscaper. With streams cascading over waterfalls, winding around perfectly manicured patches of lawn and beds filled with flowering plants, and spilling into ponds full of koi and frogs, their property was often featured in the annual Coeur d'Alene Garden Tour. More importantly to me, it was isolated and well protected. Getting there involved a long and complicated drive, and the driveway had an inconspicuous entrance obscured by a bend in the road. If anyone did come down the driveway, Dan and Vern's German shepherd Bo would alert us. Before I went to bed that night, Vern handed me an aluminum baseball bat and told me he'd keep a rifle close to his bed.

Franklin and I stayed with Dan and Vern until we moved into an apartment in Coeur d'Alene in early 2005. As supportive as my uncles were, they were the exception. Everyone else in my family and most of my Christian friends thought divorce was an unforgivable sin. When I told them my plans, I was met with scorn. "God hates divorce," they told me. And, "Jesus can forgive." They didn't mean *they* would forgive me for getting a divorce; they were saying that, if only I tried a little harder, *I* could forgive Kevin. Any attempts I made to get them to understand what it was like to live in fear for your safety and that of your child fell on deaf ears. Believing that God is on the side of the husband in any domestic conflict, they supported Kevin, who they'd embraced as a born-again Christian, even though they hardly knew him and had known me my entire life. I knew that divorcing Kevin would mean losing my entire family and many of my friends, yet I was willing to do it because I loved my son more than anything else and believed it was best for him.

The divorce was finalized in April 2005, with me getting to keep Franklin most but not all of the time. I was on my own at the age of twenty-six with very little in the way of steady employment and a three-year-old to support. And yet I felt liberated! The prevailing mindset in the house I grew up in and the one I shared with Kevin—that if it's not in the Bible you can't do it—had precluded me from ever fully discovering or claiming my own identity. Living in a new city where no one knew me, I was free to express who I was on my own terms—religiously, sexually, and racially.

I stopped attending church for the first time in my life and began a process of redefining my faith in more spiritual terms. Up until that point, the power of religious guilt had me firmly in its grasp and the possibility of eternal punishment was omnipresent. I often found myself atoning for merely existing and hating my body and myself. Now, no longer! After a year of therapy, during which I was diagnosed as suffering from post-traumatic stress disorder (PTSD) from all the physical and sexual abuse I'd experienced in my life, I started dating, men and women, and I once again embraced my inclination toward Black aesthetics. Perched on the edge of a picturesque lake, Coeur d'Alene is a resort town with an avid beach scene. I often sunbathed on the shores of the lake during the summer, and my skin darkened as a result. I didn't get melanin-stimulation shots or take drugs or surgically alter my body or skin as some would later suggest. I simply liked to get my "glow" on in the summer and keep a tan as long as I could in the winter. I also started expressing myself again through hairstyles, wearing my hair in box braids, Senegalese twists, and faux locs.

With the braids and my natural tan came the same questions I'd been bombarded with in college: "So, what are you?" and "Are you white or Black?" and "What are you mixed with?" I began answering more vaguely and letting people make their own judgments. I stopped allowing other people to dictate my identity or make me feel guilty about who I was, and when they made assumptions about my ethnic origins, I made no effort to set them straight. Now for the first time in my life, I was truly owning who I was: a woman who was free, self-reliant, and, yes, Black.

There was just one hitch. In Idaho, it's the court's general policy to make divorced parents sharing custody of a child remain within a two-hour drive of each other to prevent drop-offs and pickups from being overly burdensome. With Kevin still in Bonners Ferry, my choices as far as where I wanted to live next were extremely limited. Coeur d'Alene was the closest place to Bonners Ferry that could be called a city and, thanks to Dan and Vern, it was a place where I felt safe, so I decided to settle there. As happy as I was to be free of Kevin, the solution came with a steep price: to retain my custodial rights, I had to remain in this cultural backwater for the next fifteen years.

Chapter Seventeen

San Francisco

DURING THE ENTIRE FIVE YEARS I was married to Kevin, I never had a single orgasm while having sex with him. I'd discovered how to give myself one when I was ten years old and had continued to do so ever since, but I didn't receive one at the hands (or genitals or tongue) of another person until the summer after my divorce was finalized, when I was commissioned to create an artistic water fountain for the Fountains of Wishes fundraiser in Coeur d'Alene.

The fountain I designed depicted a steel column of figures struggling against a never-ending stream of water that fell into a pool, into which spectators were encouraged to toss their pocket change. That money, when it wasn't being pilfered by derelict teenagers, and the eventual sales of the fountains themselves, raised nearly $180,000 for twenty-one local charities that year. The fountain I made featured a globe of reinforced concrete floating above the steel column on a thin steel rod. All the steel needed to be welded together, but I didn't have any welding tools or much experience. Rodney, the owner of a local welding shop who was wealthy enough to own his own plane and have free time to share, helped me finish the piece and install it downtown.

Rodney and I became good friends while working on the project together and continued to hang out after it was done. He was married, so I felt safe around him. I wasn't something for him to control or abuse. He made me laugh. He even taught me how to fly his plane. On one of our outings I pointed vaguely to the southeast and mentioned that Josh was working as a trail manager in the Selway-Bitterroot Wilderness that summer, stationed twenty-six miles into the 1.3-million-acre slice of untouched nature. Rodney offered to fly me there, and I took him up on it. He dropped me off at a cluster of cabins that served as Josh's base camp. There I met Tony, the only person left on Josh's crew after the other guy quit. Tony had long blonde hair, tan skin, and muscles everywhere.

On my way to the bathroom one night, I noticed the door to Tony's cabin was slightly ajar. I tapped on it. Tony was smoking pot and listening to music. He offered me a hit. It was the first time I'd ever smoked weed, and it burned the back of my throat. I soon found myself talking about my divorce. He told me stories about his own troubled past. Throughout his childhood his stepdad had abused his mom. I appreciated that he seemed to understand my pain. Before long we were rolling in the sheets. I was dumbstruck and, as soon as the shock wore off, elated when I had an orgasm, my first while having sex with a man.

The first orgasm I ever had via oral sex was a present given to me by Paul Arnoti, a thirty-something white guy who'd met on Match.com and who had a license plate that read—I'm not kidding— **I R NOTI**. As in, "I am naughty." Call it a rebound. But it was a rebound that stuck. We dated for more than a year, despite a fundamental disagreement about kids. He didn't want any; I had one.

Paul and I had been dating for just a couple of weeks when I flew to San Francisco hoping to sell some of my artwork to Lloyd, a longtime client from Virginia I'd met during my first year at Howard when he bought one of my pieces. In the years that had passed he'd purchased several more. A successful businessman, he had much more money and vacation time than I did, so he offered to meet me in California to discuss some of my pieces. He picked me up at the San Francisco airport and took me out to dinner. While we were eating, he started flirting with me, which I found strange and uncomfortable on a number of levels. He was nearly twice my age, his wife had just died from leukemia, and this was supposed to be a business meeting. In desperate need of an art commission to help me get back on my feet financially, I didn't want to anger him. But I didn't want him to get the wrong idea, either. When I told him I was dating someone, he stopped hitting on me, but our conversation grew noticeably chillier after that.

After dinner, we went to a bar to get a drink. I didn't think twice when he handed me a shot of Grand Marnier. I threw it back and joined some ladies on the dance floor who were having some sort of dance-off. I hadn't been on the dance floor fifteen minutes when I suddenly couldn't stand up straight. I was stumbling and dizzy. When I went to sit down, I almost missed the chair. Lloyd grabbed my arm, told me it was time to go, and led me outside to a cab. My vision was beginning to blur. I told him I wanted to go to my hotel room. He said I'd "had a little too much to drink" and took me to his. In keeping with his financial status, it was a deluxe suite.

I was so far gone he had to carry me inside the room and set me down on the couch. I looked on helplessly as my hand slipped off the couch and hit the floor. I tried to move it, but it wouldn't budge. All I could do was stare at it. I'd lost all muscle control. I fought to stay conscious. As he fucked me, first on the couch, then on the bed where he'd dragged me, my awareness of what was happening flickered on and off.

"Stay awake," I told myself. "Stay alive. Do whatever it takes to get back home to Franklin."

When my body started going into convulsions, Lloyd threw cold, wet towels on me. Eventually, I passed out.

When I woke the following morning, Lloyd was perky, almost chipper. "What a fun night," he said. "We should do this again. Maybe take a trip to Hawaii together."

The dissimilarity between our perspectives was disturbing. He was acting like nothing had happened, while I knew I'd experienced something I'd never be able to forget. All I could do was nod as I made my way to the bathroom, where I showered for what felt like an hour, cried as quietly as possible, and formulated a plan. I couldn't let on that I knew I'd been raped. I didn't want to put him on the defensive, or—who knows?—I might not make it back home. I needed to get to the airport as quickly and safely as possible.

During the flight home, I kept running to the bathroom to cry. Paul picked me up at the airport, and I couldn't stop sobbing and hyperventilating as I told him what had happened. He drove me straight to the hospital where doctors gave me a rape kit exam. Confirming what I suspected, they said my symptoms indicated I'd been given GHB, the notorious date-rape drug. Unfortunately, they couldn't prove it definitively. It doesn't take long for all traces of GHB to vanish from your urine and blood, and more than enough time had already passed for it to completely disappear from my system. They pumped my body full of drugs to protect me from HIV, other STDs, and the possibility of getting pregnant. They also lobbed a million questions at me, which I did my best to answer during the brief moments I wasn't passed out from shock.

As I recovered, I felt like I should tell someone about what had happened. I was no longer seeing a therapist, so I called Josh. Given his molestation of me when I was younger, I thought he might understand how I was feeling and be sympathetic. Boy, was I wrong. "What were you thinking?!" he yelled into the phone. "Why did you go out to dinner all alone with a guy you barely knew? Why were you even in San Francisco?" Although he didn't say it in so many words, the message he was giving me came through loud and clear: This was my fault. I'd asked for it. I deserved it. It was time for me to stop acting like a victim.

I took yet another step back from him. We didn't talk for at least a year after that. After discussing my situation with a counselor from the women's center at the college in Iowa where he worked, Josh reached out to say that the way he'd responded had been wrong and acknowledged that he'd made an already horrific experience that much worse. He succeeded in relaying the sentiment the counselor told him he should have originally expressed to me—that he was sorry for my pain and couldn't imagine what I was going through. The gesture was thoughtful but way past due. I'd already stopped caring about his opinions and had effectively cut him out of my life.

When I reported the rape to the San Francisco Police Department (SFPD), the case worker I was assigned was sympathetic but honest. Geography wasn't working in my favor. The fact that the rape had occurred in California, Lloyd lived in Virginia, and I'd done the rape kit exam in Spokane, Washington, while officially residing in Coeur d'Alene, Idaho, added a layer of complexity to a case that already would have been difficult to win. The lack of physical evidence directly tying Lloyd to the rape didn't help. Lloyd's semen couldn't be found anywhere on me or the pair of jeans that I'd worn that night and later mailed to the SFPD's lab.* Thanks to the long, cleansing shower I'd taken the morning after, I'd washed away all the evidence. The case worker leveled with me: the odds of a jury ruling in my favor were at best fifty-fifty.

Making the situation even more difficult, I was in the middle of an ongoing custody battle with Kevin—do these things ever end?—that had flared up once again after Franklin had been injured during one of his every-other-weekend visits with his dad. I was trying to get sole custody of Franklin or at the very least ensure that Kevin's visits were supervised. After everything I'd endured during my divorce proceedings, the last thing I needed was to get embroiled in another lengthy and costly court case.

That a case against Lloyd would be precisely that—lengthy and costly—was confirmed when I emailed him to tell him that I hadn't consented to have sex with him and that I believed he'd drugged and raped me. He not only denied it but sent a very lengthy response that appeared to have been drafted by an attorney. I knew that he was rich, possibly a millionaire, and I also knew, having gone through divorce litigation while unemployed, that in court, money is often more powerful than evidence. Adding to my hesitancy—the optics. I didn't want to cast a spotlight on myself, knowing that many people would think of me as white and fixate on the idea that a *Black* man had raped a *white* woman, when the rape had clearly been about power, money, and gender, not race. I dropped the charges.

Being raped succeeded in ripping the Band-Aid off the wound from my childhood that had yet to fully heal. PTSD isn't an ailment reserved for those who've fought in Iraq or Afghanistan.

---

* In August 2016, I received a call from the SFPD informing me that the Spokane Police Department had finally released the results of the rape kit exam I'd taken eleven years before and it showed that Lloyd's DNA had been found inside of me. However, I had no recourse because the statute of limitations had expired.

The particular type of PTSD I suffered from had several triggers. Anything having to do with religion—church in particular—was one. Men who leveraged money or physical strength to gain power and control was another. As a poor single mother, I was about as low on the economic totem pole as you could get. Buoyed by a consistent salary that dwarfed my sporadic income, Kevin didn't back down when I took him to court; he fought me with everything he had, and in the end won—if there are ever any real winners in such disputes. The judge didn't grant me sole custody of Franklin or the supervised visitation for Kevin I was seeking.

I may not have been rich, but what I lacked in wealth I made up for in integrity. My moral compass was properly aligned. I'd always known the difference between right and wrong and justice and injustice, and I'd worked hard to stay on the correct side of those lines. I'd grown up wanting to help others and change the world for the better, and now after surviving one of the more difficult stretches of my life, this sense of purpose returned full force. It also came with a very specific focus. I not only wanted to help create a more just society, to fight for human rights, to narrow the gap between the haves and the have-nots, and to make the world a fairer and more compassionate place; I wanted to devote all my attention to a specific group, the group that had too often drawn the short straw (although luck had nothing to do with it), the group I identified with most, the group I considered my own: the global Black community.

Chapter Eighteen

Thirteen II

AFTER LOSING HIS SEAT AS COUNTY COMMISSIONER and failing to land another job in the area, Larry prayed for help finding his way and got it in 2000, when God called him and Ruthanne to do missionary work for the fundamentalist Christian organization Answers in Genesis (AiG). They rented their house in Troy to some equally zealous religious fanatics and moved to an AiG outpost in Evergreen, Colorado, with all my siblings. Even Josh lived with them for a short spell while he contemplated what to do next after earning his masters from the University of Nebraska.

The missionary life suited Larry and Ruthanne. When God called them two years later to move to Durbanville, South Africa, a rural suburb of Cape Town, they didn't hesitate. There, Larry taught Young Earth Creationism and served as director of the South African office of the faith-based organization Creation Ministries International.

I still wasn't on good terms with Larry and Ruthanne, but I made a point of staying in touch with them so I could maintain relationships with my younger siblings. I regularly sent my younger brothers and sister care packages while they were living in South Africa and called them every couple of weeks. I was happy that they still felt connected enough to me to confide in me during our phone conversations. But as pleased as I was, I was also concerned about their safety and well-being. Some of the stories they told me were even bleaker than the ones they'd relayed from Montana and Colorado.

What was an ideal situation for the white adults was far less so for their young Black children. Since 1652, when the Dutch East India Company established a settlement at the site of what would one day be Cape Town, the class system in South Africa has been based on race. In 1948, the racial segregation the South African government had supported for nearly three centuries was given a name: "apartheid," an Afrikaans word meaning "apart-hood," or "separateness." The apartheid era was dismantled in 1994, yet the country remained largely segregated when Larry and Ruthanne arrived. They lived in an all-white gated community where the only people my siblings regularly saw who looked like them were Julia, a Black servant hired to help maintain their three-story house, and the people who sneaked into the neighborhood during the day to beg for food.

During one phone call Izaiah told me that while he and our siblings were playing outside, one of their neighbors mistook them for vagrants, yelled at them to get out of the neighborhood, and called them *kaffirs*—the South African version of the N-word. During another call, he shared a story about Larry taking the entire family with him to a colleague's home. Izaiah and Zach got to the door first and rang the bell. When the woman of the house opened the door and saw them, she shouted, "Get off our property, Black trash, or I'll call the police!" Larry waved from the car and explained that they were his kids. As scary and degrading as these experiences must have been for my siblings, Larry and Ruthanne laughed them off as "misunderstandings."

The intent of another misunderstanding my siblings were sub-jected to in South Africa was impossible to misconstrue. During apartheid, the South African government established a racial hier-archy that had "Whites" sitting all alone at the top. "Indians" (which included Asians) came next. Then came "Coloureds," or people of mixed ethnicities. And mired at the very bottom were "Blacks." This meant that at the Christian private school my younger sib-lings attended, Ezra, with his light complexion and loosely curled hair, received far better treatment than his darker siblings—that is, until a gang of white children discovered that Ezra's brothers and sister were Black and used it as an excuse to beat him up. When

Izaiah intervened to help his older but smaller brother, the white kids grabbed sticks from the schoolyard and began beating Izaiah with them. The abuse continued even after Ruthanne arrived to pick up my siblings, with the white kids throwing rocks at them as Ruthanne rushed them from the school to the car. They were homeschooled after that.

Esther had always received worse treatment than her brothers, because, I have to assume, of her gender. Just as they'd done to me, Larry and Ruthanne made her wear "modest" clothes, including bloomers under her dresses. When she was ten, Larry forced her to eat an entire watermelon—I'll leave it to you to decide if any racism was involved—and, reprising the oatmeal incident with me, demanded that she eat any parts of it she threw up. Ruthanne directed her own brand of cruelty at Esther when, just before moving to South Africa, she made Esther leave behind most of her toys, including the Black Raggedy Ann and Andy dolls I'd passed down to her. Whether out of ignorance or malice, for Christmas that year Ruthanne replaced the dolls that had been discarded with *white ones*. Before she went to bed every night, Esther prayed to God that she would wake up in the morning and be white, just so her life would be better, easier, closer to normal.

Ruthanne's cruelty revealed itself once again after she and Larry returned to the United States and settled in Douglassville, Georgia, a three-exit town along the interstate, twenty miles west of Atlanta. One day, while taking out Esther's braids prior to redoing them, Ruthanne got frustrated with the tangles. "Your hair is impossible!" she yelled. "I'm just done!" Using kitchen shears, she cut off Esther's braids one by one. Stunned by Ruthanne's insensitivity, Esther could only sit on the stool and cry as her hair fell to the floor. By cutting off Esther's hair, Ruthanne was not only maiming Esther's natural beauty but also diminishing her self-worth.

This wasn't the only callous behavior aimed at my younger siblings while they were living in in Douglassville. On several occasions Larry and Ruthanne removed every item from their bedrooms except mattresses and Bibles and changed the locks on the doors so they only locked (and unlocked) from the outside.

For days—sometimes weeks—on end, they kept my siblings (with the notable exception of Ezra) confined to their prison-cell-like bedrooms, only letting them out to eat and use the bathroom.

As my younger siblings became teenagers, Larry and Ruthanne's noble experiment of adopting four Black babies began to fall apart. Suddenly the cute little Black children who could be kept in line with a glue stick had grown much taller than their tiny parents and outnumbered them two to one, and the do-as-you're-told-no-questions-asked discipline tactics no longer worked. When Zach briefly fell in with the Crips, the notorious gang that started in Los Angeles before spreading nationwide, Larry and Ruthanne realized they were out of their league entirely.

In a 2014 study, Phillip Atiba Goff, associate professor of social psychology at UCLA, determined that Black boys as young as ten are considered "less innocent" than their white counterparts, and that by age thirteen are viewed as adults by many white people. Two years later at the University of Iowa, a team of researchers led by Andrew Todd concluded that people were more likely to associate violence—misidentify a toy as a weapon, for example—after seeing an image of a Black person than they were after seeing an image of a white person, even when the boys in the images were as young as five. These two perceptions form a deadly combination, as innocent Black children often get treated like and suffer the same consequences as violent adults.

In our family, only Ezra was immune to being viewed so unfavorably. I credit his light complexion as well as his size. Suffering from constitutional growth delay ever since he fell down the stairs as a toddler, even fully grown he was shorter than his diminutive parents. When he turned thirteen, he was the size of an eight-year-old. His skin color and size meant that he not only received preferential treatment, but also that he never had to worry about being sent away—something that couldn't be said about his less fortunate siblings.

Once their adopted children turned thirteen, Larry and Ruthanne started getting rid of them one by one. They turned Zach in to the police for being aggressive and violent; as a result, he either had to go on probation or to a reform school. They chose the latter, sending him to Lives Under Construction, a Christian residential treatment center in Missouri that reforms boys through manual labor. While they were there, they heard about Shiloh Christian Children's Ranch, a group home for abused and neglected children, and thought it would be a good fit for Esther after a girl at church had accused Esther of stealing her phone, which was later found under a couch. Zach and Esther spent their remaining middle school and high school years in these institutions, and I was rarely able to communicate with them during this time.

Izaiah saw the handwriting on the wall. He told me he felt increasingly uneasy and out of place living with Larry and Ruthanne, especially with his siblings getting sent away. Before Zach was cast out, he and Izaiah had gotten into a fight, and Larry had once again called the police and asked that they be arrested—something almost no Black parent would ever do, thanks to a well-reasoned distrust of the police. With Black males having to endure escalated rates of arrest and brutality by the police and longer sentencing by the court system, handing your Black sons over to the cops is like throwing them to the wolves. Yes, this would be bad for any kid, but it's ten times worse for Black kids, particularly males.

Although the matter was settled out of court as an informal adjustment, the fact that Larry had called the cops frightened Izaiah. He knew that, because he was a Black boy, the police rarely would be on his side. He'd heard about what had happened to Rodney King and others like him. Scared it might happen again, he wanted to get out of there. He wanted to be part of a Black family, a family that taught him Black history and Black consciousness, that valued education, and that would set and enforce appropriate boundaries instead of turning him over to outside authorities. When he was thirteen, he asked Larry and Ruthanne if he could live with me for the summer. They'd made their disdain for my divorce and liberated lifestyle perfectly clear, so I was shocked—but overjoyed—when they agreed to let him visit me in Coeur d'Alene.

Once I'd agreed to host Izaiah, Ezra expressed a desire to come, too, but I didn't have enough space in my small apartment for both and wasn't thrilled at the idea of leaving the two of them alone with Franklin while I went to work because they frequently fought. When I told him that I was sorry, but he couldn't come, Ezra stopped talking to me for a while. The grudge he held against me would last for years.

Izaiah arrived at the Spokane International Airport wearing a Hawaiian shirt tucked into high-water khaki pants and white sneakers so dirty they'd turned gray. We drove straight to a men's clothing store so he could get some clothes that fit correctly and matched his style, then to a Black barbershop to get a haircut. After I'd gotten a home-cooked meal in him, we caught up on the events of the past several years. He told me how it always made his day whenever I included a pack of Hubba Bubba bubble gum for him in the care packages I sent when he and our siblings were living in South Africa, how he always tried to get to the phone before the others whenever I called, and how his favorite Christmas present when they were living in Georgia was the *The Lion King 1½* DVD I sent.

Izaiah's happy memories were overshadowed by horrific ones. While we were talking, he stood up and took off his shirt. His back was crisscrossed with scars. He explained how the glue stick Larry had used to punish him and our siblings in Montana had been replaced with a rubber-tipped baboon whip in South Africa. Such a whip is used to drive cattle, kill snakes, keep aggressive dogs and baboons at bay, and, during apartheid, keep Black people in line. My precious little brother, who I'd rocked to sleep as a baby, looked like a product of the slavery era, and he wasn't the only one. All my siblings except for Ezra bore the same scars on their backs.

I hugged Izaiah as tears and anger blurred my vision. I could never forgive Larry and Ruthanne for what they'd done to my siblings. After seeing my brother's back, I could no longer in good conscience claim Larry and Ruthanne as family. That concept— family—clearly meant something to me that it didn't mean to them. To me, it meant love, trust, and safety, not neglect, danger, and abuse.

For my own health and sanity, I severed as many ties with Larry and Ruthanne as I could while still being able to maintain contact with my siblings. I was also hesitant to completely turn my back on them due to the misguided hope that they might still harbor some love for me. My growing independence came at a price, however, as members of my extended family on both the maternal and paternal sides renounced me. Entire limbs fell off my family tree, but I wasn't afraid or discouraged. I received more than enough love from Franklin. He was my family. And that summer Izaiah became a part of it. The three of us formed an entirely new family tree, one that had less to do with blood and more to do with shared experiences, healing wounds, and true love.

Izaiah was seven years older than Franklin, but they bonded like brothers that summer. When I went to work, Izaiah would strap a bike helmet onto Franklin's head, help him onto a bike held upright by training wheels, and walk him up and down the sidewalk. They'd spend hours at the park, playing on the slides and swings. Izaiah would even make Franklin lunch from time to time. PB&J sandwiches were his specialty.

As summer was winding down, Izaiah asked if he could stay with us permanently. Franklin loved the idea, so I ran it by Larry and Ruthanne.

They said no.

Chapter Nineteen

Adopting a New Dad II

TO SUPPORT FRANKLIN AND MYSELF after the divorce, I had to rely on the poverty-induced resourcefulness I'd developed as a child. I worked in the photofinishing lab at Uncle Dan's camera shop on and off for a year and a half. I apprenticed as a sushi chef at Bonsai Bistro, an Asian fusion restaurant located just across the street from the Coeur d'Alene Resort. And I converted styling Black women's hair from a hobby to a job.

A walking billboard for braids, twists, and locs, I got many of my clients from chance encounters in public. In the summer, I liked to wear braids and dreads as carefree, low-maintenance, beach-ready options. In the winter, I preferred a weave because wefts insulate the scalp, negating the need for a hat in the chilly Northwest. When Black women saw me in the grocery store or bumped into me on the street, they often complimented my hair and asked where I'd gotten it done. Most were impressed to hear that I'd styled it myself, a habit I'd adopted to save money, and asked if I could do theirs. These conversations led to a steady stream of clients and a small supplemental income for my family.

My extensive background in art ultimately pulled me—just barely—above the poverty line, although not quite the way I'd imagined. After I finished the fountain Rodney had helped me put together, I was commissioned to paint a mural and sold a few small collages of landscapes at exhibits in Coeur d'Alene and Spokane, but the money I made from these sales wasn't even enough to pay for my art supplies and framing. There simply wasn't a market for

Black art in North Idaho. To me, art is a conversation, and without an audience to respond to my work, continuing to put images into the world that might never be purchased or even seen didn't make much sense. Besides, I had a kid to support. Bread and butter were more important than canvases and paint.

As much experience as I had making art, it was an easy transition when I started teaching it. I worked as a full-time art and science teacher at a Christian prep school as well as a substitute art teacher at a magnet elementary school. In 2005, I made the jump to North Idaho College (NIC), where, as an adjunct professor, I taught illustration and design classes and, starting the following year, an art history and art appreciation course. Because I received the lowest possible pay and no benefits, I took on a similar role at Eastern Washington University (EWU) in 2007. Between the two colleges, I taught full-time but at a lower rate of pay and with less job security than full professors.

The first course I taught at EWU was African and African American Art History, which had been revived after a five-year hiatus created by a lack of qualified teachers. I tried but failed to keep the course alive by cross-listing it with the Africana Studies Program, a department I was completely enamored with. I loved stopping by Monroe Hall, where the program was based. The faculty who had offices there and the students who could be found studying in the lobby were all Black. It was like the Black table at Belhaven, a miniature Howard, and it quickly became my favorite hangout spot on campus.

My interest in Africana Studies was well-received. The following year, the Africana education director, Dr. Bob Bartlett, wanted to expand the program, and, after looking over my résumé and taking note of the scholarly research I'd done and the significant number of graduate credits I'd obtained—from an HBCU no less—he found several courses in his department I was qualified to teach, including African American Culture and African History. During my time at EWU, a succession of program directors came and went, but I stayed and flourished, writing the curriculum for such classes as The Black Woman's Struggle, African American History: From 1877 to Present, and Introduction to Race and Culture Studies.

For me, the most enjoyable aspect of working at NIC and EWU was getting to interact with the students. I mentored several of them and always looked forward to the "Aha!" moments they had when discovering African history's impact on humanity's broader story, the contemporary realities of racism, and the science that proves race to be a social construct with no basis in biology. At NIC, only twelve out of the approximately six thousand students were Black, but in my mind that was an argument for—not against—creating a Black Student Union. This demographic of students was so small and isolated it desperately needed a support group. After getting the Black students on campus excited about the idea of forming a BSU, I guided them through the process of making it an official student organization. Those offended by the idea soon made their opposition known, including "Anonymous," who wrote a letter to the editor of the *Coeur d'Alene Press* expressing the opinion that Black people shouldn't be allowed to congregate alone because they needed the civilizing influence of white people.

As much as I enjoyed working on these campuses, my two part-time teaching positions, even when combined, still didn't provide the salary or benefits of a full-time position, forcing me to take on a third job. In 2007, I got my foot in the door at the Human Rights Education Institute (HREI) by guiding an art series exploring children's responses to the United Nations Declaration of the Rights of the Child. It went so well the executive director, KJ Torgerson, asked me to stay on. Under her watch, I organized exhibits and continued to work with kids. When Bob Bennett, NIC's former president, replaced her later that same year, he added to my list of duties, asking me to develop several new programs.

Bennett was an older white man who wasn't afraid to be politically incorrect. When the entrepreneur and philanthropist Greg Carr, whose million-dollar contribution helped launch the Human Rights Education Institute, paid a visit to HREI, Bennett introduced me to him by saying, "Isn't she sexy?" On another occasion during a board meeting he turned to HREI's secretary, Donna Cork, and asked, "Rachel's a colored gal, right?"

As disturbing as it was to have racist and sexist terminology used to describe me, I'd never felt more fulfilled than when I was working at the HREI. If every step toward Blackness was a step away from whiteness, I was running full steam ahead. I was a Black-Is-Beautiful, Black liberation movement, fully conscious, woke soul sista. Finally allowed to bloom, I blossomed fast, going from an unknown adjunct instructor at a community college making sushi on the side to being a prominent civil rights leader and defender of human rights in the region. I didn't work for the Cause from the outside as a white ally, but from the inside as a Black leader, someone who was eager to not only model the philosophy of a great activist like Angela Davis but sport similarly textured hair as well.

I wasn't merely "passing" as a Black woman. Passing has existed in the United States as long as white people have oppressed people of color, which is to say for its entire history. Typically, it's been light-skinned Black people who have passed for white in an attempt to accrue the same advantages white people enjoyed: to acquire gainful employment, avoid discrimination, and preclude the possibility of being lynched. But why would a white person ever want to pass for Black when doing so would involve losing social and economic benefits? One reason: love. In perhaps the best-known example of white-to-Black passing, bestselling author and famed geologist Clarence King passed for a Black Pullman porter named James Todd in order to marry a Black woman named Ada Copeland. King died before his secret was discovered, but others who have made the same leap, including Reverend L. M. Fenwick, the pastor of an African Methodist Episcopal church in Milwaukee at the start of the twentieth century, reclaimed their original racial identity after being found out. My situation was different. Just as a transgender person might be born male but identify as female, I wasn't pretending to be something I wasn't but expressing something I already was. I wasn't passing as Black; I *was* Black, and there was no going back.

Living as a Black woman made my life infinitely better. It also made it infinitely harder, thanks to other people's racist perceptions of me. The Blacker I became—not just in the clothes I wore or the books I read but in terms of how I was being seen and treated—the more distant and isolated I felt from white people. It had taken me a couple years after my divorce to stop feeling obligated to check WHITE on medical forms, and once I started claiming my identity and checking BLACK, any whiteness I possessed became invisible to the people collecting the forms and even to the doctors examining the most intimate parts of my body. Due to the higher rates of HIV in the local Black community—eight times higher for Black women than white women—nurses started testing me for it every time I went to the health clinic. While getting a bikini wax, I once had an esthetician complain about my "African American hair" as she struggled with a hair that refused to be removed. On another occasion a Latina beauty consultant described my eyelashes as "nappy." While driving, routine police stops took on a hostile feel, and I got so many traffic tickets I had to go to online driving school to keep my license.

The microaggressions I'd once worked so hard to protect my younger siblings from were now being directed at me. Countless strangers touched (or attempted to touch) my hair, commenting about its texture or asking bizarre questions about how often I washed it or whether I even did. While I was shopping in the produce section at Albertson's, a white man told me my hair looked like a mop. While listening to a lecture at HREI about human trafficking, a white lady sitting in the row behind me reached forward and patted my bare shoulder. "I've been looking at your skin all evening," she said, "and I just had to touch it. You people have such smooth skin." The list of racist comments and behavior I experienced could fill its own book. If I had enough energy at the time these incidents occurred, I would try to use them as teaching moments to educate people about their behavior, what they shouldn't do and why. If I didn't have the energy, I'd often throw out a flippant response. To people who asked, "Is that your *real* hair?" when I wore long faux dreadlocks, I'd say, "Some of it!" To those who asked how long I'd been growing my hair, I'd say, "My whole life!"

As wearying as experiencing the social stigma and hardship that comes with being Black was, I didn't regret it for a second. Beyond the police harassment and low social standing, I'd never been happier. To live as anyone but yourself is to live in a prison.

To live openly as yourself—in my case, not the self that Larry and Ruthanne had defined and attempted to shape but my own self-determined existence—is to be free.

When Bob Bennett stepped down from his position as HREI's executive director in 2008 to retire, he recommended to the board of directors that I replace him. His endorsement made sense, as he'd been subcontracting many of his duties to me, but his support came with a discouraging and disrespectful proviso. He suggested that in the future the position should be part-time and come with a much lower salary of $24,000. Much to my chagrin, the board agreed.

That I was young, poor, bisexual, nonreligious, Black, and female were undoubtedly factors in my being given such a lowball offer. According to the theory of intersectionality proposed by law professor Kimberlé Crenshaw in the 1980s, all members of a group aren't treated equally. They're discriminated against to varying degrees according to their gender, race, religion, class, sexual orientation, age, and nationality, and all aspects of their identity are inextricably linked with one another. Because of this, certain individuals can be victims of multiple forms of discrimination at once, which meant I was six steps behind the older, rich, straight, religious white man I was tapped to replace.

Offended by the offer—every previous executive director, including Bennett, had made $70,000—I decided to negotiate. The board responded by keeping the position full-time and increasing the proposed salary to $36,000. When the secretary, Donna, who was white and had no higher education, heard the news, she threatened to quit. She told the board that she refused to make less money than me and to have to report to me. She proposed instead that we be made "co-directors," with her as "director of operations" and me picking any title other than executive director.

I wasn't pleased with the way Donna handled the situation, but I also understood. She had an abusive husband and was trying to figure out how to leave him. To do that, she needed to become more assertive and empowered and to make as much money as she could. Having been in her shoes, I wanted to support her, even if that meant I had to take a hit. As a survivor of past trauma, I usually recognize when others are suffering and feel compelled to help them if I can.

I bit the bullet and accepted the board's revised proposal. As HREI's "director of education," my duties were nearly the same as those once performed by the executive director. In fact, Bob Bennett's job description had literally been copied and pasted onto mine. Meanwhile, Donna's role didn't change all that much—but her salary sure did. She was given a more than $10,000 raise.

I started working as HREI's director of education in November 2008. It was a heady time. That same month, Barack Obama became the first Black man to be elected president of the United States. Prior to his victory, forty-three presidents had occupied the Oval Office, and every single one of them had hailed from the same demographic: white and male. Obama ended that ignominious streak in emphatic fashion, obtaining 365 out of a possible 538 electoral college votes to defeat John McCain. For millions of Americans, Obama's presidency reignited a sense of hope that had nearly been extinguished by centuries of oppression. It was hailed in the media as a breakthrough, a repudiation, a national catharsis. In his victory speech at Chicago's Grant Park, he tapped into that hope, opening with these words: "If there is anyone out there who still doubts that America is a place where all things are possible, who still wonders if the dream of our founders is alive in our time, who still questions the power of our democracy, tonight is your answer." The only ones who weren't cheering wildly were those weeping quietly.

Oh, how I wish I could have been in Chicago to hear Obama's speech or in DC two months later for his inauguration, but I couldn't afford the plane fare or the time away from my new job. Despite the way the board had treated me, I was determined to excel at HREI. I was only required to work thirty-six hours a week, but, fueled by passion and commitment, I often worked sixty or seventy, even though I didn't get paid for working overtime.

Some of those who regularly attended the programs I created were every bit as passionate about civil rights as I was. One of them was Albert Wilkerson, a retirement-age Black man who had served as an Obama delegate in Idaho. He and I hit it off almost immediately. Despite his being nearly forty years older than me, we were alike in almost every other way. We enjoyed the same foods. We were both passionate about art and social justice. And we both enjoyed teaching others about Black history. One day, while talking about areas where Coeur d'Alene was deficient, Albert and I noted its failure to celebrate Juneteenth.

A portmanteau of "June" and "nineteenth," Juneteenth is a holiday that started in Texas to celebrate the end of slavery. Its origins hint at just how entrenched slavery was in the South (and how poor communications were at the time). Abraham Lincoln's Emancipation Proclamation declared that all slaves in the Confederate states were to be freed starting January 1, 1863, but the news didn't arrive in the Lone Star State, where there were more than 250,000 slaves, until June 19, 1865. When Major General Gordon Granger and his Union soldiers landed in Galveston and informed its Black community that the war was over and they were now free, former slaves danced in the streets. The celebration became an annual tradition in Texas after that, although some cities banned it from their public parks. The Black population of Houston and Austin responded by raising money, buying land, and creating so-called Emancipation Parks. The holiday quickly spread from state to state all across the country, but it wouldn't be celebrated in Coeur d'Alene for another 144 years.

In 2009, I added a line item to HREI's budget for a Juneteenth program, and, working together, Albert and I organized the first Juneteenth celebration ever held in North Idaho. We succeeded in attracting more than three hundred people that first year. I handled the advertising, press, signage, food purchases, and T-shirt design, while Albert cooked chicken on his truck-sized barbecue grill in HREI's parking lot and led Buffalo Soldier presentations on horseback.

The more time Albert and I spent together, the closer we became. One day he asked me about my family. "Is it just you and Franklin? You don't seem to have much other family involved."

I nodded.

"Well, I don't need to know all the details, but it seems like you could use a dad and Franklin could use a grandpa."

That he recognized there was a void in our lives meant a lot to me. That he was volunteering to fill that hole meant even more. I started calling him "Dad" soon after that, and he referred to me as his daughter when being introduced to my friends and colleagues. To Franklin, he was always "Grandpa Albert," and Albert thoroughly embraced the role. He took Franklin fishing. He invited us to his house for holiday meals. He even celebrated his birthday with Franklin, as their birthdays fell in the same week in October. With one out of every six Black men being sent to prison at some point in their lives, Black children—especially Black boys—need as many male role models as they can get.

Albert was so good with kids I invited him to speak about civil rights issues at a summer camp I organized at HREI called "Young Advocates for Human Rights." He'd been an instructor most of his adult life, teaching in the Marines and at several high schools and a community college in San Diego, and his experience as an educator came across in his presentation. While listening to him, an idea occurred to me. As someone who was alive during both the Jim Crow and civil rights eras and who was so knowledgeable and entertaining, he'd make a great guest lecturer for some of my classes at EWU. I was delighted when he agreed to do it.

When I introduced my classes to my dad and he spoke about Black history in the United States, he took events that might have seemed dull and antiquated when students read about them in a textbook and, by sharing his personal experiences, made them come alive. He talked about the day-to-day difficulties—eating at a restaurant, seeing a movie—of living under Jim Crow. He described how as a child he'd fled the South for the North with his father and brother as part of the Great Migration after his dad had an altercation with a white police officer. As a former drill sergeant in the Marines, he could also speak with authority about what life was like in the military before desegregation. Not easy, according to him. On three separate occasions, he'd had his life threatened by white subordinates who refused to acknowledge his superior rank. EWU was a PWI—a predominately white institution—but many of the students who listened to him loved him. Even those who could barely remember a single thing I'd taught them could recall Albert's stories.

My relationship with Albert felt perfectly natural. We already related to each other as father and daughter, so using those terms changed almost nothing. Nobody ever asked me if Albert was my biological dad. They just assumed he was, based on my appearance and his, which was a mix of Black, Native American, and Scottish. Visually, we made sense. The fact that his wife Amy was white may have lent even more credibility to the idea, although, just as I'd done with Spencer's wife Nancy, I never referred to her as "Mom," and she never called me her daughter. Family is a private matter, just as one's identity is, so I didn't feel obligated to explain the situation to other people. People saw my identity and my family correctly, even if what was "correct" to me would be considered rare, nontraditional, or unreal to others. This was my life, not theirs.

From time to time people I didn't know very well would ask me if my mom or dad was Black. I'd usually say that my mom was white because to say that neither of my biological parents was Black, that my chosen father was Black, and that I identified as Black would have created a long conversation that, to be honest, I didn't feel obligated or comfortable sharing with total strangers or casual acquaintances. I had learned from my time in Mississippi that most folks, if not all of them, who asked this question didn't want a longwinded answer. Even for people who became my good friends over time, it felt awkward and unnecessary to have to explain the very complex evolution of my identity and my unique family. Between raising a small child and working nearly every minute of the day, I didn't have very many close friends, and I didn't want to risk losing the ones I did have by oversharing. I was content with them seeing me as me, and if they were ever to hear the details of how I'd come to be that way, I trusted that, given all that I'd been through, they would understand why I'd chosen not to share everything with them. As for everyone else—strangers who only knew me as an increasingly public figure in a very small city—it really wasn't any of their business, was it?

If you're hoping to protect those you love from the judgment of others, as I was, you have to be cautious with whom you share all the intimate details of your life. To that end, I tried to answer questions about my identity with the greatest degree of accuracy while not compromising my need to protect Franklin and myself. By doing this, I hoped I could shield our small family from people's misunderstandings, conflicting definitions, and beliefs about race, identity, family, and love.

Understanding how miseducation about race and the cultural boundaries and codes that have been put into place in American society might conflict with my true nature, I decided that the most honest and real way for me to live was to be Black without any explanations, reservations, apologies, or room for negotiation. It had taken me so many years to finally embrace who I was and love myself that I didn't want my understanding of myself to be muddled by other people's perceptions or misunderstandings. I wasn't trying to be anyone else. I wasn't copying someone else's life as a way of escaping my own. All I wanted was to be the most beautiful shade of myself I possibly could.

And yet, as at home as I felt being Black, bonding with other members of the Black community, and being recognized not as an outsider who was "down" but as an insider who was truly in the know, I had a nagging fear that the wonderful and beautiful maturation of my identity I'd enjoyed balanced on a precariously thin precipice. Every job I took on, every relationship I entered, every word out of my mouth was a risk. I was stuck in an awful limbo. I'd never been entirely comfortable in white settings, but I also knew I couldn't fully relax and reveal everything about myself in Black settings, either. Scientists and scholars knew race wasn't a biological imperative, but many people still clung to old-fashioned beliefs, and if they were ever to see the parts of my extended family I'd turned my back on, my entire world could come crashing down.

Chapter Twenty

Malicious Harassment

JUST AS SOUTHERN CALIFORNIA is known for attracting starlets with big-screen ambitions, North Idaho has earned a reputation as a breeding ground for white supremacy groups. When I moved to Coeur d'Alene, at least five of them were headquartered in the area, including the Aryan Nations, a neo-Nazi hate group founded by Hitler enthusiast Richard Butler. After retiring as an aeronautical engineer in 1974, Butler moved from California to Hayden Lake, Idaho, a small town just north of Coeur d'Alene, where he bought twenty acres of land and turned it into a military-style compound complete with a two-story guard tower and armed guards.

The compound served as a factory of propaganda and violence. In 1981, Butler hosted the first Aryan World Congress, an annual gathering of the most influential racist leaders in the country and the white supremacists, neo-Nazis, and skinheads who followed them. The Aryan Nations made its presence known in Coeur d' Alene that year when one of its members harassed and threatened a biracial family and defaced the exterior of a restaurant owned by Sid Rosen, who was Jewish, with a swastika and other hateful graffiti.

Responding to these incidents, Dina Tanners invited seven other local activists to join her at the First Christian Church to figure out how to thwart such hate crimes, and together they formed the Kootenai County Task Force on Human Relations (KCTFHR). Two years later, the task force was instrumental in getting Idaho's Malicious Harassment Act passed, making hate crimes a felony offense punishable by up to five years in prison and a $5,000 fine. Working hand in hand with local law enforcement agencies, it also created a Victim Support Committee, which advocated for victims of harassment and hate crimes and sponsored human rights rallies like the one that drew more than a thousand people to Coeur d'Alene's City Park on July 12, 1986. Two months later, Order II, a domestic terrorist organization affiliated with the Aryan Nations, responded by bombing the home of Bill Wassmuth, KCTFHR's president and a popular local pastor, and, later that month, three other sites around town, including the Federal Building.

Such violence would ultimately lead to the group's undoing. On July 1, 1998, Victoria Keenan, a Native American woman from nearby Sandpoint, was driving home from her niece's wedding when her son Jason inadvertently tossed his wallet out one of the car's open windows. The bizarre incident occurred right outside the entrance to the Aryan Nations' compound at a time when the security guards were particularly jumpy. When the Keenans' 1977 Datsun backfired, the guards mistook the sound for a gunshot. Two of them along with a skinhead from California jumped into a pickup and chased after the Keenans for two miles, shooting at their vehicle until they succeeded in hitting one of its tires and forcing the car off the road. One of the guards grabbed Victoria Keenan by the hair and put a gun to her head. Another hit her in the ribs with a rifle butt. When asked if she was "an Indian," she swallowed her pride and lied, saying, "No, I'm just a poor white farmer girl. I'm on your guys' side." Only after a car approached did the men decide to let the Keenans go.

Afterward, the Keenans contacted KCTFHR's attorney Norm Gissel, who teamed up with Morris Dees of the Southern Poverty Law Center and prominent local attorney Ken Howard, and filed a civil lawsuit against the security guards and Richard Butler. When a jury awarded the Keenans $6.3 million in damages, it bankrupted the Aryan Nations, forcing Butler to sell the compound. Greg Carr—the same Greg Carr who'd go on to contribute a million dollars to help establish HREI—bought the property, demolished the compound, and donated the land to the North Idaho College

Foundation, which turned it into a peace park. Butler died in 2004, the same year I moved to Coeur d'Alene.

With its headquarters destroyed and its leader gone, the Aryan Nations struggled to survive, but their brand of hate never completely disappeared from the area. Splinter groups formed, and they grew particularly enraged after Barack Obama became our country's first Black president. The furor Obama's election aroused wasn't limited to North Idaho. The hope his ascension to the White House engendered in people of color was tainted by a harsh reality: Americans, by and large, were racist as fuck. Seeing a Black man in the Oval Office inspired those who'd previously contented themselves with making snide comments at the dinner table to start openly spewing their racially charged vitriol in public. During his two terms in office, President Obama would be called "tar baby," "that boy," and the "food-stamp president" by a succession of Republican politicians, all of whom were white and male. He was also treated with a level of disrespect—Representative Joe Wilson of South Carolina called him a liar as Obama was delivering a speech before a joint session of Congress, and Arizona Governor Jan Brewer shook her finger in his face on the tarmac of the Phoenix-Mesa Gateway Airport—it's hard to imagine he would have received if he'd been white.

Much of the anti-Obama backlash in North Idaho was directed at HREI and—because I was the face of the organization and was commonly perceived as Black or biracial—at me. After settling into the job, my first big opportunity to expand the institute's reach came in February 2009. For Black History Month, I developed curriculum guidelines, prepared handouts, and made suggested reading lists for local teachers. I also helped school libraries create displays that featured Black-conscious books. My efforts helped HREI's audience grow, but they also attracted unwanted attention.

Donna Cork and I were HREI's only full-time employees, and when she went to lunch one day I was left alone in the building. I was writing thank-you cards to those who'd donated money during a recent fundraiser when the front door bell rang, announcing a visitor's arrival. HREI was partly a museum, so it was common for people to drop in unannounced to view the exhibits. As I made for the front door, I was rehearsing the spiel I typically gave visitors when I rounded the corner and came face to face with two scary-looking white men with shaved heads, piercings, black leather vests, and swastika tattoos, and an equally tatted, pierced, and menacing white woman. The three of them stood like a wall in front of me.

"We just want to let you know we don't like what you're doing here," the man in the middle said.

My heart sounded like a drum in my head. The institute didn't have a panic button, an alarm system, or security cameras, forcing me to improvise. "Well," I said, handing each of them a manual and doing my best to remain calm, "maybe you're just not familiar with all the great new programs we have going on here. Welcome to the Human Rights Education Institute. Let me give you a tour."

Refusing to let on that I knew who they were, I guided them through the political power and human rights exhibit while silently praying that another visitor would stop by or that Donna would return early from her lunch break. When one of the men rolled his eyes and the other one saluted the swastika on a poster for the Social Democratic Party of Germany, which actually denounced Hitler's Nazi regime, I pretended not to notice. My plan was to keep distracting them until I'd succeeded in leading them outside the building.

As we were walking through the lobby on our way to the next exhibit, the man who first spoke up stopped me with a question that sent chills down my spine. "Where does your son go to school?"

Shaken, I almost tripped on a crack in the cement floor. "I didn't realize you knew I had a son." I knew I needed to be vague. "He goes to school . . . in the north part of the city."

He crossed his arms and faced me, striking a pose that showed he felt like he had the upper hand. "And where do you live?"

"A couple miles from here. Why do you ask?"

"We don't like what you're doing here," he reiterated before motioning to the others with a jerk of his head that it was time to go. Before walking out the door, all three of them gave the Nazi salute.

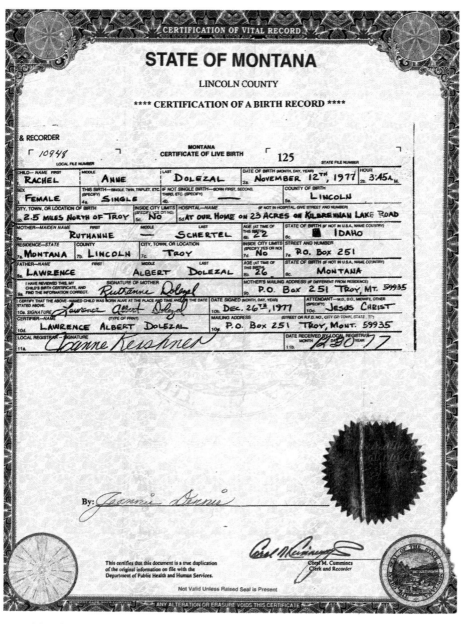

My original birth certificate, which lists Jesus Christ as the attendant to my birth and no address, because Larry and Ruthanne were living in a teepee at the time.

Josh standing in front of the teepee that served as our residence the year I was born and that, in television interviews, Larry and Ruthanne denied existed.

Me, at one month old, with dark hair.

Me and Josh. Notice the difference in our hair colors and skin tones.

A self-portrait I drew when I was four years old.

Me and Ruthanne in our "modest attire."

Izaiah, Ezra, Esther, and Zach in 1996.

Ezra, Esther, Zach, and Izaiah entertaining Larry and Ruthanne's houseguests in Montana during my college years in Mississippi.

Me with Izaiah and Ezra during a trip home from college for Christmas in 1998.

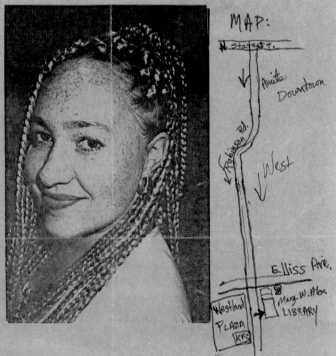

The Margaret Walker Alexander
Library Staff

cordially invites you to join

MAP:
N. State St.
↓ Amite
Downtown
Robinson Rd.
↓ West
Elliss Ave.
Westland
PLAZA
KFC
Marg. W. Alex.
LIBRARY

Artist Rachel A. Dolezal

at the discussion and showing of
POETRY PERFORMANCE
"Pieces of You, Pieces of Me"

Thursday, September 17, 1998

5:30 pm, Margaret Walker Alexander Library

Refreshments will be served.

A flyer advertising an exhibition of my art in Jackson, Mississippi, in 1998, back when I was rocking *Poetic Justice* box braids.

The Antioch community, with Spencer holding his daughter April Joy and wife Nancy beside him (top right), and Uncle Ron and Aunt Joanie holding their daughter Vera (bottom right), circa 1997.

The cover of the last *Reconcilers* magazine, featuring a portrait I drew of Spencer that was also displayed at his funeral.

Me graduating *summa cum laude* from Howard University in 2002 when Franklin was just a baby.

Me, reduced to size 0 from eating disorders caused by stress, just weeks before leaving Kevin and filing for divorce in 2004.

"Uncle" Vern and Franklin after collecting chicken eggs together during our post-divorce stay in his and Uncle Dan's basement in 2005.

Me and Franklin goofing off at his preschool, North Idaho College's Early Childhood Center, in 2005.

Me and Franklin, Christmas 2006.

Me with my dad Albert Wilkerson at Studio 66 in Spokane, Washington, where I displayed some of my art in 2012.

Amy Wilkerson, Albert Wilkerson, Franklin, me, and Izaiah, Christmas 2013.

Izaiah and Franklin bonding during a visit to Montana in the summer of 2006 after Larry and Ruthanne returned from South Africa.

Me, Izaiah, and Franklin after Izaiah's high school graduation in 2013.

CLERK OF DISTRICT COURT
SUSAN FARMER

2010 DEC -6 AM 11: 36

FILED

BY:_____
DEPUTY

1 **MICHAEL C. PREZEAU**
2 District Judge
512 California Avenue
3 Libby, MT 59923

4

5

6

7 **MONTANA NINETEENTH JUDICIAL DISTRICT COURT**
LINCOLN COUNTY

8

9 IN RE THE GUARDIANSHIP OF)
)
10 IZAIAH ALLEN DOLEZAL,)   DG-10-16
)
11)
A Minor.)
12

13

14 **LETTERS OF GUARDIANSHIP**

15

16 On December 6, 2010, the above matter came on for hearing before the
Honorable Michael C. Prezeau, District Court Judge. The Court heard testimony and
17 entered an Order appointing the Petitioner, Rachel Anne Dolezal, as Guardian of the
above-named minor, Izaiah Allen Dolezal. These letters are issued as evidence of the
18 appointment, qualification, and authority of the said Guardian, who was granted full
and complete guardianship of the minor.
19

20 WITNESS my signature and the Seal of this Court.

21 DATED this 6th day of December, 2010.

22

23   Susan Farmer
                                        Clerk of Court
24   By: Tricia Brook
                                        Deputy Clerk of Court
25

26 CERTIFICATE
(STATE OF MONTANA)   ss.

(County of Lincoln)
I hereby certify that the letters to which this certificate is affixed is
a true, correct and compared copy of the original on file in the office
of the Clerk of the District Court and that the date of the appointment
was 12-6-10 and that the same are in full force and
effect.
WITNESS my hand and seal this 06 day of Dec 2010
                     Susan Farmer
                     Clerk of Court
(COURT SEAL)   By Tricia Brook
                         Deputy Clerk

The court order giving me full legal and parental custody of Izaiah in 2010.
Some online sources still list Izaiah as my brother (possibly due to Larry and
Ruthanne repudiating my right to claim him as my son) and do not acknowledge
me as his legal parent.

Franklin, Izaiah, and Esther, Christmas 2015, two years after Esther moved in with us in Spokane.

Esther and me, poolside during the summer of 2013, when she started living with us in Spokane.

Izaiah, Franklin, and Langston outside our house in August 2016, just before Izaiah left to study abroad in Spain.

Me leading an executive committee meeting as Spokane's NAACP president, February 2015.

"*Keepers of the Dream*"

Certificate of Outstanding Achievement & Service

Awarded to

Rachel Dolezal

In recognition of your teaching, work, service and dedication to Africana Students at Eastern

On this 25th day of February in the year 2015

_____
Dean of Social & Behavioral Sciences & Social Work

_____
Director of Africana Studies Program

EASTERN
WASHINGTON UNIVERSITY
start something **big**

Keepers of the Dream Award I earned in 2015 for outstanding teaching and mentoring in the Africana Education program at EWU.

Me and Maryland state's attorney Marilyn Mosby, whose office I visited while I was participating in the Justice for Freddie Gray protests, May 2015.

Me and Rev. Jesse Jackson Sr., at the University of Idaho, when he spoke there in 2011.

Black Art and Identity:
One Woman's Personal Journey

with **Rachel Dolezal**
EWU Assistant Professor of Art

Wednesday, Feb. 27
4-5 p.m.
Monroe Hall 207

Rachel Dolezal, MFA
EWU Assistant Professor of Art
is a mixed media artist who holds her
Master's Degree from Howard University
and a Bachelor of Arts from
Belhaven College. Dolezal
cultivated a resourceful
creative process while
growing up in Montana prior
to her formal training. She
has since exhibited her
awarding-winning work in
13 states and at the United
Nations Headquarters in New
York. Dolezal will show a
number of slides of her work
while sharing stories and insights into her
ongoing identity journey both as a person
and an artist who specializes in Black
artistic expressions.

"Visitation of Light"

EASTERN
WASHINGTON UNIVERSITY
start something **big**

Persons with special needs please contact Lynn at 359.2205 by Tuesday, February 26

A flyer from a lecture I gave at EWU in 2013.

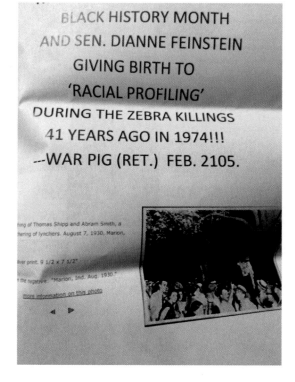

BLACK HISTORY MONTH
AND SEN. DIANNE FEINSTEIN
GIVING BIRTH TO
'RACIAL PROFILING'
DURING THE ZEBRA KILLINGS
41 YEARS AGO IN 1974!!!
---WAR PIG (RET.) FEB. 2105.

Hate mail sent to me at the NAACP P.O. box by "War Pig" in the spring of 2015.

Me with the Spokane Gospel Choir at Bethel A.M.E. after I gave the keynote speech for Martin Luther King Jr. Day, January 2015.

Me directing Transformations, a summer camp for preteen and teen girls of color, at the Spokane YWCA as part of its Empowering Women and Eliminating Racism initiative.

Linking arms in solidarity with protestors during the march for justice for
Antonio Zambrano-Montes in Pasco, Washington, spring 2015.

Gathering photos, flowers, and candles before the memorial march I helped organize for Lorenzo Hayes, May 2015.

Me and Franklin with students from EWU's BSU marching in a Martin Luther King Jr. parade, 2014.

Me and EWU students at a Black Lives Matter rally on campus in 2014.

"Irma Leah," the sculpture I made when I was seventeen to win the Tandy Leather art scholarship.

"Tatters of Time," the mixed-media collage I made when I was seventeen to win the Tandy Leather art scholarship.

A three-panel painting I did in 2004, the year I left Kevin. It's an interpretation of William Turner's "Slave Ship" painting, with the ship representing a sinking parent ship and the two figures in the side panels and middle panel representing a conversation between pessimism and optimism. Critics online accused me of plagiarizing, rather than commenting on, Turner's work.

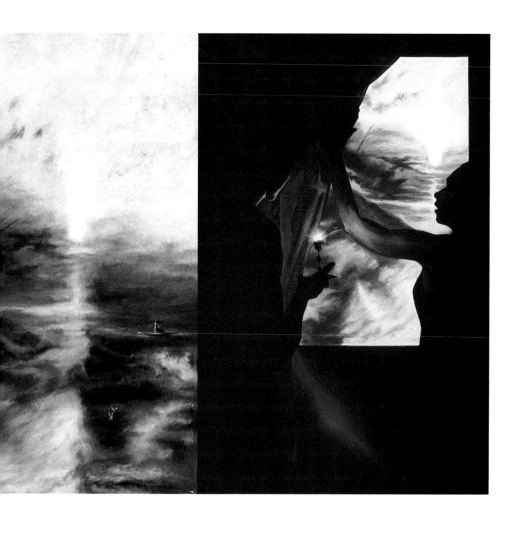

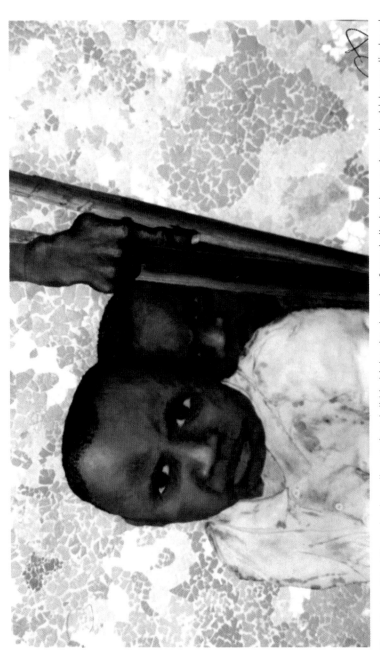

"In a Broken World," a mixed-media art piece I did in high school, made of eggshells, leather, and wood, which was displayed at the United Nations headquarters in New York City for a year.

R A C H E L D O L E Ž A L

Taraja Acrylic on Eggshells

"Taraja," a portrait I made using eggshells in 1998 when I was at Belhaven College of a little girl from the Mississippi Delta. "Taraja" is Swahili for "hope."

RACHEL DOLEŽAL

My Place Acrylic on Puzzle

"My Place," a painting I made in 2004, using recycled puzzle pieces and acrylic on panel. The model is a little girl from South Africa, and the setting is a sunset on the mountainside where I was born in Montana.

Two weeks later, one of my neighbors called the police when he spotted a white male in a hoodie trying to break into my house while I was at work. A year passed. The hate persisted. Another white male in a hoodie approached Franklin at his school and tried to lure him into his car with candy. The police investigated both incidents but never found the culprits. Their response—"Sorry, we didn't find any suspects"—would become a common refrain.

I was terrified. Surely there was a connection between these incidents and the incident at HREI. I bought a gun, took shooting lessons, and moved across town with Franklin. The problem moved with us. Soon after we'd settled into our new place, our neighborhood was littered with white supremacy leaflets. Even more discouraging, our neighbors blamed us for it in televised interviews, describing how unsafe they felt now that we lived near them.

When my new boyfriend, Dexter, invited us to come stay with him in Spokane, just across the border in Washington State and just inside the boundary established by my custodial agreement with Kevin, I quickly accepted. Dexter was a corrections officer at the Airway Heights Corrections Center. He was also six foot three and built like a linebacker. People didn't mess with Dexter. I had hoped his house was beyond the hate groups' reach. He'd lived there for eight years and, despite being Black, said he felt safe in the neighborhood. But within six weeks of our arrival his house was burglarized. Thirteen thousand dollars' worth of property was stolen. Once again, no suspects were found, but I felt confident I understood why we'd been targeted. I wasn't just perceived as Black but Black and "uppity," thanks to my growing profile in the community. I was a human rights, social justice "troublemaker." My suspicions were confirmed the next morning when we walked outside to get the newspaper and found a rope twisted into a shape all too familiar to America's Black population. A noose lay on our front porch.

My anxiety skyrocketed. I winced every time I turned on my car, suspected that cars in my rearview mirror were following me, and diligently investigated anything that seemed even remotely suspicious. Never able to fully relax, my health deteriorated. I became ill with mononucleosis, strep throat, and a rare kind of rash called viral exanthemata, *all at the same time*, and landed in the ER.

The tension drove an irreparable wedge between me and Dexter. More than anything, I needed to be in a safe place full of love and support, but I was no longer getting that from him. We began arguing. He'd led a quiet life before meeting me and didn't enjoy being associated with what was an increasingly public situation. The police actually hosted a "noose viewing," letting the press come to the police station to examine the noose, and some members of the media didn't seem to believe it was a noose at all. Dexter thought I was talking to the press too much, while I believed I was just running damage control, trying to make sure the story the media was telling was accurate. After Dexter and I decided to go our separate ways, Franklin and I moved back to Idaho, where we stayed with a friend until we could find our own place.

Responding to the hate crimes directed at me, HREI's board of directors had security cameras installed in and around the building. Unfortunately, they weren't working correctly when Donna arrived at the institute the morning of November 19, 2009, and found a swastika sticker that had been affixed to the front door sometime during the night. When I got to work a half an hour later, I asked Donna, who as director of operations was responsible for the security cameras, if she'd looked at the video feed from the night before to see if the culprit had been captured on film. She apologized and explained that she hadn't set the cameras to save mode. They'd been on but hadn't recorded anything. The police arrived, removed the swastika as evidence, and scoped out the perimeter of the building, but without any video footage they had no leads to follow.

In June 2010, Franklin and Izaiah, who was visiting us for the summer, ran through the back door one morning, yelling that I needed to come see what they'd found while picking strawberries in the backyard. I threw on a robe and followed them outside. My heart sank when I saw what had spooked them. From the rafters of the carport hung a noose, and like the first one, the message behind it was clear. I called the police. The officer who arrived wrote up the incident as a hate crime. It didn't matter how many times we moved; the hate always found us.

All the publicity these hate crimes generated didn't sit well with HREI's board of directors. They wanted to know what I was saying and doing to upset the local white supremacists. I didn't have an answer for that beyond, "Promoting human rights causes and being myself?" At board meetings, I was asked to carefully examine the words I used while making statements to the press because, the board members implied, perhaps something I was saying was causing the antagonistic responses. Having already been blamed for my own rape, I couldn't believe I was being blamed for having hate crimes directed at me and my family. The implication added a considerable amount of stress to an already nerve-racking situation.

Some of the board members suggested that the "negative press" was bad for tourism, a complaint that was anathema in a tourist town like Coeur d'Alene. Others worried that it might hurt our donor base. Soon I began hearing talk about the board wanting "a different face" for the organization, one that was less controversial and less upsetting to the opposition. It didn't seem to matter that in just two years I'd succeeded in transforming HREI from a local organization with little influence to a regional one with a noticeable impact.

I was blindsided when the board hired Dan Lepow, an older white man, to be HREI's development director in July 2010. During his first day on the job, Dan sat me down and told me I was too focused on Black rights. "I want you to know that, although I'm part Jewish, when it comes to the Black and white issue, I'm a white man." I heard him loud and clear. Within two weeks of hiring him, the board made a motion to promote him to executive director, the position I'd effectively been filling for the past two years and the title I'd been working so hard to attain. Adding insult to injury, the board asked me to train Dan to be my boss. Having documented all my achievements at HREI and stored them in a packet, I gave it to the board and asked them to name me executive director instead of Dan; otherwise I would resign. They responded by having the locks on all the doors rekeyed that night and, when I showed up for work Monday morning, giving me one hour to clean out my office.

My jobs in academia kept me afloat financially, but the sporadic nature of the work was trying. As a quarterly faculty member at EWU, I got courses added to my schedule (and consequently more pay) when full-time instructors didn't want to teach them or new ones were added to accommodate demand. By the same token, I often had courses taken from me (along with the income I would have received) by full-time instructors who were unable to fill their own classes. Sometimes these changes would come with as little as two days' notice before a semester began. I once picked up a course I'd never taught before just two hours before it began on the first day of classes, and I wasn't even given a syllabus. I had to write the curriculum as I taught the class. Hoping to gain some stability, I applied for a full-time position in EWU's Africana Studies Program twice during my time there, but both times it came down to me and another person—and the other person always got the job.

The career setbacks I experienced didn't detract from my passion for human rights, and in many ways they actually fueled it. I recognized the way HREI's board had treated me as a common form of institutionalized injustice. I'd worked twice as hard as all the previous executive directors had and received half the pay. I'd also outperformed all of them, but because I was viewed as a poor young Black woman, how was I rewarded? I'd been slapped in the face with a series of isms—racism, ageism, classism, and sexism—which, combined, delivered the force of a punch. My leadership had been stifled, my voice had been suppressed, and in the end I had been replaced, but I refused to give up.

The normal instinct in such a situation is to want to change the aspects of your character that are holding you back, but the only thing I could possibly fix was being penniless and, trust me, I was doing the best I could there. Everything else involved a permanent aspect of my being, something that couldn't be changed or removed. If I was looking to live an easier life, this would have been a great time for me to opt out of being Black. Simply by untwisting my braids and staying out of the sun, I could have crossed back over the color line. This assumes, of course, that Blackness describes little more than racialized physical features. But to me, Blackness is a permanent part of who I am, an aspect of my character that had taken me a lifetime to have the courage to publicly claim and openly embrace, and I wasn't about to give up on *me*. So I responded to the series of isms society had forced upon me with one of my own: activism.

As an "academic activist," I lived and breathed my research and endeavored not just to educate my students but also to change their lives. I also grew more vocal in response to racial injustices in the local community. When a pipe bomb was found in a backpack along the route of the MLK Day march in Spokane in 2011, I pressed authorities to find the culprit. As a member of the Spokane chapter of the NAACP—there wasn't a North Idaho chapter—I attended the press conference about the incident and called out the FBI as the news cameras rolled. I said I'd lost faith in the process. How hadn't they found any suspects? When they said, "We're doing all we can," was this really true? Or was this going to be just like all the other incidents, many of which I had personally experienced, where the local police and FBI dropped the ball and failed to find the culprit? Finally, two weeks later, the FBI succeeded in tracking down the perpetrator, Kevin Harpham of the National Alliance, a violent group of neo-Nazis who would do just about anything in their effort to establish an all-white homeland.

The failed bombing attempt was big enough news to attract the attention of the national NAACP leadership. Its president and CEO, Benjamin Jealous, traveled to Spokane to lead a protest march that doubled as a commemoration of the anniversary of Martin Luther King Jr.'s death. It was refreshing to see Jealous in person, for not only was he a greatly admired Black activist but also one whose complexion was even lighter than mine. DNA testing he once underwent on PBS's *Finding Your Roots* showed that he is 80 percent European and only 18 percent sub-Saharan African, prompting the show's host (and Harvard professor, author, filmmaker, and critic) Henry Louis Gates Jr. to jokingly refer to him as the "whitest Black man we've ever tested."

Jealous identified as a Black man, but would it have mattered if he didn't? Not according to the NAACP, which, 108 years after its founding, remained the foremost civil rights organization in the country. On its website, it says, "The mission of the National

Association for the Advancement of Colored People is to ensure the political, educational, social, and economic equality of rights of *all persons* [emphasis mine] and to eliminate race-based discrimination." One of its creators, Mary White Ovington, was white. Walter White, its president from 1931 to 1953, was technically Black, but with his white skin, blue eyes, and blonde hair, he could have easily passed as white, which he often did in order to infiltrate KKK meetings. And, although most of its chapter presidents are Black men, more than a few of them throughout its history have been white.

On April 3, 2011, Jealous led a protest march from the Spokane Veterans Memorial Arena to Riverfront Park, where he spoke about the need to embrace diversity and come together as one nation. I was honored to be invited by the president of the NAACP's Spokane chapter, V. Anne Smith, to speak as well. That day I publicly called out racism, white supremacists, and institutionalized injustice in the North Idaho and Eastern Washington communities. I specifically focused on addressing the apathy of people "with good intentions" who were sitting idly by and the dangers of the good-ole-boy network, including the police, business owners, and even leaders of some local nonprofits, which was preventing the possibility of any significant change occurring in the region. I also talked about how so many hate crimes in the area had gone unaddressed and unsolved because institutions cared more about keeping up appearances than about protecting Black citizens.

"We wear race, disability, religious, and gay blinders to edit out what we do not want to see," I told a reporter from *The Fig Tree*, a local monthly newspaper. "Our goal is not color blindness because blind love is weak love. We need to see the differences and appreciate them. We need to take off our blinders and love our neighbors as ourselves. This means loving especially people who are different or 'other.' Racial hatred exists. We can start to overcome it by taking off our blinders. The greatest tragedy is when good people are silent."

Standing up to injustice and hate became my mission. There was plenty of it in the area, but there were also plenty of educated responses to it. One of them was the annual Dr. Martin Luther King Jr. Children's Program, which the KCTFHR, NIC Popcorn

Forum, and NIC Human Equality Club started in 1986 as a way of educating every fifth grader in the Coeur d'Alene and Post Falls school districts about civil rights. I first attended in 2009 when I was director of education at HREI, then worked with the schools themselves to find speakers in 2011 and 2012, helping to recruit performers like Living Voices' Dior Davenport, who reenacted scenes from the civil rights era.

As I was leaving the Children's Program in my car in 2012, I was confronted by eight members of the White Knights branch of the KKK. They wore military fatigues, had guns on their belts, and waved Confederate flags and signs with vile slogans such as "Martin Luther King Was a Nigger Terrorist," "If Diversity Wins, We Lose," and "Honk to Keep Idaho White." I knew they were with the KKK because I recognized their Grand Wizard, Shaun Winkler, who was one of Richard Butler's understudies. As I was rounding the corner of Northwest Boulevard in my black Pontiac Vibe, Winkler and his minions spotted me and yelled, "We know where you live, Rachel!"

Furious that they that would call me out by name and threaten me like that, I did a U-turn and sped home. Unable to find any poster board in the house, I grabbed a thirty-six-inch print of my "AFRIKA" collage, wrote, "Malcolm X is My Hero" on the back with a Sharpie, and drove straight back to where the KKK were protesting the MLK Day festivities. Standing directly across the street from them, I held my poster in front of my chest, flipping it around so they could see both sides, while intermittently texting friends asking them to join me. Standing there all alone, I flinched every time a car honked in response to the KKK's sign, but I held my ground. I was relieved when "Juice," one of my good friends, finally showed up. With a Black man standing next to me, the shouting from across the street died down quite a bit. Then another friend, Virgil, arrived, and he got them all riled up again by yelling things like, "You're so stupid K is the only letter in the alphabet you know!" Some of my students from North Idaho College took an even bolder approach. Two of them, both white males, stood on either side of the KKK protestors with signs that had arrows pointing toward them and read "I'm not with stupid."

Nearly twenty-five people showed up to support me, and once the KKK protestors saw how badly we outnumbered them they packed up their stuff and went home.

Afterward, some people said I was wrong to counter the KKK protest with one of my own. They said it would have been better if I'd just ignored them. But from my experience dealing with hate groups I can tell you that ignoring them is not the best strategy. Threats that get ignored don't go away. They fester. They gain momentum. And soon the little problem you once casually disregarded has turned into an enormous one you'll never be able to forget.

Chapter Twenty-One

Raising Black Boys
in America

AFTER LARRY AND RUTHANNE refused to allow Izaiah to live with me and Franklin, he returned to Atlanta with them. His homecoming didn't last long. One night, as Larry and Ruthanne were clearing his bedroom of everything but a mattress and a Bible as punishment, they found the copy of *The Autobiography of Malcolm X* and several books by Noam Chomsky and Howard Zinn I'd given him. The books were a source of inspiration and reason in a house that lacked both—he'd been forced to hide them behind a ceiling panel in his room. Now they'd been confiscated. Tired of being treated this way, Izaiah's desire to escape Larry and Ruthanne's household resurfaced.

More than anything, Izaiah wanted to live with a Black family, and fate seemed to have rescued him when his biological parents, Cedric and Wanda Bates, made a request through the adoption agency to meet him. They lived southeast of Chicago in Merrillville, Indiana, a town that doesn't have the same bad reputation as nearby Gary and Chicago's South Side do but isn't exactly considered Pleasantville, either. Larry had a Creation Ministries conference in North Chicago coming up and offered to take Izaiah along, but he wasn't willing to venture down to Merrillville. When I heard this, I volunteered to fly to Chicago and facilitate the process. Larry suggested we meet Cedric and Wanda at the Field Museum of Natural History, a neutral spot in the heart of Chicago, but it turned out to be a very uncomfortable place to meet someone for the first time and have any sort of relaxed conversation, so we followed Wanda's suggestion and went to a nearby Dave & Buster's instead.

After lunch, Larry returned to his conference in North Chicago. When Izaiah told me he didn't feel comfortable taking off with his biological parents minutes after meeting them, I offered to go along. When he and I pulled up to the Bates' house in Merrillville, it was like a scene lifted from the movie *Antwone Fisher*. All the relatives—cousins, aunts, uncles, half-siblings, grandparents—and some neighbors as well had packed themselves into Cedric and Wanda's little house and spilled into the yard to greet Izaiah. Wanda sat with her aging mother, while Cedric manned the barbeque. There were so many people in the house it was hard to hold a conversation with anyone for more than a minute. Family trivia flew at us from all directions: Morgan Freeman was Izaiah's fifth cousin, someone's brother played professional basketball, one of the cousins just had a baby, and on and on.

I received just as much love as Izaiah. Wanda's best friend Boo was particularly friendly. A light-skinned Black woman, she kept referring to me as her twin sister and took several selfies of me and her together to show how similar we appeared. Some people there said we looked exactly alike, while others mentioned how they had family members who had similar "high yellow" or "redbone" complexions as mine—the same kinds of things I'd grown used to hearing during my time in Mississippi. The weekend we spent with the Bateses reminded me how much I missed living in a Black community. Even when the subject of the conversation was race, it never felt awkward. The Bateses had seen photos of me as a child and knew that Larry and Ruthanne were white, and yet they saw me for who I really was, making me feel right at home. "Girl," Boo said at one point, "you're really more Black than you are white anyway." I didn't disagree.

After Izaiah returned to Georgia, he and the Bateses kept asking Larry and Ruthanne to let him live in Merrillville, until they finally agreed. This was a compromise on both sides. Izaiah and I figured that living in Merrillville would be better for him than living with Larry and Ruthanne, while Larry and Ruthanne thought living in Merrillville would be better for him than living with me, the disgraced divorcée.

But the experience didn't turn out the way Izaiah had hoped it would. After living in Merrillville for just a few months, he was on the phone with me nearly every single day, saying he felt extremely uncomfortable there. Kids at school called him a faggot for playing violin and liking baseball and teased him for being a virgin and "talking white." Being continually compared to his biological brothers created an awkward tension that grew worse with time. Izaiah wanted out, but he didn't want to go back to Larry and Ruthanne. He begged me to fly him to Idaho, so he could live with me and Franklin.

I called Cedric and Wanda and asked them to let Izaiah come visit me for his sixteenth birthday. I assured them it would only be for a week or two, but I'd already made up my mind: I only bought him a one-way ticket. Several weeks later, when it became clear to Cedric and Wanda that Izaiah wouldn't be returning to Indiana, all hell broke loose. They threatened to sue me, but without legal custody of Izaiah they didn't have any recourse. Larry and Ruthanne, however, did. Threatening to charge me with kidnapping if I didn't return Izaiah to them, they told me they were moving from Atlanta back to Montana and were going to stop in Coeur d'Alene along the way to pick him up. I had no choice but to let him go. As I was hugging him goodbye, I shoved a cell phone into his pocket so he could talk to me whenever he wanted to.

Over the course of the next several months, I took a step back and let Izaiah figure out what he wanted to do. This was his life, after all. I wanted him to be sure about the choices he made and to feel empowered about charting his own course. He may have only just turned sixteen, but he'd been through a lot more than most people twice his age had, so I was confident in his ability to decide whatever he thought was best. When he asked me to help him petition the court for emancipation, I drove to Montana, picked him up at his high school during his lunch break, and took him to the courthouse, where he filed the paperwork. We were careful not to betray our intentions to Larry and Ruthanne, but the law thwarted our efforts. Because he'd never held a job and couldn't support himself, Izaiah's request for emancipation as a minor was denied. Needing someone to look after him for three more years and help him get into college, he turned to the one person who'd always been there for him ever since he was two weeks old—me.

Izaiah and I filed to have parental custody and guardianship transferred to me. He wrote a lengthy and heartfelt essay detailing his desire to be part of a family that took education seriously, was connected to the Black experience, and supported his identity as a Black male. The judge fairly shrugged. But when he described the abuse he'd experienced at the hands of Larry and Ruthanne, *that* got the court's attention. And Larry and Ruthanne's as well. They'd initially fought the custody transfer, but when the court ordered an investigator to go to Missouri to interview Esther about the abuse she'd suffered, they backed down and agreed to grant me custody of Izaiah. Had they continued to fight and the abuse been verified, I could have been awarded custody of all four of my adopted siblings. They opted to lose a battle instead of the war and moved on. Franklin had already been referring to Izaiah as his big brother for three years. Now it was official. The court awarded full custody and parenting responsibilities of Izaiah to me on December 6, 2010.

Soon after I was awarded custody of Izaiah, he and I sat down in the living room of our house and had a heartfelt conversation. After all that he'd been through during his traumatic childhood, he wanted a fresh start. Moving to a new town and enrolling at a new high school, he didn't want to be known as a Black kid who'd been adopted by a white family or a kid who'd been adopted by his sister. Like most teenagers, he wanted to blend in. He was Black. He wanted to be part of a Black family. He told me that I was the only one who'd always been there for him, that he felt like I was his real mom, and that he wanted to start calling me that. He didn't want to have to tell kids at his new school about Larry and Ruthanne, the adoptions, the religious fanaticism, and the abuse.

I could feel how much the pain of his past weighed on him, and I wanted nothing more than for him to be free of it. He had all the potential in the world, and I wanted to see him realize it. Maybe our solution wasn't typical, but his life up to this point hadn't been, either. Together we decided it would make the most sense and raise the fewest questions—and eyebrows—to tell people that before arriving in Coeur d'Alene he'd been living with his dad in Chicago, which was technically true, and that now he was living with me, his mom, which was also technically true. We knew that people would assume we meant that I was his *biological* mom, and that was fine with us. The details were nobody's business. Izaiah had described to me a life that would make him happy, that would allow him be a normal kid, and I was happy to help create that for him. I hugged him, then clasped his shoulders and looked him in the eye. "Welcome home, son."

Within the spectrum of skin color created by the amount of melanin one possesses, Izaiah was mid-tone in complexion and Franklin was light-skinned. When people asked me if they had different dads, I'd say, "Yes, Izaiah looks like his dad and Franklin looks like me," another true statement that could only be construed as a lie by people who were making certain assumptions. It was a clever way of telling the truth without spelling out all the details. I thought of it as "creative nonfiction." It made sense to the three of us, and in the end that's all that mattered to us. Izaiah had made it clear that he wanted to be part of a Black family, and with Franklin as his brother and me as his mother, that's exactly what we were.

Before that conversation, I'd often, but not always, worn my hair in traditionally Black styles, and I hadn't paid much attention to my skin color beyond sunbathing on the shores of Lake Coeur d'Alene in the summer. After that conversation, I never wore my hair straight or unaltered in public, and I consciously maintained some warmth of color in my skin, whether through sunbathing or bronzer sprays. I'd already been identified by the media and other people as Black or biracial countless times, so it wasn't hard for me to go one step further and fully commit to a look that made visual sense to people who knew me as Izaiah's mom.

This was the final piece of the puzzle surrounding my identity. I now felt completely free and secure in who I was. I'd learned to love myself and trust myself and do whatever I felt was right instead of doing what I felt others expected me to do. I'd finally claimed the identity I'd always felt was true to who I was, and in the process I distanced myself from anyone who'd known me as a child and made an entirely new set of friends and connections. Although there were some challenging days, it was still the happiest time of my life. While I was helping Izaiah shed the cocoon that had been holding back his growth, he helped me blossom into who I really was.

The joy of being Izaiah's mother, legally and practically, was mitigated by the fear of having to raise him in a place like North Idaho. At the start of third grade, Franklin returned home from school with a disappointed look on his face. "Mom, I'm the only Black kid in my class *again*," he said.

"I thought there were two girls in your class who are biracial."

He sighed. "It's not the same. They don't *know* they're Black."

I understood what he meant. Most of the Black kids you came across in Idaho were usually either biracial—often being raised by a white mom with an absent Black dad—or had been adopted by white parents. While they may have appeared Black, culturally they were being raised with a white mindset. These kids tended not to know any Black history, were ill-informed about Black culture, and weren't offended by racial slurs, including the N-word.

That's not how I raised Franklin, and while I believe it was the right thing to do, it also made living in an all-white area more complex for him. His attitude as much as the color of his skin made him a habitual target of racism. He was called a "monkey" and, during one bitter winter day, a "Black snowman." A white classmate, who had undoubtedly overheard someone talking about wanting to kill President Obama, once told Franklin that if Franklin ever became successful he'd hunt him down and "assassinate" him. Another classmate, also white, picked up Franklin and threw him over his shoulder one day, causing Franklin to hit his head on some concrete and get a concussion. The kid who caused the injury wasn't punished or even made to apologize.

On another occasion, four white kids held Franklin down during recess and kicked him in the gut, but the only one who got in trouble was the kid who'd uttered racial slurs as he was doing it. His punishment? He had to walk one lap around the playground. After hearing about the incident, I stormed into the school and—no doubt being viewed as an Angry Black Mom—was made to sit and wait for over thirty minutes so I could "calm down" before the principal would see me.

During a field trip with his class, Franklin was standing on the side of a road when a white kid pushed him, causing Franklin to lose his balance and nearly fall into oncoming traffic. The result? The teacher wrote *Franklin* up for "violent/aggressive behavior." Knowing that tagging little Black boys with a violent label was the first step in the school-to-prison pipeline, I raised hell at his school until it was expunged from his record. After failing to get any sort of apologies or justice after these incidents, I reached out to the NAACP for help, but to no avail. The sad reality in that part of the country was that, when it came to their education or even their safety, Black kids simply weren't a priority.

The anxiety I felt about Franklin's welfare extended beyond school. One day I took him to an orientation session for a Cub Scouts troop he wanted to join. I sat at a table with all the other parents as the troop leader went over the basics of Scouting. As I looked around the table at the other parents, my eyes locked on a man with a shaved head and lots of piercings who looked oddly familiar. When he saw me looking at him, he nodded in a way that made it clear that he knew me. Where did I know him from?

As he passed the sign-in sheet to me, he said, "Just write your current address and phone number on this line," then rolled up his sleeve to make sure I didn't miss the large swastika tattoo on his pale, meaty forearm. His voice and the tattoo hit me like a bucket of ice water dropped on my head. He was one of the neo-Nazis who'd threatened me at HREI three years before. I felt momentarily paralyzed, then my stomach tensed as I glanced around the room. Everyone was white. I was the outsider here, not him.

Not wanting anyone to see how badly I was shaken, I excused myself from the table and ducked into the bathroom to compose myself. I was on the verge of tears but also determined to expose this man. Taking a deep breath, I returned to the meeting room where I took the troop leader aside, told him about the incident at HREI, and explained why I felt that Franklin, and possibly other children of color, wouldn't be safe in this man's presence. The troop leader smiled at me and explained that they were an inclusive troop, which meant that it included parent volunteers as well as children from all backgrounds, whether they be people of color or neo-Nazis. The man with the swastika tattoo and his son had been members the previous year and the Scouts had had no problems with them. I started to explain that being inclusive of hate was by definition not being inclusive, but I could see by his smug smile that I wasn't getting anywhere, so why bother?

I found Franklin in the kids' playroom and told him something had come up and we needed to go. During the car ride home, I explained the situation to him as best as I could. I apologized that he had to grow up in a part of the country that was so alienating for Black people, and I let him vent. He told me he hated that his friends didn't have the same worries he did. His life basically sucked. He was a Black kid in North Idaho with a mom who was passionate about human rights, and, as far as making and keeping friends went, what could be worse than that?

I understood his pain because I felt it, too. I wished we could live somewhere he could be a Cub Scout without me having to worry about his safety, but the court wouldn't allow us to move more than thirty miles away until he was eighteen. In the meantime, I was determined to never back down from the fight I'd started to think of as my life's purpose. The struggle to attain equal rights for all wasn't an abstract subject for me but a description of my sons' daily lives.

Huddled between me and his cat October, Franklin slept in my bed that night, a habit he'd developed ever since he'd nearly been abducted from his school two years before. I remained awake long after he'd fallen asleep, listening to the walnut tree branches scratching at the window in the wind and cherishing the faint puff of his breath on my shoulder.

As stressful as it was to raise Franklin in that environment, raising Izaiah there was even more nerve-racking. He had entered that critical age—too young to know how to fully take care of himself but too old to be seen as an innocent child by most white people—that makes mothers of Black sons toss and turn in their beds at night.

Having seen studies that suggested that nice clothes might be a defense against racial profiling, I encouraged Izaiah's budding interest in fashion, buying him shoes and clothes whenever I could afford to—and many times even when I couldn't. He had a great sense of style, and it paid off in the way people responded to him. The better he was dressed, the nicer they treated him. He was voted Best Dressed in his high school, but for him, maintaining a nice wardrobe wasn't fueled by vanity alone. It was an act of self-respect as well as survival. To this same end, I didn't let him stay out late or party. As a Black boy, it simply wasn't safe for him to be out on the streets at night in Idaho, where people openly carried guns, proudly displayed them on racks in their trucks, and weren't afraid to use them.

And, of course, Izaiah and I had The Talk. I sat him down and explained the concept of DWB—Driving While Black—and the many other perceived "offenses" Black boys and Black men in the United States commit simply by being themselves. The list of things they can't do without attracting the attention of the police or "concerned citizens" is shocking and embarrassing and sad. For Amadou Diallo, it was pulling out his wallet in response to the police's request to show them his identification in front of his Bronx, New York, apartment building in 1999; he died after the police shot him forty-one times. For Harvard professor Henry Louis Gates Jr., it was entering his own home just a few blocks from Harvard Square on July 16, 2009; when Sergeant Crowley of the Cambridge Police Department said he didn't believe Gates lived there and Gates protested, Crowley charged him with disorderly conduct. And for Trayvon Martin, a seventeen-year-old high school student, it was carrying candy while walking through a gated community in Sanford, Florida, on February 26, 2012; he died after George Zimmerman, the neighborhood watch coordinator, confronted Martin and shot him in the chest.

When Trayvon Martin was shot—and even more so when George Zimmerman was later acquitted—mothers of Black boys nationwide went into a state of emergency, and I was no different. Izaiah was the same age, height, and weight Trayvon was when he was killed. For all intents and purposes, he *was* Trayvon. They even enjoyed the same candy. When he was shot, Trayvon was carrying a bag of Skittles, and in the wake of his death that candy took on new meaning, highlighting his youth and innocence and becoming a symbol of racial injustice. Feeling compelled to protest this senseless death, I designed two commemorative hoodies. One read, "Got Skittles? Never forget Trayvon Martin," and the other, "Am I . . . Suspicious?" To get the sweatshirts made, I invested about a thousand dollars of my own money—money that, as someone who'd never made more than $37,000 a year, I couldn't spare—and then distributed them at local protests and rallies. Some people paid for them at cost, but I gave most of them away and ended up losing money on the deal. I didn't care. This wasn't business. It was activism.

Trayvon Martin's death had another unfortunate result. While Uncle Dan, his partner Vern, and I had always found common ground as pariahs of the Doležal family, we didn't see eye to eye about everything, and racial justice activism was one of those things. Vern didn't get why I'd made the hoodies in Trayvon's honor. Having been raised in North Idaho, he didn't understand that much about Black consciousness or Black culture. As the mother of two Black sons, I felt the urgency. Vern did not. He attacked me on Facebook. Upset, I blocked him. I stopped speaking to the uncles. My family grew even smaller.

That love and support, even from close family members, is often conditional has been a difficult realization for me and led to a succession of unfortunate breakups in my life, but some good has come from these rifts. Rather than dwell on them and allow them to cause me additional pain, I've come to see them as a series of moments that ultimately led to my liberation—from patriarchy, religion, white authority, and fear—and this freedom has allowed me to provide a safe and nurturing environment for those who need it. My family may have been growing smaller, but that only made those who remained that much more important to me.

Chapter Twenty-Two

The Third Strike

IZAIAH STARTED GOING TO LAKE CITY HIGH SCHOOL in Coeur d'Alene when he was sixteen, and, as one of the few Black students in a predominantly white high school, ignorance and harassment followed him everywhere he went. He couldn't walk down the hall without getting a racial epithet slung at him. As he was putting his books in his locker one day, a white male student pointed at Izaiah's brand-new Air Jordans and said, "Those are some real nigger shoes." What was most disturbing about this incident was that it wasn't an aberration but a regular occurrence.

As much as I hated hearing about these ugly encounters, I had to walk a fine line, making sure Izaiah was safe while at the same time letting him decide the most socially beneficial way to handle each situation. As much as I wanted to intervene and fight every battle for him, I knew that I also needed to let him stand up for himself and develop healthy conflict resolution skills. He was too old for me to run to the principal's office every time he got picked on. Even doing that himself had consequences. Unless schools exercise a zero-tolerance policy for harassment of any kind, the kids who report it are the only ones who ever really get punished. They get called "snitches" (and worse), and their social lives are forever tainted by the stigma that they're somehow cowardly and weak.

Izaiah had read many of the books about Black history I had on my bookshelf, and we'd watched films on the subject together, so he understood the history of the Struggle and the good judgment that successful solutions required. But one day he told me he'd had enough. "I need you to buy me some headphones," he said. "I hear the N-word in the hallway every day, and I'm getting to the point where I'm afraid I'm going to hurt somebody."

I understood his anger and felt his request was not only reasonable but wise. That night, I drove to the closest entertainment store and bought him a pair of headphones. As clever as Izaiah's response to the problem was, he also seemed to understand that it didn't fix the core issue or provide any sort of systemic solution. Toward the end of his sophomore year, he adopted a new strategy— killing them with kindness. He'd always been a good-natured kid, but now he was Mr. Congeniality. He went out of his way to be polite and friendly to his teachers and developed the ability to strike up a conversation with just about any student from any clique, whether it was a cheerleader, a geek, a jock, or an emo kid. It was a successful campaign. By the end of his junior year, everyone at his school knew him by name and nearly all of them liked him, which, considering this is high school we're talking about, is saying a lot.

Unfortunately, the racism that was so prevalent at Lake City High didn't magically disappear. It continued to be directed at other kids of color. Out of the roughly 1,600 students who attended Izaiah's high school, only about fifty of them were Black, and, just as Franklin had once observed about the two biracial girls in his third-grade class, most of the Black students didn't *know* they were Black. Izaiah on the other hand most certainly did, wearing his identity like a badge of honor, speaking up in classroom discussions when the Black perspective was missing or misrepresented in history or literature, proudly displaying his hair texture with fresh bald fades and edgy lineups, and wearing spotless kicks from his extensive collection that always matched whatever shirt he was wearing.

Izaiah's classmate Julian also ran counter to the norm. Julian's family had moved to Coeur d'Alene from Virginia, and both of his parents were Black. Being from the East Coast, he wasn't used to the demographics of Idaho, and he certainly wasn't used to white students freely issuing disrespect. As he was walking down the hall one day, a white male jock called him the N-word, and

Julian wheeled around and punched him in the jaw. A fight broke out, with both kids landing punches, but Julian was held solely responsible. He was suspended for "violent and aggressive behavior," while the white kid and those who'd cheered him on suffered no consequences.

When Izaiah told me about this incident, I remembered something the Reverend Jesse Jackson once said before he spoke at the University of Idaho in 2011. I'd been included among the local dignitaries selected to have dinner with him before he delivered his speech, and what he had to say about diversity education—that it was not only for white students but that it was *especially* for white students—had stuck with me. He explained that most Black people were already very adept at interacting in multicultural settings—going from their homes to school or work and back each day, for example—but many white people who lived in predominantly white areas like Idaho simply didn't have the experience, training, or skills to know how to appropriately interact with people from other cultures.

With this in mind, I pitched an idea to the administrators at Izaiah's school. When racist incidents or harassment went unpunished, I explained to them, it was not only an injustice to the Black students but to the white ones as well. Because the jock who'd called Julian the N-word hadn't been punished, he'd effectively been taught that what he'd done constituted acceptable behavior, so he was likely to do it again. If the jock did the same thing as an adult, he could get sent to prison for as long as five years, even if the person he'd directed the slur at responded by punching him in the face. In states like Idaho where malicious harassment is a felony offense, a racial slur is considered violent and aggressive behavior, essentially the first punch thrown in a fight. Certainly, the parents of the school's white students didn't want their children to grow up to be criminals, did they? What if the entire incoming freshman class each year could get a "vaccine" that would prevent the diseases of racism and bullying from spreading through the school?

My idea didn't gain any traction with the school administration until Izaiah's senior year, after he made a video about online bullying for his capstone research project. Filled with interviews with kids from his school telling it like it really was, his video gained a lot of attention. An article about the issue made it onto the front page of the local newspaper and featured a quote from Izaiah and a photo of him talking to other students about his project. When word of it reached the administrators, they said they were shocked to learn about the many hurtful ways students had been treated on social media and at school, and they gave Izaiah and me the green light to put on a joint presentation about diversity training as part of freshmen orientation. Izaiah opened the event with his video and a brief talk that challenged the incoming freshmen to embrace all their peers as if they were part of "a four-year family." I followed with a lecture about the need for reducing prejudice, highlighting the practical benefits of doing it and revealing ways in which intercultural sensitivity would help them in various careers as well as life in general.

Izaiah's video and capstone project were just a few of the many achievements he enjoyed at Lake City High. When I got custody of him, his GPA had nearly hit rock bottom, but by the time he'd graduated he'd raised it high enough to obtain a college scholarship. In addition to Best Dressed, he was also named Homecoming Royalty and Prom Prince his senior year, and when the principal handed him his diploma and hugged him, tears welled in her eyes. He definitely left his mark on that campus. Watching from the bleachers in the sweltering gymnasium packed with white families, I smiled at Albert and squeezed Franklin's hand as Izaiah raised his diploma with an ear-to-ear smile. As his mother, I couldn't have been any prouder.

Izaiah's graduation coincided with Franklin's graduation from elementary school. With both of them slated to change schools in the fall, I was presented an opportunity to do something I'd wanted to do for a while—move back to Spokane, this time for good. While it certainly wasn't New York or Paris, Spokane was a real city in ways that a tourist town like Coeur d'Alene was not. It had six times as many people as Coeur d'Alene, an international airport, and, with four universities, far more opportunities in the world of academia.

I'd always liked teaching at EWU (and Whitworth University, which was also in Spokane) more than at North Idaho College, but I hated the long commute from Idaho. The move solved that problem. I stopped teaching at NIC, where my focus had always been art, and took on more work at EWU, where my focus was Black studies. At EWU, my academic life and my activist life began to come together as one. In some of the classes I taught, such as African American Culture, Research Methods in Race and Culture Studies, and Black Women and Hair, I was able to discuss issues that had an immediate visceral impact on my students' lives. I didn't just make them read about *Brown v. Board of Education* in a textbook; I had them go to a local high school and tutor twelve students of color who weren't on track to graduate on time, eight of whom graduated that year as a result.

And when it came time to teach my students about "white privilege"—the idea that white people enjoy "an invisible package of unearned assets" compared to people of color—I didn't simply have them read Peggy McIntosh's essay "White Privilege: Unpacking the Invisible Knapsack" and call it a day. We did exercises in class that made it easier for them to visualize this somewhat abstract concept. One of the exercises was called the "privilege walk." All my students started out at the back of the room, and if a certain privilege, such as being white or male or straight, applied to them, they would take one step forward. Along these same lines we developed a "privilege scorecard," awarding one point to all the historically dominant groups in the main seven categories that shape identity: gender, race, class, sexual orientation, religion, disability, and age. You got a perfect seven—the numerical equivalent of an extremely privileged life—if you were a straight, Christian, white man between the age of twenty-one and forty with no disabilities who had enough or more than enough resources growing up. Any Muslim Black women over the age of forty who grew up poor, had a disability, and were bisexual weren't so lucky. Getting a low privilege score meant the person receiving it would likely have a far more challenging life than those with higher scores.

When teaching classes where most of the students were white, I often heard some very passionate opposition to the notion of white privilege. This sort of resistance is common in our society. There are actually people who talk about "Black privilege," as if a program such as affirmative action overly compensates for the horrors of slavery, the legally entrenched injustice of the Jim Crow era, and the inequitable treatment of Black people that continues to this day. White students who grew up poor were usually the biggest critics of white privilege. Exercises like the privilege scorecard were helpful in acknowledging the challenges that poverty brings, regardless of other demographic factors.

My empathy for students from economically disadvantaged backgrounds came from a very personal place. Despite picking up several new classes at EWU, I was still struggling just to get by. The house Franklin, Izaiah, and I moved into in Spokane was a rental, and it only had two bedrooms. We knew it was going to be tight, but we also knew Izaiah would be leaving for the University of Idaho in the fall, so we were prepared to make it work. What we hadn't foreseen was the addition of another family member.

When Esther completed her senior year at Shiloh Christian Children's Ranch in May 2013, Larry and Ruthanne signed her out and brought her back to Montana. In the five years she'd spent in Missouri, I was never allowed to talk to her on the phone and I'd only seen her in person once. I was able to visit her for Christmas in Montana the year before but only under the supervision of Larry and Ruthanne. Whenever I tried to contact Esther on my own, they intervened to block my efforts. The one time they relented proved to be a disaster. With their permission, I purchased a plane ticket so I could visit her at the ranch and braid her hair, but the day before the flight they changed their minds and said I couldn't see her, forcing me to eat my nonrefundable ticket.

Now that Esther was home and free to do as she pleased, I reached out to her online to see how she was doing and what she planned to do next. She told me she wanted to get out of there ASAP and would love my help. I was delighted that she trusted me enough to seek my help and that our relationship remained just as strong as it had been when I'd last seen her. (Unfortunately, the same couldn't be said for my relationship with Ezra and Zach, from whom I'd grown distant after they kept posting what I viewed as racist images on their Facebook pages, including Confederate flags and President Obama as a monkey.) When Esther came to Coeur d'Alene with Larry and Zach, while Zach was looking into a wrestling opportunity at NIC, she asked me if I could help her move out of Larry and Ruthanne's house, assuring me she wasn't going to be telling them about her imminent departure. The following week, I drove to Larry and Ruthanne's, knocked on the door, and announced I was there to pick up Esther. They couldn't stop her from leaving now that she was eighteen, but Ruthanne's steely glares and Larry's game of Twenty Questions made their unhappiness with the situation clear. Esther and I shoved all her belongings—except her baby book, which Ruthanne refused to let her take—into large trash bags, loaded the bags into my Pontiac Vibe, and raced back to Spokane.

On the drive home, I noticed how damaged Esther's hair was. During my holiday visit with her the previous year, I'd done her hair in microbraids, hoping they would last a while, but the Shiloh staff had cut the braids out well before the end of their lifespan. Such braids were considered to be extravagant and violated the group home's modesty policies. The home also didn't have a single Black hair care product available the entire time she was there, and using Ivory soap and Dove shampoo had left her hair so dry that most of it had broken off. Before I'd graduated from college, I had continued to do her hair every time I came home, but I hadn't seen her more than twice since she'd gone to and returned from South Africa, and the long healthy head of hair she'd once had was now all but gone.

As damaged as her hair was, it was a problem that could be fixed with time, attention, and a little TLC. I was glad to help, as my doing Esther's hair had always been an integral part of our relationship. In fact, the first memory both of us have of each other includes me braiding her hair. The first week she stayed with me I deep-conditioned, hot-oiled, masqued, and hydrated her hair until it was finally able to hold a good braid. Working in a spiral pattern, I braided her hair into one long cornrow, sewed on a weave net, and gave her a nice weave in a style she'd picked out. Over the course of the next year I moisturized and styled her hair, from weave to box braids to cornrow up-dos, to encourage it to return to its healthy state. Within eighteen months, she had about eight inches of healthy new growth, and each time I did her hair she would run to the mirror after I unbraided it and shriek with excitement, "It's so long!" as she stretched it out.

When Esther and I arrived home after moving her out of Larry and Ruthanne's house, I moved Franklin into the basement with Izaiah and let her have the second bedroom upstairs. After she'd gotten all her stuff moved in, she and I sat down in my bedroom and had a talk. I wanted her to set some short-term life goals that could be achieved within a year. After being institutionalized for five years, she needed some help getting back on her feet. Clearly she'd already thought this through because she didn't hesitate before telling me her four-part plan.

"First, I want to get a driver's license."

She explained how the staff at the group home had burned her learner's permit after she'd taken the house parents' car for a drive around the block without permission when she was seventeen. The police charged her with grand theft auto, but as a minor she was able to get the charge dropped after being on probation. This problem had an easy fix. I took her to driver's ed classes, and as soon as she'd gotten her license I let her drive my car whenever she needed to.

"Next, I want to go to college."

She told me that Larry and Ruthanne had enrolled her in Flathead Valley Community College in Lincoln County, but, according to Esther, the entire "campus" consisted only of a one-story building, a tree, a tiny gravel parking lot, and a picnic table. She wanted to go to a "real" college, where she could study music performance. Esther could play the piano and the saxophone, and she could also sing exceptionally well. With all the connections I had at NIC after teaching there for eight years, I was able to facilitate her enrollment process, and I helped her fill out the paperwork for the financial aid she needed.

"I also want to get a job."

Esther had never been employed before, but this aspect of her plan was no more difficult to achieve than the others. One of my hair clients managed a used auto parts business just off Interstate 90, and she helped Esther apply for a position at the company. Despite her complete lack of knowledge about cars, Esther was soon working as a cashier at Pull and Save Auto Parts.

"And I want to sue Josh."

The final part of Esther's plan puzzled me. "Sue him for what?"

"For molesting me when I was a kid."

Hearing those words felt like a dagger to my heart. I gave her a long hug. "I'm so sorry it happened to you, too."

When I told her what Josh had done to me, it freed her up to talk about her own experience. She was eerily matter-of-fact as she relayed the story. Esther never cries. While talking about being flogged with a baboon whip or forced to eat her own vomit, she'll use the sweetest tone of voice you've ever heard. She employed the same incongruously saccharine tone as she told me how Josh had sexually assaulted her more than thirty times while he was living with Larry and Ruthanne in Colorado after getting his masters from the University of Nebraska. She described two occasions when Josh forced her to perform oral sex on him and seven or eight instances when he performed oral sex on her. "Don't tell anyone or I'll hurt you," she told me he'd once said to her. These assaults occurred when she was six and seven years old. Now that Josh had a two-year-old daughter, Esther was worried he might do the same thing to her. I agreed to help her.

As upset as I was for Esther, I also wasn't that surprised, given what Josh had done to me and his boyhood fantasies about the topless African women in *National Geographic*. For me, this was the third strike against Josh. I vowed that I would never forgive him for what he did to Esther and hoped never to see him or speak to him ever again. Not allowing people who have wronged me or who have hurt those I love to occupy space in my mind is my way of coping with trauma. It's simply too painful for me to think about them. While I will never forget what they did, I quarantine the memories I have of them and put all traces of their existence out of my mind. I just had one last thing to say to Josh before I terminated our relationship. I went on Facebook and sent him a message: "I can't believe what you did to Esther. Fuck off and get the fuck out of my life. I don't want to ever speak to you again." Then I unfriended him and blocked him for good measure.

It took a while for Esther's claim to get processed; the assaults had taken place in Colorado, Esther reported them to the police in Washington, and Josh lived in Iowa. When it finally was, Larry and Ruthanne made their unhappiness toward me for helping Esther clear. Years earlier, in an attempt to heal our relationship and pay back the inheritance money she and Larry stole from me, Ruthanne began sending me fifty-dollar checks each month with "Inheritance" written in the memo line. Immediately after I helped Esther file her case against Josh, those checks stopped coming.

Their displeasure escalated into a threat during Esther's first semester of college. Assisted by Zach, who was also attending NIC at the time, Larry and Ruthanne showed up at Esther's dorm and demanded to speak with her. Hoping to avoid being part of an embarrassing scene, Esther agreed to go to lunch with them at Bonsai Bistro. Drop the case, they warned her, or they would ruin my life and hers. Esther recorded the conversation on her phone and sent it to me, but the district attorney I spoke to didn't seem to think it amounted to much. If he'd predicted a blizzard in Miami in July, he couldn't have been more wrong.

Chapter Twenty-Three

Black Lives Matter

AFTER ESTHER PRESSED CHARGES AGAINST JOSH, he was arrested in Iowa, brought to Colorado, and indicted on four felony counts of sexual assault. Larry and Ruthanne bailed him out by posting a $15,000 bond and accused Esther of lying. The Doležals had become the Hatfields and McCoys.

As large a role as Esther's case against Josh played in my life, I was so busy I didn't have much time to dwell on it. Between raising Franklin, teaching at EWU, writing part-time for the local weekly newspaper *The Inlander*, and braiding hair, I barely had time to breathe. I felt like I was constantly chasing after a ball that was rolling downhill, its speed always just a bit faster than mine. So when a local activist asked me in the spring of 2014 to apply for one of the open seats on Spokane's Office of Police Ombudsman Commission (OPOC), a watchdog group for the local police, I brushed off the idea. But after two more people made the same suggestion I started to pay attention.

Everyone who recommended I do it said much the same thing: the current applicants were mostly older and white, and Spokane needed my voice on the commission. Translation: Spokane needed a strong Black leader who wasn't afraid to stand up to the police department, denounce police brutality, and demand transparency. Having concluded that the need to reform the culture of policing was at the heart of racial justice activism and seeing that no one else was stepping up to the plate, I filled out the application.

My decision to apply for the position soon took on greater significance, as that summer was reminiscent of the one in Spike Lee's *Do the Right Thing*: hot, violent, and filled with racial tension. On July 17, 2014, officers from the New York City Police Department approached Eric Garner, a forty-three-year-old Black man who was standing outside of a bodega on Staten Island, and accused him of illegally selling "loosies," individual cigarettes sold on the street. When Garner protested his innocence and frustration at being harassed, Officer Daniel Pantaleo put him in a chokehold and took him to the ground. As Pantaleo shoved Garner's face into the sidewalk and four officers assisted, Garner pleaded with them, saying, "I can't breathe" over and over again. An hour later, Garner was pronounced dead.

Less than a month later, Darren Wilson, a white police officer in Ferguson, Missouri, while responding to a call about a theft at a convenience store, approached Michael Brown, an eighteen-year-old Black male, and his friend Dorian Johnson as they were walking down the middle of the road. When Wilson confronted them, he and Brown reportedly engaged in a struggle and Wilson shot Brown in the hand. Brown and Johnson tried to run away. Wilson got out of his vehicle and pursued Brown. Even though Brown was unarmed, and, according to some, had his arms in the air as if trying to surrender, Wilson shot him at least six times. Brown died in the street in a pool of his own blood, where his body remained for several hours before any medical personnel examined it.

When people in Ferguson took to the streets to protest, the local police responded with what a Justice Department report later classified as "excessive force," deploying military weapons and armored vehicles and firing tear gas and rubber bullets into the crowds. What ensued seemed like a never-ending feedback loop, with the police continually failing to respond to the protests appropriately and protestors responding to the police's botched efforts with increasingly angry demands for justice. A week after the shooting, protestors in Ferguson and all around the country were still marching through the streets chanting, "Hands up, don't shoot!" and carrying signs that read, "Justice for Mike Brown" and "Black Lives Matter."

I'd first become aware of the BLM movement when #BlackLivesMatter emerged on Twitter the year before in response to George Zimmerman's acquittal. Like a lot of people, I'd been hopeful that it might blossom into an ongoing movement for justice and not just be a hashtag moment. The response to Michael Brown's death showed just how much the movement had grown in a year. Relying on grassroots activists, Black Lives Matter made its presence felt all around the country in the weeks that followed as it transformed the dying words of Garner and Brown into posters, chants, and T-shirts, and reignited the conversation about police brutality against Black men that had risen to national attention with Rodney King's beating in Los Angeles on March 3, 1991, then lay dormant for more than two decades without being adequately addressed. The Black Lives Matter movement arose as a response to this dereliction.

Working with community organizers, I helped coordinate BLM vigils and protest marches in Spokane, hoping to make more people aware of the implicit bias against Black people in our nation's police departments. According to a study released by *The Guardian* in 2015, Black men were *nine times* more likely than other Americans to be killed by police officers that year. Three hundred and seven of the 1,134 people killed by the police in 2015 were Black men, despite their making up only 6 percent of the U.S. population. So many young Black men were gunned down that some might just see the victims as a long list of names on a website. Not me. Every Black life that was taken mattered to me, and as names kept getting added to the list I felt more and more devoted to the cause of demanding police reform and promoting community vigilance. Every time I shouted, "Not one more!" at a rally, I was protesting what had come to feel like an imminent threat against my own Black sons.

On October 16, 2014, I gave a speech to more than a hundred EWU students and community members titled, "Ferguson and Race Relations in America: Are We Headed toward a Deeper Divide or a Post-Racial Society?" At the end of my talk, I handed out copies of an extremely misguided editorial written by Tanner Streicher, the art director of the campus newspaper *The Easterner*, in which he argued that in America Black people receive the same if not better treatment than white people. Dividing the room into smaller groups, I asked each of them to discuss the article, and the feedback I got was unanimous: the article was so offensive, something needed to be done. Those who attended the forum got right to work, petitioning the paper, writing letters to the editor, and raising campus awareness about the BLM movement until Streicher was removed from his position.

I had always supported the Black students at EWU, serving as an unofficial advisor and mentor for many of them, and that fall they issued a public endorsement of my leadership by petitioning the director of the Africana Studies program to remove the Black Student Union's current faculty advisor, who they believed was doing more to hurt the club than help it, and replace her with me. The student-run coup succeeded, and I was named the BSU's new faculty advisor even though I technically wasn't qualified to advise the club because I wasn't a full-time, year-round professor.

The role meant a great deal to me—I'd been a BSU member myself during my undergraduate years and had advised the BSU at NIC, after all—and I took it very seriously. I helped the BSU members organize a protest march, and nearly two hundred people attended. We passed out BLM bracelets to be worn as symbols of solidarity. We made signs denouncing police brutality. We walked through campus wearing all black, each of us with one fist raised in the air. We read aloud stories about the long list of Black men, women, and children who'd recently been killed by the police and made memorials commemorating them in three different spots on campus. I also gave a call-to-action speech, and afterward the students and I held hands and sang "Lift Every Voice and Sing"—the Black national anthem.

Feeling more empowered, the members of the BSU organized a campus forum in November to talk about what had happened in Ferguson, racial profiling in society, and race relations on campus. Yik Yak, a social media app popular on college campuses at the time because of the anonymity it provided, had exploded with racist comments following the BLM protests on campus, so this took up much of the discussion. As part of the panel, I spoke at length, lending my support to the BSU's desire for race and culture classes to be required for all majors, more Black representation in the faculty and the student body, and a multicultural student center that would serve as a safe space for academic and social enrichment.

Organizing and attending BLM events in Spokane took so much of my time and energy, I had to be selective about what made it onto my calendar. One of the activities that fell by the wayside for me was the monthly meeting for the NAACP's Spokane chapter. I went so infrequently I was a little shocked when the chapter's secretary, who was a friend of mine, nominated me to be president. As honored as I was, I was also hesitant. With past-due fees, no active committees, and a rapidly dwindling membership, the local chapter was on the brink of being shut down, and I knew revitalizing it would be a major undertaking. Given my unique identity, I was also cognizant of the need for me to represent what the Black community as a whole wanted. I considered removing my name from the ballot. But when I was informed that only the incumbent and I were running, and I considered how much more effective my activism would be if connected to a national civil rights organization, I decided to go ahead and run.

The ratio of women to men in the Spokane chapter was about two to one, and most of the women who showed up at the next meeting in November voted for me. On the strength of their votes I won the election by a healthy margin, becoming only the third female president in the chapter's nearly century-old history. As honored as I was, I was also overwhelmed by the thought of how much time and energy it would take for me to do the job right. But my fear quickly gave way to excitement. I had a grand vision. I wanted to return the focus of the Spokane chapter to the five NAACP Game Changers, the most urgent issues facing Black America: economic sustainability, education, health, public safety and criminal justice, and voting rights and political representation.

My biggest short-term goal was simply ensuring the chapter's survival. Having read the NAACP's constitution and bylaws, I knew that without three or more active committees an NAACP chapter could be shut down. When I was elected president the Spokane chapter only had one, which was essentially just the president and his hard-working wife. I was on a mission not only to keep the doors open but also to grow the organization to the point where it would never be threatened with closure again.

Another one of my objectives was to unify the organization. While founding the Inland Northwest Juneteenth Coalition three years earlier, I'd noticed how divided Spokane's Black community was. There were lots of pastors and lots of ideas, but not very many organized groups of people getting things done on the ground. I wanted to nurture and support grassroots activism that brought about sustainable changes on an institutional level. To this end, I was hoping to serve as a bridge between the NAACP's Spokane chapter and the local BLM movement, and after being the president-elect for just one week—I wouldn't officially assume the position until the meeting in January—I was given an opportunity to do just that.

If Michael Brown's death was the flame that lit the fuse of the BLM movement, Darren Wilson's acquittal on November 24, 2014, was the explosion. Using the rapid-fire organizational capability of Twitter, Black Americans who were sick of hearing about police officers getting away with shooting innocent Black men took to the streets across the country to express their outrage. I was already a known voice on human rights issues in Spokane; being elected president of the local NAACP chapter just extended my reach. I called for a citywide rally and a "die-in" in front of City Hall, and nearly 250 people participated. While Black men and boys, including Franklin and Izaiah, lay on the sidewalk, their relatives and friends traced outlines around their bodies with chalk. Afterward, we marched through the city, chanting, "Stand up! Stand up! We want freedom, freedom! All these racist-ass cops, we don't need 'em, need 'em!" "Hands up! Don't shoot," and "No justice, no peace! No racist police!" It was very real, very emotional, and very intense. I actually had to assure a few nervous police officers that the protest was going to remain nonviolent.

My commitment to racial justice ended up costing me one of my jobs. After organizing the protest in Spokane against Darren

Wilson's acquittal, I arrived late to teach the evening session of my Race & Ethnicity class at Whitworth University. That, when combined with the dean seeing me on the news leading the protest, prompted her to call me and tell me to not bother showing up to teach anymore. Essentially, I was fired from my position teaching a class about race for leading a Black Lives Matter protest on one of the most important nights in Black American history in the past decade.

Others weren't so put off by seeing me in the news. My tenure as NAACP president still hadn't officially begun when I got a call from Lisa Johnson, a Black graduate student at Spokane's Gonzaga University. She told me she'd already talked to the current local NAACP president, who hadn't been much help, but she saw the good work I was doing and was hoping I might be more supportive. She told me her five-year-old son Jason had recently come home from school with dirt on his clothes and a bandage on his forehead. When she'd asked him what had happened, he told her that some kids at school had thrown him in the garbage and he'd hit his head. She drove straight to St. Aloysius Gonzaga Catholic School, and Jason showed her the dumpster into which two twelve-year-old white kids had tossed him. Unable to lift the heavy lid, Jason remained trapped inside until one of his classmates heard him yelling and went for help. He was taken to the school nurse, who told him not to tell anyone about what had happened. Lisa discussed what the two boys did to Jason with the school's administrators, but they denied any such thing had taken place.

I found Lisa's story completely heartbreaking and unacceptable. As the mother of two Black sons, I also found it completely believable. I couldn't think of a more salient example of devaluing a Black child's life. The two white boys literally treated little Jason like garbage! I asked her how I could help. She needed school supplies to homeschool Jason until he felt safe going back to school, and she wanted to raise public awareness about the incident so it didn't get swept under the rug. I was happy to do both. I rallied EWU's BSU, and we reached out to the BSUs at Gonzaga and Whitworth. Together we collected homeschool supplies, and on a cold day in December we marched around the school, stood on the corner where parents picked up their kids, and brandished signs that read, "Treat Our Black Kids with Respect," "School Should Be a Safe Place for Everyone," and "Justice for Jason." Even Jason was there, all bundled up in snow pants, a winter coat, and gloves, holding an "Every Student Matters" sign above his head.

I officially assumed the presidency of the NAACP's Spokane chapter on January 1, 2015. The position was unpaid, but that didn't stop me from working overtime. One of the first tasks I assigned myself was finding the chapter a new office. It was currently located in the back of the Emmanuel Family Life Center, an African Methodist Episcopal church several miles from downtown next to some shady-looking apartments. You had to park in a dimly lit parking lot, and it was always dark outside when the meetings ended. Around the same time that I assumed the presidency, an NAACP office in Colorado Springs was bombed, and it was also located in an obscure part of town. I knew from experience that the local white supremacy groups were fully capable of doing something similar, and I didn't want anything like that to happen on my watch.

When I heard that State Representative Marcus Ricelli was moving out of his office on West Main Avenue, I went to take a look. It was perfect. It had beautiful hardwood floors, access to conference rooms where we could hold our monthly meetings, and more-than-reasonable rent. It was also located in the middle of downtown, above a community theater, with a law office on one side and State Senator Andy Billig's office on the other. Those who might be tempted to direct a hate crime at this new office would probably think twice when they saw that it shared a wall with a government official who was white and male. I secured a large donation from a local businessman and prepaid our rent and utilities for an entire year. We had a ribbon-cutting ceremony on MLK Day to commemorate the office's opening.

Meanwhile, I was already hard at work in my new role on Spokane's Office of Police Ombudsman Commission, which oversaw the work of the local ombudsman and intervened as needed to recommend policy reform within the Spokane Police Department. Getting the OPOC job had been an arduous process. The application was very long and detailed, requiring me to write an essay, and unlike the ballot for the NAACP position it included an "ethnic origins" question. I checked BLACK, WHITE, and NATIVE AMERICAN. I was then interviewed by two city councilmen, a committee, and finally the mayor, David Condon. Getting interviewed three times for the job—which I believe was one or two interviews more than the other OPOC members had to endure—seemed excessive and unfair to me. But once the mayor appointed me I put that behind me and concentrated on the work that needed to be done. In December, the four other members of the commission elected me to be its chair and Kevin Berkompas the vice chair. Some people commented how funny it was to have a Black Lives Matter activist be the chair, while the vice chair looked like a white cop. Kevin had served in the Air Force and worked in the Department of Defense, but underneath the close-cropped hair and militaristic demeanor was a man with a conscience who was committed to ensuring police accountability and transparency.

Like my position with the NAACP, this one was also unpaid, but I took it as seriously as I would have if I'd earned a million dollars a year, and attacked the three-inch binder, which detailed the history of the previous ombudsman's work, with the same rigor I used for academic research. As chair of the OPOC, I went on ride-alongs with police officers to understand local policing methods and make sure they were acting aboveboard, and I presided over the commission's monthly televised meetings. I met frequently with local leaders, including city council members, nonprofit directors, and the heads of community organizations such as the Spokane Police Accountability and Reform Coalition, the Center for Justice, and the Peace and Justice Action League. I occasionally joined some of the other commissioners on trips to places like Seattle and Oakland for training sessions in civilian oversight of law enforcement. And once a month I had a one-on-one meeting with the police chief, Frank Straub.

With his moustache and gruff demeanor, Chief Straub was a cop through and through. Even in the safety of his office, he'd wear a bulletproof vest and sit with his hands on his belt inches away from his gun. He generally acted civilly toward me during our meetings, but he always conveyed an air of condescension. He would offer me coffee, which with my tight schedule and limited sleep I never refused, but once we were seated, he'd usually start off by saying something snide like, "Rachel, it must really suck to be the head of the NAACP and the chair of the Police Ombudsman Commission. Isn't that a conflict of interest? Which hat are you wearing today?"

Since my divorce, I'd gotten better at standing up to bullies and men who tried to leverage their power to intimidate me, so I never backed down when Chief Straub baited me. "I'm doing fine, Frank," was my usual response. "I'm here as chair of the commission today, and, no, I don't see my roles as conflicting but complementary since both of them address justice issues."

He'd usually have his assistant there taking notes for him, and occasionally someone else from his department would show up. I never quite understood why. I responded by bringing Kevin Berkompas, who'd also take notes for me and chime in as needed. What made it into the notes was standard commission business, me asking for things like access to certain Internal Affairs files and Chief Straub telling me why he didn't think that was appropriate. He was always very standoffish toward me, and the vibe I got from him kept me at a distance. I always felt like he was either checking out my cleavage or wishing I wasn't there. Despite our differences, we did our best to act professionally and cordially toward each other, but I'd soon come to discover the truth. I was a thorn in the man's side, and he had it in for me.

Adding this job and the NAACP job to the two I already had required lots of planning and coordination. As I took on more tasks, I had to subordinate others on my agenda. I'd become a licensed intercultural competency trainer, but I put that on the back burner for the moment. I also reduced the number of hair clients I was willing to take on. Still, I was working more than sixty hours a week. One of the students in my African history class asked me, "What do you do for fun?"

"My work *is* fun," I assured her.

Chapter Twenty-Four

Lorenzo Hayes

B EING NAMED PRESIDENT of the Spokane chapter of the NAACP had one unfortunate consequence—after a lull following my departure from the Human Rights Education Institute, the hate crimes that had been directed at me and my sons starting in 2008 resumed in earnest. In March 2015, a package addressed to me but lacking a return address and postage was delivered to the NAACP's post office box. When I opened it, I found an article about me from *The Inlander*, photos of Black men being lynched and used for target practice, photos of white men pointing guns at the camera, and handwritten notes issuing threats and signed "War Pig." Two days after I received this package, Franklin and one of his friends were accosted a block from our house by a white male who called Franklin the N-word.

A month later, I received another package from War Pig—same handwriting and signature and, once again, no return address— but this time it was delivered by the postal service directly to the NAACP office on West Main Avenue instead of our P.O. box. Still traumatized by the grisly photos from the previous package, I declined to open the second package and handed it over to the police. A week later, another package from War Pig showed up, this time in my faculty mailbox at EWU. Once again I opted not to open it and gave it to the police. These last two packages contained postmarks indicating they'd both been mailed from Oakland, California.

That same month, as I was chairing the monthly OPOC meeting live on TV, Franklin started blowing up my phone with calls and texts. "Mom, I'm hearing noises outside," one of his texts read. "Footsteps. October's fur is standing up on her neck. I'm in your bedroom with the sharpest knife I could find. Hurry, Mom. Please. I'm scared." I handed the meeting over to the vice chair, asked the police officer in attendance to send someone to my house, and raced home, where I found large boot prints in the snow right outside my bedroom window. I filed another police report and installed some surveillance cameras, which a friend had given me.

Another strange incident occurred while I was chairing the May OPOC meeting. Franklin was home and had forgotten to lock the side door. A white male and female burst in through the door. Seeming surprised to see him, they told him they were supposed to be watching someone's dog and must have come to the wrong house. The detective who came to investigate told us that the couple were probably burglars, based on their excuse, which burglars commonly used when encountering someone unexpectedly. The surveillance cameras I'd installed captured their faces, and I handed the footage over to the police. Were these incidents related? Were we safe? I tried to keep an open mind, but when the police investigations came up empty, I started to grow more concerned about our welfare.

The sense that I was being targeted returned on April 16, when an unnamed individual filed a "whistleblower complaint" against me and my fellow OPOC commissioners Kevin Berkompas and Adrian Dominguez, accusing us of workplace harassment and abusing our authority. I was surprised by the allegations. Like Kevin and Adrian, I had never had my integrity or ethics questioned in my entire career. Among other things, Rebekah Hollwedel, whose name was later revealed by a local television station to be the whistleblower, alleged that I had manipulated the minutes of meetings, when in fact Kevin had taken over the task of transcribing our minutes. Any editing was only done to ensure that the minutes were accurately transcribed and properly formatted, at which point they were passed along to Rebekah. OPOC's independent legal counsel advised us that in all likelihood nothing would come of the charges, chalking them up to personality issues. But I wasn't so sure. I couldn't help but notice the similarities of those being targeted. Of the five members on the commission, Kevin and

Adrian were the only ones who were as adamant and outspoken about enforcing transparency in local policing as I was, and we often voted the same way.

Whether it was coming from white supremacists or city officials, I felt bullied, and the local media were hardly sympathetic to my plight. That nearly all of them were white and catered to a predominately white audience was certainly a factor. I'd noticed the same bias when it came to reporting the deaths of Black men at the hands of the police. To Black people, all these deaths were news, but the media typically focused on some more than others, and I wanted to know why.

The reason for the media's bias remains a bit of a mystery to me, but I believe there could be several factors involved and one of them was the victim's age. On November 22, 2014, Timothy Loehmann, a white police officer in Cleveland, shot Tamir Rice twice after responding to a dispatch call about "a male Black sitting on a swing and pointing a gun at people" in a park next to the Cudell Recreation Center. Rice died the next day. The "weapon" he'd been holding was an Airsoft toy gun. He was twelve.

Another factor that could turn what has been almost a daily occurrence in our country's history—Black men getting killed by the police—into a media event was video footage of the incident. On April 4, 2015, Michael Slager, a white police officer in North Charleston, South Carolina, stopped Walter Scott, a fifty-year-old Black man, for a non-functioning brake light. When Scott got out of his car and started running, Slager chased after him and shot him five times, killing him. The incident might have gone ignored if Feidin Santana, a bystander unseen by Slager, hadn't recorded it on his phone and shared the gruesome footage of Scott's death—his hands were in the air as bullets ripped through his back—with the media after the initial police report differed from the events he'd witnessed.

The proximity of one incident to another also seemed to play a role in turning certain cop killings into major headlines. Just eight days after Walter Scott was killed, police officers in Baltimore picked up Freddie Carlos Gray Jr., a twenty-five-year-old Black man, for reasons that were never made entirely clear. Gray fell into a coma while he was in police custody and died a week later. Livid that yet another name had been added to the long list of Black men killed in police custody, BLM protestors once again took to the streets in major cities across the country I might have joined them if I hadn't been so consumed with a racially charged cop killing that had occurred much closer to home.

On February 10, police officers in Pasco, Washington, had shot and killed Antonio Zambrano-Montes, a thirty-five-year-old Mexican man, after he'd allegedly thrown rocks at them. When the three officers fatally shot him in the back, Zambrano-Montes had his hands up in a position of surrender. Over the course of the next several months, I went back and forth to Pasco, a six-hour round-trip drive from Spokane, multiple times to march with protestors who were calling for justice after the officers involved were put on paid administrative leave and never charged with a crime. During the first trip, I spoke at a rally and marched with Gerald Hankerson, the NAACP president of the Alaska–Oregon–Washington State Area. The police refused to issue us the proper permits for a protest, so each time we marched we risked getting arrested. The cops drove close behind us, blocked streets in front of us, and yelled at us through bullhorns, demanding that we disperse. When we didn't, they started arresting people at random. I went to at least three protests in Pasco that spring, all of them contentious.

Some incidents of police brutality had occurred in Spokane in the past, and most of them received very little attention. The same was initially true after the local police arrested Lorenzo Hayes on May 13, 2015. A thirty-seven-year-old Black man and father of seven children, Hayes was charged with illegally possessing a firearm and, curiously, violating a no-contact order, even though Hayes was at his own house at the time. According to witnesses, Hayes cooperated with the police as they handcuffed him, put him in the back of a police car, and took him in for booking. When they arrived at the jail, thirteen white male officers surrounded the car and, later claiming Hayes was uncooperative, yanked him out of the car and dragged him into the building. Inside, the officers threw him on the floor and held him down as he suffocated on his own vomit, went into cardiac arrest, and died from asphyxiation, just as Eric Garner had.

Moments after Hayes died, Chief Straub called my cell phone and told me he was assembling Black community leaders for an emergency meeting. He didn't provide any details. All he would say was that a critical incident had occurred, and we'd learn more at the meeting. I left work early to be there, as did a handful of Black pastors and organizers of local youth groups and community programs. We sat around a large oval table as Straub, whose officers had taken Hayes into custody, and the local sheriff, who had jurisdiction over the jail where Hayes died, told us that Hayes' death needed to stay quiet and asked us to, in effect, keep the local Black community in line. With racial tensions still high after the deaths of Walter Scott and Freddie Gray, he didn't want there to be any protests or bad publicity. He told us that our constituents needed to understand that this was not "a media moment," that the highway patrol would be handling the investigation because the police department and the sheriff's department were both being investigated, and that we should reserve judgment until the investigation had been completed.

Straub went on to say that Hayes was high on drugs at the time of his arrest and that his death was likely the result of an overdose. He said he hadn't read any reports about the incident and was relying on his memory of a single conversation he'd had with the officers who'd been present, so he didn't want us to feel like he was being misleading if the autopsy contradicted what he was telling us.

Since I regularly rode around with police officers as the OPOC chair, I knew that they were required to keep notes about every call they were assigned by the Computer Aided Dispatch (CAD) system, so I asked him if he'd read the CAD notes. He said he had, but in a tone that let me know he wasn't pleased with the question.

I pushed harder. "Did any of the officers have a body camera on?"

He said they didn't, although I later found out that one officer who came to the jail with the ambulance after Hayes died did have a camera, and the footage it captured revealed a clear racial bias. When the officer was told the victim's name was Lorenzo, she assumed he was Hispanic. When she was corrected and told that he was Black, she said, "So how many priors does this guy have?" After hearing that Lorenzo had gone into cardiac arrest, she said, "That's what happens when they come in here all doped up."

"How do you know for sure that he overdosed?" I asked Chief Straub.

He said the toxicology report would confirm it.

"When will that be completed?"

He admitted it could take several weeks.

The other people in the room, who'd been mostly silent up to this point, began asking questions of their own. The chief impatiently answered a few of them before ending the meeting and asking us to keep the information he'd shared confidential until after he'd discussed the incident with Lorenzo's family. I later learned that while we were sitting in that meeting getting debriefed, Lorenzo's family didn't even know that he'd died. The police had returned to his house, forced his family to stand outside in the rain while they searched it, and towed Lorenzo's car without telling any of them what had happened. It wasn't until that evening that they finally learned that Lorenzo was gone.

Admittedly, I was in an awkward position, being both the OPOC chair and having access to confidential information, and being the local NAACP president and having a duty to serve the needs of the community when civil rights issues were involved. As NAACP president, I reached out to Lorenzo's family and asked them if I could assist them in any way. Did they want help dealing with the media? Did they want to do a protest march or a memorial rally? Did they need legal advice? Lorenzo's sister told me her concerns. She was upset that the local media was portraying her brother as a drug dealer. She told me how unfair his being falsely described as a criminal was to his children. She asked me to be a liaison and spokesperson to the media and expressed her hope that I could do something about the smearing of her brother's reputation.

She wasn't the only one bothered by the bias of the local media, which depicted the white world as normal and the Black one as other. Sandra Williams moved with her family to Spokane when she was twelve, graduated from nearby Cheney High School, and earned a bachelor's degree in psychology from Washington State University. Except for a six-year hiatus working on the all-Black TV show *City of Angels* while living in Los Angeles, Sandy, as I would come to know her, had spent most of her adult life in Spokane working for social service nonprofit organizations such as the Youth Suicide Prevention Program, the Odyssey Youth Center, and, most recently, EWU's Pride Center. As she was watching the local news on television one day, it struck her how much different—and how much more accurate—some of the stories would have been if they'd been told by a Black journalist. She was tired of seeing the media depicting people of color only as criminals, entertainers, or athletes, highlighting negative aspects about them, and supporting existing stereotypes. In January 2015, she did her part to rectify the situation when she produced the first issue of *The Black Lens: News from a Different Perspective*, a monthly publication that focuses on the news, events, people, and issues that affect Spokane's Black community.

I first met Sandy at an NAACP meeting in Spokane back when I was still living in Coeur d'Alene, but I got to know her much better at EWU's annual Drag Show when she was the head of the Pride Center. I was dating Dr. Kim Stansbury, a sociology professor at EWU, at the time, and Sandy was a lesbian, so we bonded over the difficulty of having to balance our Black identities with our LGBT identities in terms of knowing where and when it was okay to be "out" and when it would be more strategic to put our sexual orientation on the back burner. NAACP meetings and Black churches weren't always LGBT-friendly, and even when they were, there was an understanding that this issue shouldn't be brought up or flaunted out of respect for the older churchgoing folk.

As I got to know her better, Sandy asked me if I'd like to write a column for *The Black Lens*, and I agreed to do at least one piece per month, relaying news from the NAACP to the local Black community. The opportunity to write with an unapologetically Black voice without having to filter myself for a white audience more than made up for the fact that, once again, I'd taken on work that produced no pay. Having come to trust Sandy's vision, I went to her first when Lorenzo Hayes' sister asked me to speak to the media on her family's behalf. "There is a similar pattern that we have seen over and over again, with the death of Trayvon Martin, Michael Brown, Eric Garner, Walter Scott, Freddie Gray, and others," she quoted me as saying in the article she wrote about Lorenzo's death. "The first thing that happens is that the Black male is criminalized. They are implicated in their own death. And there is a loss of humanity, both for that individual and for an entire population of people."

The Hayeses also asked me to help them get in touch with a lawyer and told me they wanted to do a memorial rally for Lorenzo. I recommended an attorney at the Center for Justice and helped organize a march and candlelight vigil. On the march, we carried signs, flowers, and photos of Lorenzo to the jail where he'd died. There Lorenzo's children released thirty-seven blue helium balloons—commemorating his age and his favorite color—I'd purchased from a party supply store. His family members and friends shared memories of him, gave tributes to him, and spoke lovingly about him. I held back tears as a preschool-age child picked up the bullhorn that was being passed around and quietly said, "I love you, Daddy." Lorenzo's family also expressed the need for an honest investigation and answers about his death. If the investigation was done thoroughly and effectively, I was certain that one or more of the police officers would be convicted of homicide.

In the days that followed, I continued to ask Chief Straub many tough questions about the handling of the investigation. He responded by canceling our regularly scheduled monthly meeting. By this point, my relationship with him and his department could most charitably be described as strained.

While Lorenzo's death was barely covered in the local news, Freddie Gray's death remained national news a month later. Knowing I wanted to go to Baltimore to support the Justice for Freddie Gray protests, Albert bought me a plane ticket for Mother's Day. On May 19, I flew to Baltimore to meet with Freddie Gray's friends and family, talk with members of grassroots organizations such as Baltimore United for Change and Baltimore Bloc, share stories about what was going on in the social justice front in Spokane, meet with the NAACP's Washington Bureau Director and Senior Vice President of Advocacy Hillary Shelton, and hear from the BLM protestors on the ground how the NAACP was helping them. As invigorated as I was talking to those from the Black Lives Matter movement, I was dismayed and disillusioned to hear that the NAACP hadn't shown up to support their efforts, even though its national headquarters was located right there in Baltimore.

Refusing to let this affect my determination to participate in the protests as much as I could while in Baltimore, I marched in a #BlackWomenMatter rally that started at the iconic Billie Holiday statue on Pennsylvania Avenue. When I got back to my hotel room, I took a shot in the dark and emailed Baltimore's state's attorney Marilyn Mosby, the youngest chief prosecutor of any major city in the country and a courageous Black woman who'd given Baltimore's Fraternal Order of Police a slap in the face when she held six officers accountable for Freddie Gray's death. I asked her if I could meet her while I was in town, and after I'd given her secretary my credentials Mosby graciously fit me into her schedule. When I asked her how she was faring being the center of a media firestorm after her indictment of the police, she shared with me some wisdom imparted to her by her grandma: "People will always talk, so give 'em something to talk about!" I'd recently won the bid to host a regional NAACP conference in Spokane in September, and as our meeting was coming to an end I invited her to speak at it. She agreed, although, thanks to what was about to transpire in my life, she never made it to Spokane.

While I was in Baltimore, a reporter from the *Coeur d'Alene Press* called to tell me that he was working on a story about me being born white and that all the harassment directed at me and my family weren't actually hate crimes. I had to be Black for them to be hate crimes, he said, ignoring the fact that KCTFHR's president Bill Wassmuth and others like him who had been attacked by hate groups in North Idaho had been white. He also informed me that he'd been talking to my parents and my ex-husband. At first, I thought the call was a prank, an idea supported by Kevin's assertion, after I called to discuss it with him, that he hadn't talked to anyone about me. Knowing how private Kevin is about his personal affairs, I believed him.

I knew that at some point in my life I would have to reconcile my self-identification with the various notions people have about race, particularly the idea that it's biological. I was aware that my view wasn't embraced by the mainstream. I was also conscious of the fact that my being born to white parents but identifying as Black would at first glance sound crazy to some people and be downright offensive to others. Not wanting to offend anyone, and not believing that an interview with a reporter in North Idaho would adequately contribute anything toward educating the masses about the origins and evolution of the idea of race and our common human ancestry in Africa, I opted to say nothing. I guess I was being optimistic when, after three weeks had passed, I felt certain nothing would come of the reporter's call.

Much of my reluctance to talk about the admittedly rare way I identified myself came from a desire to shield my sons from the possibility of receiving undue negative attention. I didn't want them to be put in a position where they would have to constantly explain my situation to other people. I hoped (once again, optimistically) that someday, after my sons had graduated from college and were living on their own, I'd be able to write a memoir that gave my unique racial identity (and the notion of race in general) the serious and measured consideration it deserved. Until that day arrived I wanted to live my life the way that felt most comfortable to me without having to answer a million questions about it. I wanted to focus my energy on more important issues like the work that needed to be done to create a more just society.

And there was so much to do! In May, I started hosting a weekly panel discussion on justice issues called Moral Mondays Northwest at Spokane's Community Building. It borrowed its title from the grassroots movement the Reverend William Barber started in 2013 in response to Republicans taking control of the North Carolina state legislature the year before and attempting to, in his words, "crucify voting rights." As president of the state chapter of the NAACP, Barber called for protests in the form of civil disobedience. Our version of the movement he started was essentially a talk show designed to create a discussion about the NAACP's five Game Changer issues and deliver a weekly call to action in seeking justice in the Northwest. We filmed local citizens airing their grievances and allowed the local officials who were responsible for each issue to say what was being done about it, and we aired the resulting discussion afterward on YouTube.

For the June 8 show, I had a bunch of guests talking about education reform, including several retired Black school teachers, a young Black man who'd been pushed out of school via the standard school-to-prison pipeline and ended up on the streets despite having been a straight-A student, the assistant principal of his former high school, and the school superintendent. The discussion grew contentious at times, and I looked forward to having an equally powerful one when we covered public safety and criminal justice, including police brutality, in the next segment of the Moral Monday Northwest series on June 15. But I'd never get the chance.

On June 9, I was interviewed by the international news organization Al Jazeera. During the interview, I was very critical of the Spokane Police Department and the city administration, wondering aloud how much accountability they really wanted local law enforcement to have. I aired my frustrations about ongoing resistance to the OPOC's efforts toward greater transparency and the limitations of our ability to reform policing, while explaining all that I'd done, including initiating monthly meetings with the Department of Justice. I said I wasn't confident that justice would be served in the Lorenzo Hayes case. I also added that I wasn't too happy with Chief Straub after he'd canceled our monthly meeting three months in a row. I stuck my neck out in that interview. I was real and raw and honest. I did the interview on a Tuesday and it was scheduled to air that Friday, but thanks to the uproar that ensued in the days between, it never made it on the air.

Only later would I find out just how upset Chief Straub was at me. For the past two months, he'd had a private investigator following me and looking into my "integrity issues." Because I wasn't hiding anything and didn't have a criminal history, there wasn't much to dig up about me other than standard background information such as where I'd grown up. The investigator's search led him to Larry and Ruthanne's house in Montana. Most parents would have told the investigator to mind his own business, but of course Larry and Ruthanne weren't like most parents. They were still furious at Esther for pressing charges against Josh and at me for supporting her.

Esther's case against Josh was proceeding as so many in our justice system do, which is to say glacially. A preliminary hearing was scheduled for June 15, 2015, but the actual jury trial wouldn't be taking place until August 11. When Esther asked me if I would testify in support of her, I assured her I would be there for her in any way she needed. The trial promised to be a he-said, she-said affair, with the exception of my testimony, which could possibly break the tie. The district attorney's office seemed to believe the same, sending me a letter dated June 9, 2015, informing me that my testimony was going to be critical. It would almost take a miracle for Josh to wriggle out of the trap he'd created for himself with his disgusting behavior years before.

That miracle arrived in the form of the private investigator Chief Straub had assigned to look into my past. When he arrived at Larry and Ruthanne's door asking about me, they saw an opportunity to discredit me before Josh's trial got underway. Instead of telling the investigator to get lost, they invited the man inside to have a little talk.

Chapter Twenty-Five

Ambushed by Reporter

CHIEF STRAUB WASN'T THE ONLY ONE who had hired a private investigator to dig into my past. Josh's legal team had one of their own, and he was responsible for telling Shawn Vestal, a columnist for *The Spokesman-Review*, during the first week of June that I wasn't born Black and that Larry and Ruthanne could confirm it. With this knowledge, Vestal, who had been writing about the spree of hate crimes directed at me and my sons, had been handed the scoop of a lifetime, but, as he later claimed, he'd had no interest in doing any "racial vetting." The dubious honor of dissecting my life story in print went to Jeff Selle and Maureen Dolan of the *Coeur d'Alene Press*, who, after getting tipped off about my background, called Larry and Ruthanne to ask if I was Black. Their article "Black Like Me?" was available to read online and in print the morning of June 11.

Selle and Dolan's story remained mostly a local phenomenon until video was attached to it later that day. Having heard through the area's media grapevine about the imminent publication of "Black Like Me?" Melissa Luck, the executive producer at the local television station KXLY, had sent senior reporter Jeff Humphrey to interview me on June 10. He'd come to my house while I was proctoring final exams at EWU and left his business card with Izaiah, who was home from college. When I got home from work that afternoon, Izaiah told me about the reporter, and I called the number on the card. Humphrey informed me that the Spokane Police Department had completed its investigation into the packages sent by War Pig as well as the other incidents for which I'd filed a police report and that they'd found no suspects. He asked me if I would discuss it on camera. One of my duties as the local NAACP president was to comment on such things, so I agreed. He offered to come to my house. I had plans to meet Esther that afternoon at the Starbucks on the downtown mall to discuss the upcoming hearing in her case against Josh, so I told Humphrey it would be better if we met near that location.

When it came to his career in journalism, Humphrey had some big shoes to fill. His father was Don Harris, the award-winning NBC News correspondent who was killed on November 18, 1978, during the notorious Jonestown Massacre. One of the stories that helped solidify Harris' reputation as a hard-nosed journalist concerned airport security—in 1972, he filmed two people carrying guns through the security checkpoint at Dallas' Love Field Airport and did a piece about it that attracted a lot of attention. As an eighteen-year-old college intern a decade later, his son Jeff tried to one-up his father by filming people smuggling explosives through security at the Fort Myers Airport in Florida but only succeeded in getting his photographer fired and himself barred from the state by the FBI. Now middle-aged with gray hair and hanging jowls, he'd settled into a career at KXLY covering crime and safety.

In Eastern Washington, the press generally skewed right-wing conservative, so its coverage of human rights issues was never as thorough as I would have hoped, but I was surprised at just how unsympathetic Humphrey's line of questioning during the interview was. From the outset, his body language and attitude indicated he was unmoved by my plight, and he only grew more insensitive the deeper into the interview we got. First, he told me the noose my sons had found on our property when we were living in Idaho was actually a rope meant for hanging a deer carcass. He made this implausible scenario—that someone would butcher a deer on someone else's property using what was clearly a noose—sound perfectly normal. Then he suggested that a "key holder"—presumably someone who had a key to the NAACP's P.O. box—had planted the first package sent by War Pig, a notion I found equally absurd. Then he took it a step too far, albeit in a very passive-aggressive way.

"What do you say to the folks who say maybe *you* put that letter in there because you were one of the people who had a key to do so?"

I was momentarily stunned speechless. There's a long history of Black Americans being vilified by the press, hate crimes aimed at them going unsolved, and, in some cases, guilt being placed on the victims of the crimes instead of the perpetrators. In this moment, as Humphrey essentially accused me of perpetrating hate crimes against myself, all these injustices came to mind. His cavalier attitude and contemptible insinuations angered me. He was so smug and condescending I considered ending the interview but continued because I felt it was my responsibility as the OPOC chair and NAACP president to let people know when justice wasn't being delivered.

"I don't even know that I have any words for them," I finally managed to say, doing my best to control my anger. "Because as a mother of two Black sons, I would never terrorize my children, and I don't know any mother personally who would trump up or fabricate something that severe that would affect her kids. My son slept for two weeks in my bed after we received that particular package, and he's thirteen years old." Thinking about how upset Franklin had been nearly made me cry. "That's the kind of terror that I as a mother and my son as a Black male, a thirteen-year-old in Spokane, never needs to experience. And the slightest implication that I would perpetrate terror toward my kids is at best offensive, but . . ." I was so mad it took all my focus to stay on point and complete my thought. "I don't know how that could be a conscionable statement that anybody could live with or believe."

Seeing that I was upset, Humphrey toned down his rhetoric. "Rachel, despite these threats that started many years ago, you continue to go out and fight for equality and civil rights and you're not going to be scared off from doing this."

"No, I'm not. This is actually something I've cared about since I was a young child, and I've been involved with social justice work since middle school, high school, college. It's part of my life work so . . . I've heard some people say, 'Oh, you get publicity from these hate crimes,' and I think that's very sick as well because that's not the kind of publicity anyone wants. It's publicity of a negative and terrorizing scenario, especially death threats and photos of lynchings. As a Black Studies professor, I know what these images mean and take them very seriously, given the history of racism in the United States."

There was much more I wanted to say. I wanted to ask him how he would feel if someone accused him of doing something analogous. But he barely let me finish my sentence before he asked, "Speaking of that, did your dad ever make it to Spokane in January for the ribbon cutting?"

It was an odd segue from the discussion we'd been having. The ribbon-cutting ceremony for the NAACP's new office had taken place six months before, so why was he bringing it up now? And what did that have to do with hate crimes? I was a little confused. And very annoyed.

"No, actually," I responded, hoping we'd come to the end of the interview. "Unfortunately, he has bone cancer and was not able to get cleared for surgery yet."

In the heat of the moment I misspoke. Albert was actually suffering from prostate cancer and was scheduled to have surgery on the bones in his leg, and I conflated the two. Not that it was any of this guy's business. Albert was a very private person, particularly about his health, and I immediately felt bad sharing this information with a reporter.

Humphrey pulled out a photograph of Albert. Despite wearing dirty white sneakers that looked even shabbier next to my black Nine West heels, Humphrey literally looked down his nose at me as he pointed at the photo. The vibe I was getting from him was a mix of smugness and disdain.

"Is that your dad?" he asked.

I recognized the picture of Albert from my Facebook account. Why had this reporter been snooping around there? I couldn't believe how unprofessional he was being. When I'd agreed to do this interview, it was with the understanding that we'd be discussing the fact that, once again, the Spokane police had closed a hate crime investigation after failing to find a suspect.

As confused as I was by Humphrey's question, it was easy to answer. "Yes, that's my dad."

He pointed at the photograph again. "This man right here is your father?"

Somehow a serious discussion about hate crimes had shifted to an examination of my private life. It felt like I was walking into a trap, so I pushed back a little. "Do you have a question about that?"

"Yes, ma'am, I was wondering if your dad is really an African American man?"

I wish I'd been able to steer the conversation back to the issue I'd agreed to discuss, but his question had thrown me off balance. It was becoming clear that this man knew something about my background and that was a little scary. Why was he prying into my private affairs? Whatever the reason it couldn't possibly be good.

"That's a very—I mean, I don't know what you're implying."

I knew *exactly* what he was implying, but after watching him tiptoe around the subject I wasn't about to help him get there any quicker.

"Are you African American?"

And there it was. That's what this was all about. His question put me in an impossible situation. I knew any answer I gave could be used to ruin my credibility. If I said yes, I'd be asked to prove it. If I said no, I'd be tried in the court of public opinion for how I'd been identifying on and off since my college days. The idea that my reputation might be damaged because of this bothered me but not the way you probably assume. I'd never had any sort of job security or financial stability so in that regard I didn't have all that much to lose, but I was frightened about the prospect of people no longer seeing me for who I was and I was even more concerned how this "news" might affect my two sons and baby sister. Esther would be arriving at the coffee shop any minute and I was scared that if I said the wrong thing it might ruin my credibility as the key witness in her case against Josh.

I was also enraged by Humphrey's adversarial tone. I wanted to slap the smug grin right off his face. There was a long, awkward pause as I made myself hold my tongue—and my hands—in check. I told myself to calm down and be professional. It wasn't easy. I felt cornered, and his snide tone convinced me that anything I said could and would be used against me. If I could have pled the Fifth, I would have. Instead I said, "I don't understand the question. I did tell you that, yes, that's my dad, and he was unable to come in January."

Out of the entire twenty-minute-long interview, "I don't understand the question" would be the one sentence people would remember most. My uttering it would be transformed into countless Vines and memes online, quickly supplanting the popularity of Lucille Bluth, the snobby mother on *Arrested Development*, uttering the same phrase in response to a waitress in a kid-friendly diner asking her, "Plate or platter?" For me, that sentence contained much more defiance than humor. I didn't understand—or want to endorse—the relevance of these personal questions to the very public matter of hate and terror being allowed to spread in our community.

Beyond this, in my scholarly circles, "African American" specifically referred to Americans whose ancestors were taken from Africa and enslaved in the United States. When used as a catchall term for Black Americans, however, it often caused confusion. For example, there were significant cultural and identity differences between someone who was born in, say, Kenya and voluntarily emigrated to the United States and a Black American who was a descendant of slaves, but both might be called African Americans. For this reason, I preferred "Black," a much broader term that denotes a connection to the Pan-African Diaspora. "Pan," of course, denotes inclusion and unity, which I found apt, as I'd always considered myself part of this movement.

The reporter pressed me. "Are your parents, are they white?"

I'd had enough. Out of the corner of my eye I saw Esther walking into the Starbucks. Hoping Humphrey and his cameraman would clear out of the area before they caught sight of her and—who knows?—started digging into her personal life as well, I did an abrupt about-face, walked in the opposite direction of the coffee shop, and ducked inside a Lululemon Athletica store. When the film crew finally left, I joined Esther at a table inside the coffee shop and vented. I was pissed off at the reporter for not being straightforward with me about what his true intentions for the interview were. I was upset about what sort of impact the footage was going to have on my standing in the community, my sense of identity, and my family. But I was most concerned about how it would affect Esther. The reporter had told me that he'd spoken with Larry and Ruthanne and was clearly on a mission to sully my reputation, so I knew the fallout from his investigation couldn't possibly be good for her case.

I went to bed that night with an awful sense of foreboding, and it was confirmed when I woke up the next morning. Izaiah turned twenty-one that day, and when I knocked on his bedroom door to wish him a happy birthday he relayed the news to me: the *Coeur d'Alene Press* had published its story about my racial identity during the night, and *everyone* was talking about it. His friends from high school had been calling him all morning, saying things like, "You lied to us!" and "That's not your real mom!" The exact situation we were hoping to prevent—Izaiah having to deal with the awkward stigma of having been adopted twice—had occurred, and it nearly broke my heart.

Like Esther, Izaiah rarely cried, but he did that morning. "Can someone just call and wish me a happy birthday?" he asked, as he slumped on the couch with his head in his hands.

When I looked at my phone, any hope I'd had that this story might stay under the radar was destroyed. It was only 8 AM, but I'd already gotten more than twenty texts and voicemail messages, all of which said nearly the same thing. People wanted me to explain myself to them. They said they felt shocked and betrayed. They were confused. They were angry. A few of my friends reached out to make sure I was doing all right, but they were the minority. Many more people, who I'd once considered friends, told me they no longer wanted to have anything to do with me.

The initial wave of messages was a trickle compared to the tsunami that was coming. Over the course of the next four days I would receive hundreds, maybe even thousands, of emails and direct messages on Facebook, Twitter, Instagram, and LinkedIn, so many I quickly gave up trying to respond to them. My voicemail box kept filling up within hours of me checking and erasing my messages. When it became clear that I'd never be able to keep pace with the barrage of incoming calls, I gave up and turned off my phone. There was simply no way I could have replied to everyone who contacted me, much less appease them.

As overwhelmed and heartbroken as I was by the way my life was being dissected and my reputation destroyed, I knew I needed to focus my energy on protecting my sons and my sister. Izaiah seemed to take it the hardest. He said that he didn't see any way forward for me and that he would understand if I needed to leave the country and disappear for a while. I was pretty sure he didn't mean that and I was *positive* Franklin wouldn't be fine with the idea, but I was touched that, after his bid to escape his past had failed, he was more concerned about my welfare than his own. He asked me what I was going to do, and when I told him I was going to find a way through this ordeal, he said, "You're the bravest person I know."

Esther was also worried about how the news would affect me but wasn't initially concerned about it having an impact on her case against Josh. After all, it was her bid for justice, not mine. Her response to the growing media frenzy was to lie low and not talk to anyone, particularly reporters, about what was going on. Only after several days had passed did she open up about her feelings. "It amazes me how fast people are willing to tear down someone who has worked very hard to get where they are," she wrote on her blog. "It amazes me how, after all these years, and the civil rights movement, it still comes down to what color someone is . . . For something that is making a difference, someone that is making positive changes in this messed up world, why would someone want to stop the good work they are doing? Why would someone want to reverse the positivity that has been created? Why does everything have to come down to race?"

Perhaps because of his age and his inherent optimism, Franklin took the news much better. He hugged Izaiah and me and assured us that everything would be okay, that it wasn't as bad as it seemed, that it would all blow over soon. "We might as well have fun with this!" he said as he took his cat October outside, sat with her on the front stoop, and posed for the television cameras that were starting to arrive. Only later would he come to realize just how big of an impact the story was going to have.

Chapter Twenty-Six

Unemployed

THE MORNING THE ARTICLE ABOUT ME went online was extremely stressful for me, but it was practically a meditation retreat compared to the afternoon. KXLY posted footage of my awkward interview with Jeff Humphrey on its website around 3 PM. From there it was uploaded onto YouTube. And from there it went viral. Within hours, I became an internet sensation, widely lampooned for my perceived fraudulence. My story was the subject of hundreds of online news stories and made it onto the front pages of respected news outlets across the country and several places overseas. If I'd lit myself on fire and started running down the street, I couldn't have created a bigger uproar.

I found some comfort when NAACP state area president Gerald Hankerson called me that afternoon and, after expressing some incredulity about my situation, assured me that I'd sparked the perfect debate about race and not to worry, everything would be all right. He also told me that I shouldn't speak to the press, that he and the national president, Cornell William Brooks, would handle that. The NAACP has a clear chain of command. Local chapter presidents answer to the state area presidents, who answer to the regional presidents, who answer to the national president. Respecting the protocol, I did as I was told.

The next day, June 12, the NAACP issued an official press release that indicated it had my back and encouraged me to think I might be able to keep my job. "NAACP Spokane Washington Branch President Rachel Doležal is enduring a legal issue with her family, and we respect her privacy in this matter," it read. "One's racial identity is not a qualifying criteria or disqualifying standard for NAACP leadership. The NAACP Alaska–Oregon–Washington State Conference stands behind Ms. Doležal's advocacy record."

That was the only good news I received that day. In early May, the members of EWU's BSU had voted on who they wanted to be the keynote speaker at the Africana Education graduation. I was unanimously selected and very excited to do it. The graduation ceremony was scheduled for the evening of Friday, June 12. That morning, my supervisor at EWU, Dr. Scott Finnie, called me to ask if I was still planning on speaking.

"If the students want me to do it," I told him, "I'll be there."

I then contacted the BSU leaders and asked them what they thought I should do.

"Of course we still want you to do it," they said.

I relayed the news to Dr. Finnie.

Amidst all the chaos surrounding me, at least I had this to look forward to. It was important to me that I be at my students' graduation to express my appreciation for all the hard work they'd done and to send them out into the world feeling supported, inspired, and loved. I'd done much more than simply teach these students. I'd mentored them, helped them file discrimination complaints, braided their hair, and stood alongside them protesting police brutality and racial injustice. The speech I was scheduled to give that evening was my opportunity to give them the sendoff they deserved.

But when Dr. Finnie called back, he told me that the school's administration had asked him to relay a message: I wasn't going to be speaking at graduation, nor was I even to set foot on campus. The most devastating aspect of the furor surrounding my identity was the impact it had on my sons and my sister, but this was a close second. I'd known some of these students all four years they'd been in college, and I wasn't even allowed to say goodbye to them.

Following Gerald Hankerson's orders, I made no official statements to the press in my capacity as the local NAACP chapter president on Thursday, Friday, and Saturday. But on Sunday I had a meeting with our executive committee, during which its members made it known that they wanted me to address the issues at hand, namely my identity and parentage, at the general membership meeting the next day. I told them my hands were tied. Cornell Brooks had told me to cancel the meeting and wait until Thursday to say anything publicly. He was launching a new NAACP initiative called Journey for Justice the same day as our meeting, and he didn't want my situation overshadowing its unveiling in the press. Knowing the local membership wouldn't like this proposed plan, I asked him to reconsider, but Brooks backed up his command with a little muscle, telling me that if I didn't cancel the meeting by noon on Monday he would revoke our chapter's charter. When I explained this to the executive committee, they were up in arms. Their attitude was, basically, who is he to tell us how to run our local branch?

With my executive committee going rogue, unwilling to follow one of the NAACP's most fundamental rules—deference to the national president—I knew I could no longer lead the Spokane chapter. In the past six months, I'd worked my butt off to save it from losing its charter. Before I took office, the chapter had fewer than fifty members, only sixteen dollars in the bank, and just a single committee. Just a few months after I took over as president, it had more than two hundred members, its finances were well into the black, and it had eight committees. After all I'd done, I couldn't just stand by and watch the chapter lose its charter because of an internal collapse or an external shutdown. I decided to resign instead.

After I got home from the executive committee meeting on Sunday night and discussed the issue with Izaiah and Franklin, I emailed a letter of resignation to the executive committee, asking them to respect the leadership of the vice president I had appointed in January, Naima Quarles-Burnley. Quitting brought me a lot of pain and sadness. It didn't hurt because I lost a title or a line on my résumé. It hurt because it meant that I wouldn't be able to finish the work I'd started and that I'd be cut off from all the people I'd been trying to help.

I didn't have long to grieve the loss of my NAACP position. The next day, the editor of *The Inlander*, the local weekly newspaper for which I'd been writing part-time, posted an editorial online that mentioned the fact that I was no longer affiliated with it: I'd been fired. This was news to me! The editor hadn't reached out to me to let me know, but instead chose the coward's way, crucifying me in print and basically calling himself dumb for hiring me. Although the income I got for writing for *The Inlander* was negligible—a hundred dollars a month—before Sandy Williams started *The Black Lens* it had given me a platform to write about racial injustice and police accountability, and I was going to miss having such an outlet for my voice.

That same day, I found out that the investigation into the complaint Rebekah Hollwedel had made against me and two of my fellow OPOC commissioners in April had suddenly gained traction. The legal team from Winston & Cashatt, the law firm the city hired to look into the allegations, wrapped up their investigation on June 5 but didn't release their report until the day I resigned my position with the NAACP, when public opposition to me was at a fever pitch. One of the conclusions the report came to was that Kevin, Adrian, and I had "harassed Rebekah Hollwedel in the workplace by collectively and individually creating an intimidating, hostile, and offensive environment." It also accused us of altering the minutes of our meetings, calling it a breach of ethics. What their report failed to mention was that most of the alterations were related to fixing grammatical errors and inserting items that we'd covered in the meetings but that Rebekah's minutes failed to include.

The furor surrounding my racial identity provided city officials with the perfect smokescreen to distract people's attention while they led a witch hunt against the three most principled members of the commission. With the local press fixated on my story, few people even noticed that the city government had effectively turned its back on the idea of holding the local police accountable for their actions.

On June 15, City Council Chair Ben Stuckart and Mayor David Condon sent me a letter that said I'd been followed by a private investigator who'd discovered that I had integrity issues, and asked for my resignation. Knowing that Kevin, Adrian, and I had done nothing but our best, I refused to fall on my sword. The city council responded by holding a special session on June 18 during which they unanimously voted to remove me. When the media spread the news of my dismissal, people assumed I'd been forced out because of the controversy surrounding me. What they failed to notice was that I was just one of three OPOC members who were asked to step down, and for an entirely different reason. By removing three of the five commissioners, the city council succeeded in shutting down the work of the OPOC indefinitely.

I also received a letter from the City of Spokane telling me I was being sued for checking BLACK on the application I filled out to get the OPOC position, but that was the last I ever heard about the lawsuit. Maybe the city's legal team figured out that, thanks to scientific evidence that says modern humans evolved from Africa, all of us could feasibly check BLACK on forms such as theirs, which defined the category as "having origins in the continent of Africa." More likely, they were just happy to get rid of me and, once public opinion turned against me, considered their work done.

My theory that the investigation into Rebekah's complaints was a smokescreen gained credibility when I later found out that it succeeded in distracting attention from the meltdown taking place in the upper echelons of Spokane's government. In April, police spokeswoman Monique Cotton had informed Mayor Condon and City Administrator Theresa Sanders that Chief Straub had "grabbed her ass" and "tried to kiss her." Despite Cotton's claims that Straub had sexually harassed her, she refused to file a formal complaint. Instead, after a private meeting with the mayor during which she agreed to keep the scandal quiet, she walked away with a new job in the Parks and Recreation Department, a $10,000 raise, and an agreement that the $13,000 in legal fees she owed would be paid.

Three months after I was removed from the OPOC, Straub "voluntarily resigned," though his resignation had all the hallmarks of a termination. Because Straub resigned and wasn't fired, it prevented the investigation into his behavior from going public until after Mayor Condon's reelection in November 2015. Doubling down on his stupidity, Condon appointed Rick Dobrow to be Straub's successor, even though Dobrow lacked a bachelor's degree, had less than three years of experience in the upper ranks of the police department, and was on the verge of retirement. Dobrow's tenure only lasted three months, but it was enough for him to retire with a pension adjusted for a police chief's pay. Dobrow's successor, former U.S. Attorney for Eastern Washington Jim McDevitt, seemed just as ill-suited for a position that required good judgment and tact. Prior to taking the job, McDevitt had written an opinion piece in *The Spokesman-Review* that said, in effect, that Black people wouldn't get shot by police if they would just cooperate and that their welfare moms were to blame for not raising them right.

Even though I hadn't earned a cent while serving as the OPOC chair, I'd cherished the job. Along with my unpaid NAACP presidency, it had made my mission to hold the local police accountable for their actions much more effective. Without those positions, I only had my teaching job at EWU to sustain me, but that was on life support as well. Soon after resigning from the OPOC, I discovered that I could no longer access my EWU email account. Then Dr. Finnie asked to meet with me. When I arrived, he informed me that my contract wouldn't be renewed and told me to clear out my office. After working for the university for more than eight years, I was given ten minutes to grab all my stuff before being shown the door.

Losing my teaching position was the final blow to my professional career. On June 10, I'd had four jobs and, after winning a series of honors earlier in the year, including a woman in nonprofit leadership award from *Catalyst* magazine and the Bill First Human Rights Award from the Spokane County Democrats, I was starting to feel appreciated for all my hard work. But within a week, I'd lost every single one of my jobs. One minute I was working 24/7 in support of racial justice, and the next I only had one job left: explaining and justifying my very existence on the planet.

After losing my income and my reputation, I was reeling. Izaiah, Franklin, and Esther were what kept me going. If nothing else, I knew that I needed to keep breathing, eating, sleeping, and surviving for them. I'll admit it wasn't easy. I was looking at the very real possibility of never being able to find employment, love, friendship, or fulfillment ever again. When I realized that living as who I really am might never again be an option for me, my will to survive waned. Overwhelming social pressure is enough to drive people to the edge, and that's where I was—the edge. I considered killing myself and might have actually done it had it not been for my family.

I wasn't a white woman, but no one saw me as a Black woman either, so how was I supposed to proceed? If the whole world rejects you, what's the point in sticking around? Life is already too difficult and too painful to take on the added burden of being without a community, quarantined in solitary confinement psychologically, intuitively, and emotionally.

Was there a place for me in this world?

Chapter Twenty-Seven

New York

WITHIN JUST A FEW HOURS of the KXLY interview appearing on the internet and the story about me going viral, the media set up camp on my street. Cameramen hid behind trees and shrubs, hoping to get a shot of me. Whenever I dared to leave the house, reporters ran up to me, asking me questions and begging for a comment. Producers and entertainment bookers tried to convince me why I should agree to be interviewed on their shows. This one reporter from *People* magazine would run up to my car, get right in my personal space, and refuse to take no for an answer. Compared to the reporters from Fox and ABC, she was an angel. The guy from ABC would actually bang on my front door and yell, "We know you're in there!" I had no interest in talking to any of them, but that only seemed to make them more determined to convince me.

Larry and Ruthanne didn't share my apprehension about speaking to the press, agreeing to be interviewed by Fox, NBC, ABC, and CNN. On Monday, June 15, they appeared on *Good Morning America*, and when host George Stephanopoulos asked them about Esther's case against Josh, Ruthanne responded, "Of all of Rachel's false and malicious fabrications, this is definitely the worst. Rachel is desperately trying to destroy her biological family." Stephanopoulos called that "a very serious charge." It was a very telling one as well. Think about it. What had I done to destroy that family? Josh was the one who had assaulted Esther, and Esther was the one who'd filed the charges against him. All I'd ever done was support her and be myself. Larry and Ruthanne

were the ones who'd gone on the offensive. When the press contacted them, they could have declined to be interviewed. Instead,
they shared a truncated copy of my birth certificate that made no
mention of Jesus Christ being the attendant to my birth, as well
as photos of me from when I was a little girl, which, strangely,
appeared to have been altered to take on a bluish-white skin tone.
In short, they tried to ruin my credibility by dragging my name
through the mud. Why else would they volunteer to air their family's dirty laundry on national television?

Not content to carry out their smear campaign all by themselves, they enlisted Ezra and Zach to join them. My brothers made
all sorts of calculated yet no less hurtful allegations. On MSNBC,
Ezra said that I was "pretending to be Black" and that the pictures
I drew of myself as a child—long before he was born—were "not
real." On ABC News, he falsely claimed I'd once taken him aside,
told him I was going to change my identity, and asked him not to
"blow [my] cover." He even told the *Washington Post* that I "made
[Izaiah] really racist toward white people" by raising him in a pro-
Black environment. But he saved his most offensive and insulting
comments for the interview he did with BuzzFeed when he said
my transition from white girl to Black woman was "a slap in the
face to African Americans." Although he had never witnessed my
morning routine in front of the bathroom mirror, he went on to
allege, "She puts dark makeup on her face and says she Black. It's
basically blackface."

Out of everything he said, this comment brought me the most
sorrow because I was well aware of just how offensive blackface
was and was saddened that someone, especially someone I'd helped
raise from a baby, could confuse how I was living with that sort of
racism. Knowing that he hadn't been raised in a very healthy environment, I wanted to cut him some slack, but his comment made
it sound as if I were wearing a costume and making fun of Black
women instead of simply being myself. Wearing blackface is the
opposite of being pro-Black, of celebrating "Black is Beautiful," of
working for racial justice, and of trying to undo white supremacy—
all the things to which I'd dedicated my life. To mock these things

would have been to mock myself. But it made for a provocative headline, so the truth was lost in the uproar.

As hurt as I was, it was clear to me that Ezra had been brainwashed by Larry and Ruthanne and coached into making the blackface comment. He and Zach were still young and impressionable and almost completely dependent on Larry and Ruthanne, financially and psychologically. Of all my younger siblings, Ezra had always been their favorite, so it made sense when he sided with them, but I was confused about Zach's motivations. After all, he'd been treated even worse by his adopted parents than Izaiah had. Then I remembered that in the spring, just a few months before the story about me went viral, he'd asked me to cosign a loan with him so he could buy a truck. Unfortunately, I didn't have the necessary income or credit to help him out. He found another way. Not long after making his one appearance on national television to discredit me, he started driving a new truck. If I had to guess, I'd say that Larry and Ruthanne or perhaps Larry's mother Peggy had bought it for him. Regardless of what he and Ezra said about me on TV, I still loved them and held out hope that someday they would find their true selves, become more empowered and independent, and reconcile with me.

The sullying of my reputation, which Larry and Ruthanne started and the media quickly picked up on, wasn't limited to tearing my life apart; it also burrowed its way into the lives of everyone close to me. Fortunately, Izaiah was able to get out of town and avoid the spotlight that was shining on me. On Saturday, June 13, he left for a summer internship at the American Association for Access Equity and Diversity in Washington, DC. When he arrived, his supervisor took him aside to assure him that they would do their best to shield him from the media and any negativity while he was there. But no one could stop what was being said about him in the press. Few of the reporters were able to get the story straight. They kept referring to Izaiah as my brother and Franklin as my oldest son.

Other commentators mistook Franklin for Izaiah and called Franklin my adopted child. They seemed to put more trust in the words of Larry and Ruthanne, the two people who'd caused Izaiah so much pain in the past, than the official paperwork that showed I had full custody of him. Izaiah didn't see the situation getting better with time. He had the same last name I did and worried about what sort of reaction he was going to get when he returned to school in the fall. "You need to say something," he told me.

Hoping to protect my kids by pulling attention away from them and squarely onto me, I grew more open to the idea of speaking to the media once I'd resigned from my NAACP position and could freely do so. The only producer of color I saw, Devna Shukla from CNN, got my attention first. I let her inside my house, and we discussed whether I wanted to go on Anderson Cooper's show. I also discussed my options with an entertainment booker from NBC named Giselle. I told her that I wanted to talk to a Black woman about my experience and that I really respected Melissa Harris-Perry.

Unlike all the other journalists who jumped to the simplest and most popular conclusion and called me a liar, Harris-Perry seemed to understand and appreciate the complexity of my identity. "Is it possible that she might actually be Black?" she asked in a discussion about me with the author Allyson Hobbs on her June 13 show. "The best way I know how to describe this—and I want to be very careful here because I don't want to say it's equivalent to the transgender experience but there's a useful language in trans and cis, which is just to say that some of us are born cisgender and some of us are born transgendered—but I'm wondering can it be that we can be cisBlack and transBlack, that there's actually a different category of Blackness that is about the achievement of Blackness despite one's parentage?"

Wanting to engage in exactly this sort of in-depth discussion about the fluidity of race, I asked Giselle if she could get me on Melissa Harris-Perry's show on MSNBC and was a little shocked when she said, "Who is Melissa Harris-Perry?"

"Uh, just my favorite journalist and academic on television."

Giselle left to speak with her boss, and when she returned the negotiations began in earnest. If I agreed to come to New York City and talk for ten minutes with Matt Lauer on the *Today Show,* thirty minutes with Savannah Guthrie on NBC Nightly News, and sixty minutes with Amber Payne on MSNBC-BLK, I would get to speak with Melissa Harris-Perry for forty-five minutes on her show. I said I would do it on one condition. Perpetually strapped for cash and overloaded with work, I'd never taken my kids on a true vacation. Sure, we'd done plenty of fun stuff locally like hiking in the mountains, spending the day at Silverwood Theme Park, and going out on friends' boats in the summer, but all three of us had never gotten on a plane together and flown across the country. I'd been to New York several times to attend academic conferences, but Izaiah and Franklin had never been, so I asked Giselle if NBC would pay for Franklin to fly with me and Izaiah to fly up from DC. Giselle said they'd be happy to do that if I agreed to get on the next plane to New York. The next plane! This was problematic. My good friend Siobhan, who I'd met at church while living in West Jackson, Mississippi, had called me earlier in the day and told me that after hearing about my situation she'd packed a suitcase, rented a car, and started driving with her sixteen-year-old son Malique from Las Vegas to Spokane to help me through this ordeal. I explained to Giselle that I couldn't leave Siobhan hanging. If I was to leave that day, they'd need to fly her to New York as well. Giselle agreed to it all.

While flying from Spokane to New York, we had a layover in Chicago, and Franklin, Giselle, and I ducked into a spa. We didn't want massages. We just wanted to avoid being ogled by people who'd seen me in the news. We asked the staff if we could sit in the waiting area for just a moment. The Black man who was working there asked us why.

"I've been in the news a lot lately," I told him.

"For what?"

"Am I Black or white?" I asked him.

He looked me over. "Black."

"*That*'s why I've been in the news. Everyone's talking about what ethnicity I am."

After getting accosted by paparazzi at the airport in New York, we got into a town car that took us to the Park Hyatt, which, Giselle informed us, was one of the few hotels in New York with a private entrance just for celebrities. "It's where Obama and Jay Z stay," she added.

The hotel was indeed really nice, and Franklin was bouncing off the walls with excitement, pointing out the stocked fridge, the super-comfy bed, and the TV built into the bathroom mirror. The only things he was unhappy about were having to sleep on a cot and not being twenty-one, which would have allowed him to get his own room just like Izaiah, who'd checked in several hours before us. Both of them felt like they were on vacation, and I indulged their fantasy by encouraging them to make a list of all the places they wanted to see and things they wanted to do in Manhattan. Standing on top of the Empire State Building, going to Central Park, getting a slice of pizza, buying an I♥NY T-shirt, and seeing a mime all made the list.

As thrilled as they were to be staying at a five-star hotel, I barely noticed all the plush amenities. My body was numb from lack of sleep, exhaustion, and the emotional overload I'd endured in the past few days. Taking a long hot bath has always been my religion, and at that point all I could think about was the deep marble bathtub with the fancy bottle of body wash and bouquet of fresh-cut flowers sitting on the edge. I managed to get Franklin calmed down enough to allow me to melt into the tub, where I hoped to soak away my anxiety and think about what sort of answers I might give to all the questions I expected to be asked in the morning.

The bath didn't last long enough. When I got out, I only had five hours until I was supposed to wake up and find the town car that would be taking me to NBC Studios at Rockefeller Center. All I wanted to do was get some much-needed sleep, but when I opened the bathroom door I saw that Franklin had passed out on the bed with candy wrappers all around him and at such an angle it precluded me from slipping in beside him. I had to make do with crashing on the cot instead.

I woke up at 4 AM with a sharp cramp in my side. I hadn't slept well or much, but I needed to find out if Siobhan and Malique had arrived safely. The text she'd left on my phone confirmed that they had. Groggy but awake, I ironed my suit, rousted Franklin, and led him down to the lobby, where we rendezvoused with Izaiah, Siobhan, and Malique. We arrived at NBC at 6:15 AM, and I was immediately whisked into hair and makeup, where the lights were much too bright for the time of day. A staff person fetched coffee. Giselle introduced me to a bunch of people whose names I would never remember. I nodded and smiled and continued to think about how I wanted to respond when asked about working for the NAACP and the OPOC and fighting for racial justice.

After I'd taken a seat opposite Matt Lauer on the *Today Show*, it quickly became apparent that he had little interest in talking about any of these issues. I was frustrated at the direction he took. Many of his questions seemed downright bizarre to me at the time. He wanted to know what I did to change my appearance, as if I'd taken some drug as the author of *Black Like Me* had done instead of merely enjoying lots of sunshine, styling my hair, and opening my mind. That my hands and Matt's hands were very nearly the same complexion highlighted the question's absurdity for me. I wondered why he was asking me if I did something to darken my complexion when he clearly lounged on the beach, laid in a tanning bed, or had some kind of melanated heritage.

The question of whether I've ever altered my appearance to look Black bothered me because, like most women, I wanted to feel beautiful when I looked in the mirror, and how I did my hair and makeup and treated my skin was a personal decision. Many women surgically alter their bodies in ways that make them look different from how they were born. They get brow lifts, nose jobs, tummy tucks, booty shots, breast implants, and lip augmentations and reductions. Two months before I appeared on *Today*, Candice Bergen sat in the same seat I was now in and explained to Matt how she'd gotten her eyes "done" when she was forty-one and, a year later, some bands under her neck, but no one vilified her behavior.

Plastic surgeons are even capable of changing someone's "racial appearance" by performing something called race reassignment surgery. After having his skin bleached, his nose reshaped, his lips thinned, and his hair straightened, Michael Jackson became the best-known recipient of this medical procedure, and more recently, Lil' Kim had similar work done. The rapidly increasing popularity of such surgeries raises some interesting questions: Is one's racial appearance a proprietary entity? If so, who owns the brand? What does wanting to get this surgery say about the people who do it? Are the people who criticize such surgery right or wrong? What does the procedure say about the social construct of race in general? And is it fair that only those with enough resources can access these procedures?

I've never had any surgeries or alterations done to change my appearance. I didn't do any intensive makeup contouring. I'm a low-budget, low-maintenance woman. I liked to get a tan and occasionally used bronzer and I spent a lot of time on my hair, and with my somewhat broad nose, somewhat full lips, and somewhat curvy figure, that was enough to push the public's perception of me from white girl to "mixed chick."

Matt's interest in my appearance seemed to be shared by just about everyone. I tried to be understanding when people attempted to turn the modest choices I've made to beautify my appearance into a big deal, but at the end of the day I preferred to keep my morning routine private and devote my energy to talking about more serious issues. Why not say all this on camera? Because I was overwhelmed and exhausted, my brain was shutting down from being besieged by the media five days in a row, and I wasn't prepped in advance about what I might be asked. It's much easier to answer questions when you've had a little time to reflect on them.

I wasn't happy about how the interview was going, but I knew being rude to Matt wouldn't help my cause. I answered his questions with as much accuracy and respect as I could muster, and before I knew it the interview was over. There was no time for me to take stock of what had just transpired. I was immediately moved to another room, where I was told I would be interviewed by Savannah Guthrie for the nightly news. This interview would be much longer than the previous one, but it would be friendly—that's the only prep I got. I felt like I'd been placed on a balance beam and told to perform some amazing gymnastics routine I'd never been trained to do. I knew the odds of this turning out well were slim.

When Savannah brought up the interviews Ezra, Zach, Larry, and Ruthanne had done, it triggered my PTSD, and I scrambled to find my breath and my patience. I didn't think it was fair that in her line of questioning there was nothing about who I really was or the work I'd done. It was becoming clear to me just how little these mainstream white reporters knew about the idea and history of race. I began to wonder if breaking my silence on national television was the best plan after all. I fantasized about interviewing Savannah about her whiteness. How much time did she spend on her hair? How did she choose the right color of lipstick for her complexion and ultra-thin lips? Had she considered the history of how white people had come to be called white? But, of course, I couldn't ask these questions. I was the one on trial here, not her. I wanted to model respect and humility, so I forced myself to concentrate and try to make sense of all the odd questions coming my way.

Noticing how hard this interview was on me, Izaiah and Franklin hugged me afterward, and Franklin insisted he wanted to say something on camera. I was opposed to it at first but relented when he wouldn't drop it. I told the producer that I would allow him to do it on one condition: they needed to make it clear that it was Franklin's idea. Franklin took a seat on the couch, tugged on his sleeves, and said the kindest words I'd heard in what felt like a really long time. "I always knew my mom was going to be world-famous. But not like this. She doesn't deserve to be remembered as a liar, but as a hero." Izaiah and I both had tears in our eyes.

Franklin went on to talk about how he'd witnessed some of the hate crimes, how I wasn't making anything up, and how much it upset him that people thought that I had, but none of that made it onto the air. However brief Franklin's appearance on television was, it was long enough to attract the attention of some cowardly bullies, who harassed him on social media and, more alarmingly, on his cell phone, for "being a bitch." The next day, he received a text that read, "Tell your mom to kill herself and do the world a favor."

After the interview with Savannah, I was given ten minutes in the green room to refocus and prepare for my interview with Melissa Harris-Perry. When Melissa came to see me, we chatted for a bit. I'd chosen to do these exclusive interviews with NBC so I could speak with her, and I wasn't disappointed. We talked about the fluidity of identity and how power and privilege had created the current worldview about race. She told me she didn't understand why people were so upset about my identity. She even shared a story with me about her second daughter being identified as white at birth after being born via a surrogate who was white. "We thought about just leaving it that way," she said, describing the attitude she and her husband had adopted while pondering their daughter's legal racial classification.

After Melissa and I briefly discussed what she wanted to talk about during our segment, we were mic'd up and on set in no time. I felt much more at ease with her than I did with Matt or Savannah. I liked that she emphasized that my NAACP and OPOC positions were unpaid, but I was a little dismayed when many of her questions covered the same ground I'd already talked about in the previous interviews. At times, I felt like I was just repeating myself for the third time that morning. I hoped we could move on to a more academic discussion. We touched on a few interesting subjects, such as race, gender, and identity, but we didn't have a *thorough* discussion of any of these topics. In the end, it wasn't quite the synergy-filled conversation I'd envisioned.

I was told the fourth interview I would be doing was going to air on MSNBC-BLK, which focused on Black issues and targeted millennials. I went in with the hopeful idea that it might be like having a conversation with my students, but it was just more of the same. As I took a seat on an uncomfortable stool, an animated light-skinned Black woman named Amber Payne started asking me questions. I noticed that we were nearly the same complexion and her hair wasn't all that much different than mine, falling in a loose, wavy pattern with very little curl. If she'd run a flat-iron down her hair, she could have easily passed for Italian. Surely with her ethnically indeterminate appearance she would be a bit more understanding, I thought. After all, most of those who had reached out to me to express their support were people stuck somewhere in the middle of Black and white. Darker Black women, on the other hand, had become one of the primary voices of opposition against me, calling the way I identified "the ultimate white privilege."

In this instance, however, Amber, who was light-skinned, was taking the voice of the darker sistas, over-representing to underscore that she was solidly Black and not like Raven-Symoné, the Black actress/singer/comedian/talk show host who once said on her show *The View* that she would never hire someone who had a "ghetto name," or Stacey Dash, the Black actress/talk show host/Republican, who has called Black Lives Matter a terrorist group and wants to abolish Black History Month and Black Entertainment Television.

Amber's questions were adversarial and oppositional. I was frustrated and tired by now but tried not to show it. I let her lead the conversation and did my best to be patient—even though her attacks came at my expense. The only time I got visibly irritated occurred when she asked if I was "willing to acknowledge that level of white privilege that you took in choosing to be Black." She obviously didn't get it.

"So you do acknowledge that you have that ability to shift?" she went on to ask. "Because that's what really frustrates a lot of people. That's the heart of it. People in the Black community, that's what makes them angry because we can't do that." She seemed to have forgotten the long history of lighter-skinned Black people doing exactly that* and couldn't wrap her head around the idea that I wasn't passing for something I wasn't but identifying as something I was.

When she wasn't attacking me, she was patronizing me. "How do you do your hair?" she asked at one point. "Is it a perm? Is it a weave? Everybody's asking." Groundbreaking journalism this was not.

The interview was supposed to last thirty minutes, but it felt like three days in a bus station. I told the crew I needed to be done. I didn't even know what time it was. All I knew was that I was exhausted and famished and that my kids and Siobhan and Malique must have felt the same way. A photographer told me he

---

* Darker-skinned Black women obviously don't have that choice.

just needed to take a few photos of me for their website and then I could go. I tried to smile for the camera, but as I forced my mouth to turn upward I broke down and cried.

We spent two more nights in New York and Franklin and Izaiah were able to cross every item off their sightseeing wish list except visiting the Statue of Liberty. After all they'd seen and done, Franklin and Izaiah went home feeling like they'd had an amazing vacation. I, on the other hand, limped home feeling completely wiped out, emotionally and physically. I didn't need any more drama in my life but received some anyway. My period was a week late. The optimistic response would have been to chalk it up to stress and hope it arrived soon. I chose the more realistic route and called the man with whom I'd recently had a fling and asked him if he'd go to the store and get a pregnancy test for me. He did, then picked me up and took me to his apartment, where I took the test. Squatting over the toilet, I peed on the stick and watched the two red lines emerge, indicating it was positive. Unconvinced, I then used the second stick in the box. It also came back positive.

Damn, I was pregnant.

Chapter Twenty-Eight

Backlash

THAT I COULD EVEN GET PREGNANT was something of a surprise. During an OBGYN visit just after I'd gotten divorced in 2007, a Pap smear had shown the presence of abnormal cells in my cervix. A month later, I got another one done, and the result was the same: positive, which in this case meant very bad. A biopsy confirmed what no one ever wants to hear: I had cancer.

When you have something growing in your body that might kill you, you want to get it out as soon as possible, so the wait for the surgery to remove it, known as a LEEP procedure, seemed to take forever. The operation itself produced just as much anxiety, as it involved having a bit of my cervix cut out with an electric wire. As I laid back with my feet in the stirrups, the doctor cranked open my vagina with a speculum and assured me that everything was going to be fine.

It wasn't. As soon as the wire touched my flesh, I felt a searing pain unlike any I'd ever experienced before. Smoke poured out of my vagina. The room smelled like burning flesh. Evidently, the nurse had set the voltage on the machine too high. While she was being dismissed and replaced with a new one, my fingernails dug into the sides of the operating table and my teeth sunk into my bottom lip as I dealt with the excruciating pain and prepared for round two. The doctor did the procedure correctly on her next attempt, but my next Pap smear, done three months later, still came back positive.

Over the course of my next several visits to the doctor, more and more of my cervix was removed through various surgical procedures, and yet the tests still showed the presence of cancerous cells. After my last surgery, the results finally came back negative— but in the process most of my cervix had been cut away. The cervix regenerates over time, but I still didn't know if I would ever be able to get pregnant. I was also told that if I did get pregnant the chances of my miscarrying (and being subjected to life-threatening health risks such as excess hemorrhaging) would escalate unless I got a cervical cerclage, a procedure that involves having your cervix sewn shut.

Since the final surgery, I'd managed to get pregnant twice, and both times I opted to have an abortion. After my divorce from Kevin, the pro-lifer I was brainwashed to be as a child died and was replaced by a free-thinking pro-choice advocate. As in so many other aspects of my life, I'd come to understand that things are rarely so clear-cut and that the reasons for making a decision sometimes are as important as the decision itself. As before, there were many valid reasons to terminate the pregnancy this time around. The medical risk I faced if I were to try to have a baby was just one of them. The soaring levels of stress I had from being thrown into a global media firestorm also didn't promise to mix well with the hormonal challenges of pregnancy. That I no longer had any income had to be considered, too.

The father thought that we should get married or that I should have an abortion. The first option was a nonstarter. I didn't feel that we knew each other well enough or were compatible enough to get married—or even continue our romantic involvement, for that matter. He didn't take it very well when I made it clear that I was happy just being friends with him. The second option, abortion, made much more sense, especially after the father began saying that he didn't know for sure if the baby was even his, even though it was clear from the timing of the pregnancy and the size of the fetus that no one else was in the running.

Even though getting an abortion made the most sense, I took a moment to consider my options. Just because I supported a woman's right to choose didn't mean I took the decision lightly. With all the chaos in my life, I felt like it was important for me to give it my full attention and think it through. It would have been easy to make a rash decision, given all the distractions and pressure I faced. I continued to get pummeled with emails and texts directing other people's negativity onto me. Many of them began, "You're a pathetic cunt nigger," or some variation of the same. I deleted these messages without reading any further and changed my cell phone number, but I couldn't control what appeared in the media or on the internet and couldn't completely shield my kids from the fallout. Given all the negativity being directed at me, bringing another child into the world and exposing it to that hate and suffering didn't seem like such a good idea.

Thankfully, amidst all the gray clouds, there were some rays of sunshine. On June 12, Black R&B singer Keri Hilson took to Twitter to express her much appreciated—albeit somewhat backhanded—support of me. "Let's just all thank #RachelDolezal," she wrote. "Identity, pathological, & parental issues aside, she's doing more than most of us do for ourselves."

Another person who seemed to get me—or who was at least willing to give me the benefit of the doubt—was the comedian Dave Chappelle. "The thing that the media's got to be real careful about, that they're kind of overlooking, is the emotional content of what [Rachel Doležal] means," he told Soraya Nadia McDonald of the *Washington Post* on June 14. "There's something that's very nuanced where she's highlighting the difference between personal feeling and what's construct as far as racism is concerned. I don't know what her agenda is, but there's an emotional context for Black people when they see her and white people when they see her. There's a lot of feelings that are going to come out behind what's happening with this lady."

McDonald asked Chappelle which racial group should take me in the next "racial draft," a reference to a skit the comedian had created for *The Chappelle Show* in 2004. Similar to the way general managers picked newly eligible players for their teams in professional sports leagues, representatives from the main racial groups selected various celebrities to join their ranks. With the first pick in the draft, the Black delegation took Tiger Woods, the Jews took

Lenny Kravitz with the second pick, and so on. Years later, Black Twitter, a subset of the popular online social network united by issues affecting the Black community, picked up on the idea, with posters suggesting that certain Black celebrities get sent before the Black delegation for review and traded to another race, including Raven-Symoné and Stacey Dash. "I think Black," Chappelle told McDonald. "We would take her all day, right?"

The next day, he was joined by former NBA star Kareem Abdul-Jabbar, who wrote in a *New York Times* op/ed, "Whatever the reason, [Rachel Doležal] has been fighting the fight for several years and seemingly doing a first-rate job. Not only has she led her local chapter of the NAACP, she teaches classes related to African-American culture at Eastern Washington University and is chairwoman of a police oversight committee monitoring fairness in police activities. Bottom line: The black community is better off because of her efforts." He concluded, "The fight for equality is too important to all Americans to lose someone as passionate as she is and who has accomplished as much as she has. This seems more a case of her standing up and saying, 'I am Spartacus!' rather than a conspiracy to defraud. Let's give her a Bill Clinton Get Out of Jail Free card on this one (#Ididnothavesex) and let her get back to doing what she clearly does exceptionally well—making America more American."

Two days later, Allyson Hobbs also gave me some much-needed encouragement in a *New York Times* op/ed. "As a historian who has spent the last twelve years studying 'passing,' I am disheartened that there is so little sympathy for Ms. Doležal or understanding of her life circumstances," she wrote. "The harsh criticism of her sounds frighteningly similar to the way African-Americans were treated when it was discovered that they had passed as white. They were vilified, accused of deception and condemned for trying to gain membership to a group to which they did not and could never belong."

As far as the positive responses I received, that was about it. Otherwise, the press was quick to assume that Larry and Ruthanne were fine, upstanding citizens and that I was the worst kind of villain. The words journalists used to describe what I'd done, many of which were taken directly from Larry and Ruthanne's mouths, shaped the narrative. I was "masquerading." I was "faking." I was "being deceptive." While the evolution of my identity made perfect sense to me, it quickly became clear that it didn't to anyone else. Instead of delving into the complexities of my life and asking thought-provoking questions about the concept of race, the press fixated on my alleged "fraudulent behavior."

The real story, at least in my eyes, was the public's response, which showed just how divided—and confused—we remain in this country when it comes to talking about (or even defining) race. Many people simply couldn't fathom how someone who was born into the racial category known as white could ever feel Black or why that person would want to be viewed that way. They presumed I identified as Black to advance my career or make more money, and the press seemed happy to play along. There was never any mention of the fact that two of the four jobs I'd had were unpaid, that one of the paid ones barely covered the electric bill, and that the other provided only enough income to pay the rent and buy groceries. My income had always hovered around the poverty line, and in that regard I was not unlike many other Black women in the United States, who, studies have shown, make 16 percent less in the workplace than white women do.

What the press had to say about me was tame compared to what people said to me in emails or about me on online message boards. In the days following my outing, I was slapped with a long list of ugly labels so misogynistic and racist they could make a foul-mouthed comedian blush. That I was called both a "cracker-ass honky" and a "cunt-bitch nigger" showed how united Americans were in their division: Black people and white people hated me equally. I lost count of how many ugly memes were generated about me online. Another hurtful name I was called was "transnigger." When discussing it with Sandy Williams, the editor of *The Black Lens* and my good friend, she grimaced but tried to make light of it, saying, "Well, that's new!" Neither of us had ever heard that word before. Had a racial slur really been concocted specifically for me?

As offensive as most of the names I was called were, one of them invited further discussion. One of the many claims made about me was that I was the "first transracial woman." Unbeknownst to many, "transracial" had already been coined as a very specific term used to describe interracial adoptees. It would have been correct to categorize my adopted siblings that way under this definition, but not me. When I repeated this term in an interview, quoting someone else, people assumed I was using it to describe myself, and, unfortunately, doing that offended an entire segment of the population that otherwise might have been open to hearing what I had to say. On the plus side, a small fan base emerged in support of the idea of racial identity fluidity. They made me the mascot for their movement and had T-shirts printed that read, "TransRachel," a play on the word "transracial." Soon people began relaying to me their own stories of the difficulties of living with plural racial identities.

As inaccurate as the term "transracial" was, it did succeed in capturing the fluidity of my identity. There simply weren't any words available that correctly categorized my unique experience. Without the proper vocabulary, people kept comparing me to Caitlyn Jenner, the Olympic gold medalist formerly named Bruce who'd come out as a transgender woman in an interview with Diane Sawyer on April 24, 2015. Insofar as Caitlyn had been born under one categorical label and later claimed another categorical label as being closer to her true self, I could understand how the comparison was helpful. The accusations that I was sick in the head were reminiscent of the struggles endured by those in the LGBT community. Up until 1973, even homosexuality was classified as a mental illness in the *Diagnostic and Statistical Manual of Mental Disorders*. But in other ways comparing my cultural (and perceived racial) identity to gender identity didn't make much sense. Most people in the scientific community would agree that sex has always been defined to a greater degree by genetics than race, whereas race is a social construct that can't be determined by physical or genetic measures. I nonetheless appreciated the attempts at understanding my situation, as they highlighted our limited knowledge of racial fluidity and showed how little empathy we have for those who don't fit neatly in any one category.

When it comes to our understanding of gender, we've made incredible strides. Fifty years ago, you were either male or female or you were forced to hide in some closet. Now all the shades in between are recognized, to the point that an entirely new vocabulary has emerged, including female-to-male transgender, male-to-female transgender, trans*, and cisgender. On the subject of race, however, we're less informed. In most communities in the United States, you're either Black or white. Period. We barely have words to describe the large and rapidly growing population of multiracial people who inhabit the space between these two manufactured poles. Those who visibly fall somewhere between Black and white and can't be quickly categorized by physical features are frequently ostracized for not being Black enough, not being white enough, being too Black, or being too white.

I could empathize with these people, as I never comfortably fit into a single box. I certainly didn't think, feel, or act white, but at the same time few people now saw me as Black. Photos of me were analyzed on talk shows and websites, with my body shape, facial features, skin tone, hair texture, clothing, food choices, habits, and mannerisms all being racialized. Some people contended that I "must be a real sista" based on these traits, while others said I "looked so white" they didn't know how anyone could ever see me as Black. I was stuck in a surreal space that defied categorization. As Chris Stewart, aka Citizen Stewart, said on his weekly education reform podcast, I was "a nation of one."

It only takes a quick glance at the convoluted formulas that were created to determine one's race—from Thomas Jefferson's unsympathetic math to the one-drop rule—to see what a mirage race truly is. Why have we invested so much meaning in the idea of race and gone to such great lengths to ensure its existence? The notion of race was created and maintained by fair-skinned Europeans and Americans to justify the colonization and enslavement of darker-skinned people. It was used to rationalize a hierarchical system generated to leverage power and privilege and justify the resulting oppression. Simply put, racism created race.

Most white people don't take the time or effort to understand why the idea of race was created because it doesn't threaten their existence or that of their children. In fact, it is usually in their best interest to promote and maintain the idea. If Black-categorized people and white-categorized people could choose which racial identity to adopt—many Hispanic people are already allowed this privilege—it would dismantle the hegemony white people have enjoyed since this nation's birth. That I could be born white but identify as Black threatened to overturn this entire worldview (and possibly destroy white financial security and privilege as well), and white people let me know they weren't happy about it.

Liberal white folks who were happy to repudiate their white privilege were just as happy to throw me under the bus. From what I've observed, white liberals tend to believe that whatever they read in *The Root* or Huffington Post's "Black Voices" section represents the perspective of the entire Black population and that to hold any other view would be racist. For them, being called racist is the ultimate taboo, and mimicking the viewpoints espoused by these mainstream Black news sources presents a safe and defensible path for someone who hasn't experienced racism as a lived experience. By accusing me of being a cultural appropriator and a fraud, countless white liberals, including the "antiracist essayist" Tim Wise, were hoping to prove they weren't racists but rather white allies. While I appreciated what they were trying to accomplish, I wasn't pleased with the execution.

Out of the thousands of emails and hundreds of text messages I received after my story went viral, half of them were from extremely pissed-off white people who were outraged by the thought that someone born white would ever "choose" to be Black. These were the sort of people who embraced the patently ridiculous idea of Black privilege. They not only denied the existence of white privilege but also believed that programs such as affirmative action actually discriminated against white people. In the eyes of these people, I was a traitor.

The other half of the messages were from extremely pissed-off Black people who accused me of appropriating Black culture in the same way that white rappers like Eminem and Iggy Azalea had. Some felt like I'd taken jobs that should have been reserved for Black women. They were mad that I never "asked permission" to be Black. They didn't think I'd earned the right to wear Black hairstyles. In their eyes, I hadn't truly lived the experience and couldn't possibly understand Blackness, and nothing I had done or ever would do could earn me membership into their group.

I understood their anger. The racism and dehumanization they experienced daily prevented their psychological wounds from healing. Discounting my identity was a defense mechanism for many. By dissing me and invalidating my Blackness, they could underscore theirs. Colorism in the Black community also played a role. Those who said I wasn't allowed to identify as Black because they could never be seen as white were clearly referencing the pain of having darker skin while living in a society where having lighter skin brought access to privileges. When others claimed that crossing the color line was only possible for whites, they were forgetting, just as Amber Payne had, the long history of lighter-skinned Black Americans who'd passed for white. Black women in the media were particularly hard on me. By hating on me and revoking my "right" to appear with certain Black characteristics, they succeeded in damaging my self-esteem in an attempt to bolster their self-worth, which probably says more about women's tendency to tear each other down in general than it does about Black women in particular. My hope was that the furor surrounding me in the Black community was just a family feud that could be resolved with the aid of compassion, tolerance, and time.

As devastating to me as the public's reaction to my story was, it felt even worse when I saw the impact it had on others. It didn't just upend my life but also the lives of everyone around me, and had a ripple effect that prevented justice from being served in several cases that were extremely important to me. Investigators eventually ruled Lorenzo Hayes' death a homicide, but prosecutors determined that the officers and jail staff had "acted without malice, or evil intent," and none of them were charged. Lorenzo Hayes' case should have been national news. Instead, the story quickly faded away, which I guarantee would not have happened had I still been the local NAACP president and OPOC chair.

Esther was also part of the collateral damage. Because she lived in Spokane and shared my last name, she often got stopped on the street by people who would ask if she was my sister, if she thought I was Black, if she thought I wished that I was her, if it was true that she'd been molested, and many other equally personal questions about her, me, and our family. While she was at work the day after my story blew up, someone broke into her apartment and trashed the place, destroying most of her belongings, ripping her clothes to shreds, even snapping her toothbrush in half, but nothing was taken. Fearing that a police report with her last name on it would only result in more chaos, she chose to move across town instead of calling the cops.

Even more heartbreaking to me was the fact that she never got her day in court. After I'd been tried and convicted in the media, the district attorney in Clear Creek County, Colorado, dropped the charges against Josh. The DA didn't come right out and say he was doing it because my credibility had been destroyed, but what else had happened between June 9, when the DA's office sent letters to me and Esther requesting our appearances at the jury trial, and June 15, when the first hearing had been scheduled?

With so much negativity swirling around me, I tried hard to focus on the good things in my life. I was healthy. I had two amazing sons and a wonderful sister. I was loved, not by everyone, but at least by them. If I was to stay healthy, I knew I needed to limit the amount of sorrow in my life and increase the amount of love. I felt like I simply couldn't handle any more pain or loss. So as much sense as it made for me to opt out of having a baby, I simply couldn't bear the thought of having an abortion. My options in life had become very limited, but deciding to have a baby and giving him or her all my love was one choice I could make.

Aware of the impact being pregnant and having a baby would have on Franklin and Izaiah, I asked them for their opinions. Both supported the idea of me keeping the baby. I frequently sought the guidance of a counselor whose advice I respected when it came to making major life decisions. Before I'd gotten the previous abortions, I'd consulted her, and she'd confirmed what I'd felt, that I shouldn't feel guilty about terminating the pregnancies, that it was the right decision. When I spoke to her this time, she said she felt this baby's spirit was made up of pure love and would provide a much-needed place for me to devote my nurturing energies. I've always liked getting confirmation in sets of three, so her advice and Franklin and Izaiah's encouragement, coupled with my own desires, decided it for me: I was going to have a baby. The father wasn't happy with my decision and we soon lost contact with each other, but I comforted myself knowing that parenting on my own was familiar terrain and would give me the freedom to live without having to negotiate the terms of raising a child with a disinterested co-parent.

After losing my jobs, most of my friends, and, to a large extent, my ability to carry on with my life purpose, my heart and spirit were wounded. I felt worn down, vulnerable, and condemned. With so much hate being directed at me, pouring all my love into my baby was one thing I could look forward to. All the energy I'd devoted to my students, the local Black community, and the causes I believed in I now channeled into bringing a new life into the world. Focusing on this one task, I was able to push any distractions and disruptive emotions aside as I set about rebuilding my life.

Like most mothers, I wanted to keep my pregnancy a private affair for as long as possible, but in addition to questioning my identity and tearing apart my life, the press also seemed hell-bent on stealing what little privacy I had. The gossipy celebrity news website TMZ leaked news of my pregnancy by posting a screenshot that someone had lifted from my private Instagram account. If I'd been asked how I wanted to introduce my baby to the world, that wouldn't have been my first choice, but that was the life I was now living.

Chapter Twenty-Nine

Survival Mode

H AVING FAILED TO GET MY MESSAGE ACROSS in the interviews
I'd done for NBC in New York, I hoped doing an interview for
a magazine might give my story the in-depth look I felt it deserved
and help resurrect my image. *People, Elle,* and *Cosmopolitan* all
reached out to me, but I went with *Vanity Fair* because I was told
its editors wanted to do for me what they'd done for Caitlyn Jenner,
who was featured on its June 2015 cover and given a long, sympathetic article that contained many beautiful images of her. The
other reason I chose *Vanity Fair* was that a Black journalist named
Allison Samuels was going to write the piece, and I wanted to support her work in a publication that rarely features Black women as
the subject or author of its articles.

I did the interview in July, and when it came out in August,
I was devastated. I wasn't on the cover, and the article was much
shorter and much less empathetic than I'd been led to believe it
would be. The article's bias against me was apparent in its title:
"Rachel Doležal's True Lies," which fed into the "fraudulent behavior" narrative being told about me. All the photographs the magazine chose to use supported that point of view, making me look
pissed off, uncomfortable, and, by extension, guilty in the eyes
of most readers. The article itself not only failed to clear up the
confusion about me; it actually added to it by introducing new fallacies. Allison knew that I'd been braiding hair for more than two
decades and had been making money doing it for years. During our
many conversations, she even asked for my advice about her own

hair. But the article gave the impression that I'd only just started braiding, making it sound like some sort of desperate last-resort career move. With the magazine's reputation for delivering well-researched articles offering astute social commentary, I was hoping it might give my story the measured examination such a timely issue warranted and that it would help me restore my reputation, but it ended up doing more harm than good.

While the whole world was trying to tear me down, Ambassador Attallah Shabazz, the eldest daughter of one of my biggest heroes, Malcolm X, contacted me on LinkedIn, asking if she could give me a call. "Of course," I replied, not fully believing it was her. But it was. She offered me some crucial support, assuring me that not everyone was fooled by Larry and Ruthanne's televised denunciation of me disguised as parental concern. She told me about her own family's many trials with the media and how important it was for me to stay clear about who I was before the "manufactured media frenzy" had erupted in June. She consoled me by saying that she could see how passionate I was about human rights and that perhaps I wasn't meant for a small, local platform, that I was just experiencing growing pains as I moved toward a national—perhaps even international—stage. "Don't let this shape you," she said.

Offering me a safe space where I could be free from the "curiosities and funk" and speak from my experience as an activist and academic, she invited me to be on a panel at a film festival for the United Nations' International Day of the Girl forum, which she was hosting in Louisville, Kentucky, in October. I gratefully accepted and was rewarded with an amazing experience. During the panel discussion, I talked about the role of identity in the documentary *Somewhere Between*, which traces the story of four teenage girls who were adopted from China and raised in contemporary America, and the significance of the film *Skin*, which depicts the true story of Sandra Laing, a dark-skinned girl born to white parents during the apartheid era in South Africa.

Laing's story had always resonated with me. Because she was legally classified as white but appeared Black, she was shunned by the white community, rejected by nine schools, refused service at stores, mocked, abused, and persecuted. As a teenager, she eloped to Swaziland with her Zulu boyfriend. When her father found out, he threatened to kill her. She became estranged from her family and was forced to live in a sort of racial limbo, not Black, not white, just misunderstood. There were very few people in the world I could identify with, but she was one of them. I was drawn to her story because of the way it depicted being categorized in different ways by different people, feeling isolated, and struggling to finding a harmonious place in the world.

In the months preceding the trip to Louisville, I'd found myself being forced into an awkward position, with people constantly judging my hair, skin, body, and speech to decide if I passed their test for Blackness or whiteness. If my hair was too straight or my skin tone too light, people accused me of going back to being white and opting out of Blackness for convenience's sake. If my hair was too textured or my skin too tan, they faulted me for cultural appropriation or perpetuating a fraud. As a response to this sort of scrutiny, I wore my hair in a loose wavy pattern and tried to adopt an ethnically indeterminate look that underscored that I wasn't going back to looking white while not, I hoped, offending anyone who felt I wasn't Black.

Fortunately, I could be myself in Louisville, and, per Shabazz's suggestion, discuss the films as I would have before the scandal erupted. It was comforting that everyone on the panel had experience with racial identity issues. Paula Williams Madison, a former executive at NBC Universal and a half-Chinese, half-Black woman commonly seen as Black, discussed *Finding Samuel Lowe*, the documentary she made about discovering her extended Chinese family. Lacey Schwartz talked about *Little White Lie*, the documentary she wrote and directed, chronicling her experience growing up white and finding out in college that she was half Black. In an interview on the news program *Democracy Now!* in June, Lacey had spoken harshly about me, but after meeting me and getting to know me she became much more empathetic. She wasn't the only one there who came away with a better understanding of who I was. Toward the end of the panel discussion, a Black woman in the audience took the microphone and said, "I just want to apologize for being so wrong about you."

The trip was a healthy reprieve for me, but when I returned home it was back to reality. I was broke. I hadn't gotten a paycheck since June. I had no savings. I couldn't pay my student loans or medical bills. I had collections agencies calling me every other day. I had no assets I could sell, no house, no boat, no fancy car, and no relatives who would ever be contributing to my finances. With 180,000 miles, a cracked windshield, a broken side mirror, and two dents courtesy of icy roads and white supremacists, my Pontiac Vibe wasn't worth the effort required to sell it. And thanks to my abysmally low credit score, I wasn't qualified to get any new credit cards or loans.

I responded the way I always had, doing what had to be done. I cut out all unnecessary expenses, stopped paying car insurance, signed up for food stamps and state health insurance, and relied on the resourcefulness I'd learned as a child. I tried to sell greeting cards I'd made as well as some of my artwork, but it seemed that everyone was making more money off my art than I was. People who'd bought some of my pieces years before took advantage of my name recognition being at an all-time high and sold my work for inflated prices online. Larry and Ruthanne were among the vultures, selling some of my high school art pieces and telling people they were giving me the funds. Do I need to mention that I never got a cent from them? Wild accusations further dampened my spirits and dissuaded me from creating any new work. Some people had the audacity to suggest that I'd printed photographs onto canvases and claimed they were paintings. I'd once made a triptych in which the middle panel was a commentary on the famous Romantic painting "The Slave Ship," and, choosing to ignore the two side panels, people accused me of plagiarizing J. W. M. Turner. The absurd implication that I wasn't a "real artist" but a fraud certainly didn't help sales.

The only thing that generated any sort of income for me was my experience braiding and styling Black hair. I was what's known as a "kitchen stylist," working out of my home to pay the bills. In Washington State, it's legal to charge for braiding and non-chemical styling of Black hair, thanks to Salamata Sylla, the owner of Sally's African Hair Braiding in Kent, Washington, who sued the state for the right to braid Black hair without a license. The fact that the cosmetology schools in Washington didn't teach prospective beauticians how to braid and style Black hair helped her win the case and keep her shop open.

I specialized in braiding, producing a look that was somewhat more African than African American. I could do individuals, cornrows, weaves, extensions, beaded extensions, crochet, jumbo twists, hot fusion, cold fusion, sew-in, tape-in, Senegalese twists, micro twists, Nubian twists, dreadlocks, faux locs, and microbraids. About half of my clients got a sew-in weave and the other half came to me for braided styles. I occasionally maintained men's dreadlocks, but most of my clients were women or girls.

In a good week, I'd have three or four appointments; in a bad one, none. While juggling my four jobs, I'd been forced to pare down my list of clients, and with the media portraying me as a lunatic or a fraud it was hard to find new ones. Friends suggested I make YouTube videos or advertise, but having been accused of cultural appropriation I knew that the few clients I might be able to pick up from Spokane's 2 percent Black population wouldn't be worth the mockery I'd receive online. I didn't lose many clients after the media firestorm, but I didn't gain many new ones, either.

Braiding and styling Black hair in the Inland Northwest had never been very lucrative, but it was extremely rewarding. There weren't a lot of Black hair stylists in Spokane, so in some ways I felt like I was performing a vital public service, particularly when working with white parents who'd adopted Black children. These parents often didn't know the first thing about taking care of Black hair. While hanging out at an indoor trampoline park with my kids one day, I saw a white couple with four Black kids, all of whom had short, tangled, and unkempt hair. I handed the mother my business card and explained that I did Black hair, and I was glad that I did. The woman told me that her three little girls had been getting teased at school for looking like boys and had become so shy they were hardly talking to anyone anymore. The family lived in Idaho, a good two hours from Spokane, but the long drive to their house was worth it. After I gave the three girls long flowing braids, they couldn't stop hugging me. Their delight made the back pain and cramped fingers I had after fifteen hours of braiding—five hours per girl—disappear.

On another occasion a white mother brought her twelve-year-old daughter directly from the hospital to my house so I could do her hair. The girl, whose father was Black and out of the picture, had attempted suicide because she felt like she didn't fit in at school and was unhappy with her life. When she saw how she looked in the new style I gave her, she beamed. The smile on her face was priceless. She came to me to get her hair done several times after that, and it seemed to elevate her spirits each time.

There were some heartbreaking experiences as well. A white woman who'd adopted a Black girl once asked me to braid her eight-year-old daughter's hair. I did, but because money was tight the woman didn't bring her daughter back to me until nearly a year had passed. It took me nine hours to detangle the combination of dreads and braids mixed with grass and lint that had resulted from so much neglect, and I only charged fifty dollars because that's all the woman could afford. I often charged white mothers who'd adopted Black girls and didn't have much money far less than the standard rate for my services, fearing that if I didn't they might not bring their daughters back as often as is necessary to keep Black hair healthy. One of these mothers was the only client I lost because of the controversy surrounding me, telling me she felt "betrayed." All my Black women clients continued to come just the same because they knew I did quality work and liked me as a person. To them, I was just Rachel, and in their presence I felt free to be myself. But even with their loyalty I still couldn't make ends meet.

My financial situation got so desperate I started to consider some of the offers I'd been given when I was one of the most popular trending topics online. In the weeks following my public shaming, the entertainment industry was full of ideas about how I could be turned into a commodity and offered me all sorts of "opportunities." The easiest ones to dismiss were the six-figure offers from Vivid Entertainment—one for $150,000, the other for $175,000—to appear (and engage in four different sex acts) on its porn site wefuckblackgirls.com. I couldn't say no fast enough. The

British company Okon also wanted temporary use of my body, asking me to model its underwear, but I was seeking credibility-building options rather than gigs that required me to take my clothes off, so I passed.

A variety of television shows contacted me as well. I was invited to be a contestant on *The Amazing Race.* VH1 flew me to New York City to discuss the possibility of having me appear in an episode of its reality show *Family Therapy with Dr. Jenn* with either Larry and Ruthanne or Ezra and Zach. *Dr. Phil, Steve Harvey,* and Oprah's show *Iyanla: Fix My Life* also reached out, wanting to capitalize on the storyline that I was misguided and needed mental help. Knowing that none of these shows would help me rebuild my life, I turned them all down. The only offers I got that might possibly lead to me having a serious discussion about my situation came from the major networks. After my appearance on the *Today* show, CNN, FOX, and ABC expressed interest in talking with me, but respectable news organizations such as these don't pay for interviews, so I kept searching.

Running out of money and options, I agreed to be interviewed on November 15, 2015, for *The Real,* a daytime talk show whose hosts are all women of color, for $5,000. I also asked for Franklin to be flown with me and for him to be given a tour of Warner Bros. Studios. After aspiring to be a veterinarian and an author, Franklin now hoped to become an actor. Arranging this tour was one of my birthday presents to him. He'd just turned fourteen.

I was promised that the discussion on the show would focus on my art and motherhood. To ensure that this would happen, I vetted a series of questions in the weeks leading up to the taping. But as soon as the cameras started rolling one of the hosts, Loni Love, asked, "So what is it about Black culture that you love so much? Is it the *men?*" and immediately I knew this was not going to be the interview I was promised. She went on to ask, "Are you ashamed of being white?" As the audience booed, Franklin tried to walk onto the stage to tell them to stop, but the production team held him back, saying they couldn't let a minor go on camera.

Since the show's hosts wanted to talk about everything but my art and motherhood, I tried to weave in some tidbits of education regarding the convoluted worldview of race and the ways in which race isn't a biological reality, but they were ignored and the conversation was steered back to drama and mockery. When the hosts asked me to admit that I was white and I acknowledged that, yes, I was born to white parents, the audience cheered wildly. When I went on to explain that I identified as Black, they booed. The all-too-familiar blight of American society had reared its ugly head once again: applause for whiteness and jeers for Blackness. What pained me was that this time around it was being orchestrated by women of color.

This was the first time I'd appeared visibly pregnant on television, and Loni had the nerve to joke about it and ask if my baby was Black or white. After TMZ leaked the story about my pregnancy and people began speculating who the father might be, this became a sensitive topic for me. Being Black and living in an environment that was mostly white had already forced me to experience the anxiety-producing "gaze of the other," and having my body scrutinized in this way only added to my unease, to the point that I'd come to dread going to the grocery store. When Loni asked about my pregnancy, I gave her a look that clearly illustrated how I was feeling. "You really don't want to go there, bitch," my eyes said. "You'd better back the fuck down."

I later found some consolation when a few people observed online that only a Black woman could shut down another Black woman like that. Others fixated on the idea that I'd "admitted to being white" when I acknowledged that was how I was born. Much to my relief, another segment of the population expressed their dislike for the way the hosts had handled the interview. As terrible as I felt afterward, this appearance seemed to generate much more sympathy for me than the *Vanity Fair* article had. Maybe people had begun to feel that, after four months of constant abuse, I'd been hit by enough punches and it was no longer funny to see me get beat up.

Once the interview was over, I asked Franklin to bring out the portrait I'd painted of the hosts as a gift, handed it to them, then went straight to the green room, tore off my mic, and let the production team know how pissed I was. For Franklin's sake,

I managed to curb my anger enough to get through the Warner Bros. tour, but it took all my willpower to do so.

I'd gone on the show with two goals: make enough money to keep my little family afloat and turn my reputation around. I comforted myself knowing that I'd at least achieved one of them. After my attorney and agent's fees had been deducted, I had enough money to pay our rent and bills and buy food in November and December. Beyond that, who knew?

In every other regard, the trip to Los Angeles was a disaster. I was done trying to explain myself to people on television or in magazines. They didn't get me and weren't giving me a fair hearing, so why bother? I retreated to the cocoon I'd created for myself in Spokane, emerging only to run errands and turn in job applications and left wondering when or if people would ever be able to understand where I was coming from.

Chapter Thirty

Rebirth

IN HIS 1970 BLACK POWER PROTEST SONG, Gil Scott-Heron asserted, "The revolution will not be televised." He was right. If racial equality is ever to be achieved in the United States during the present era, it's much more likely to be tweeted.

The Black Twitter community has displayed its growing influence on several notable occasions in recent years. In the summer of 2013 alone, its followers succeeded in causing the loss of millions of dollars' worth of business to companies that sold the products of Paula Deen, the celebrity chef who had admitted to telling racist jokes and repeatedly using the N-word, and preventing a book deal between a literary agent in Seattle and one of the jurors in George Zimmerman's trial.

In the wake of my story going viral, Black Twitter users grew equally enamored with posing questions that, in theory, only Black people could answer correctly and signing off with an #AskRachel hashtag. Most of the questions were about Black history or culture and were meant to test one's Blackness. Many were also intended to make readers laugh. For example:

What has been left in the sink?

A. A fork

B. Cutlery

C. Silverware

D. All these damn dishes

As funny as a few of the tweets were, the humor always came at my expense. The implication was that I couldn't possibly know the answers to the questions because I hadn't been born and raised as a Black person. To those who wrote these tweets, I was just a pretender who may have been able to tell you all about the Freedom Riders or Queen Nzinga, but didn't have a clue what it was like growing up "in the cut."

These sorts of examinations of my Blackness—as well as declarations of my perceived whiteness by others—became regular occurrences after June 11, 2015. Even though I clearly had more than a cursory knowledge about Black history and culture and didn't relate to other Black people as an outsider but as someone who had also been subjected to microaggressions and hate crimes, a sista in the struggle, I still had to prove myself every time I spoke with a Black journalist. I was once a guest on a radio show featuring Pekela Riley, a celebrity hair stylist from Jacksonville, Florida, who specializes in Black hair and enjoys playing a wordplay game, where she gives two options and her guests have to choose one. For me, this turned into a not-so-subtle assessment of my Blackness.

"Idris Elba or Leonardo DiCaprio?" she asked me.

As if I'd ever pick the kid from *Titanic* over Stringer Bell. "Idris Elba."

"Mani/pedi or massage?"

Duh. "Mani/pedi."

"Black Lives Matter or All Lives Matter?"

Of course, all lives mattered to me, but Black Lives Matter was the message that needed to be heard the most at that time. "*Please,*" I said, "I was leading the Black Lives Matter rallies here."

"Biggie or Tupac?"

"Okay, now you're trying to get me into trouble. I've always been a 'Pac fan and my sons like Biggie, so we have that constant conflict going on in our household, but I'll have to go with Tupac."

"CNN or MSNBC?"

"MSNBC would be my choice, but they kind of broke my heart with the Melissa Harris-Perry thing recently. But fingers crossed they turn around—"

"And fix it. *Good Times* or *The Jeffersons?*"

"I'll have to go with *Good Times*."

While I understood the purpose of such tests, I looked forward to a day when I might not have to take them anymore. No matter how I responded they always left me feeling misunderstood, like I was on some sort of cultural probation. Being asked to prove myself over and over again after I'd already spent nearly two decades paying my dues brought me a great deal of pain and isolation. Adding to my loneliness was the distance that grew between me and my dad.

During the global media firestorm, journalists had bombarded Albert with questions. A private person, he didn't appreciate them digging into his military record and private affairs. He and his wife Amy were also dealing with some health issues at the time, and at their ages—both were in their seventies—they didn't want the stress of having nosy reporters knocking on their door. When I told Albert I was pregnant, he grew more detached from me, responding with a chilly silence. I thought he was disappointed in me, and I felt bad that he and Amy were being inconvenienced simply for knowing me. Not wanting to burden them further by dragging them into the chaos that surrounded me, I stopped contacting them. The casual "Hey, Dad" sort of intimacy I'd previously enjoyed with Albert disappeared. So did the "Dear Daughter" cards and texts I used to get from him. With his absence from my life, I felt completely adrift, unsure if I'd ever receive unconditional love from a father figure again.

Vilified by both the Black and white communities, I felt as isolated as I'd been growing up on the side of that mountain in Montana. I credit the baby I was carrying inside me for helping me get through that rough patch and taking care of myself. Being pregnant encouraged me to avoid self-destructive tendencies I might have been tempted to engage in and to be as healthy as possible. I made myself eat nutritious foods, drink copious amounts of water, and get lots of rest, things I probably wouldn't have done while under this much stress had I not been pregnant. There were days—quite a few, to be honest—I wanted nothing more than to down a nice Olivia Pope–sized glass of cabernet to help me unwind from all the tension I was carrying, but, being pregnant, I obviously couldn't do that. In loving my baby, I was loving myself. I felt like he and I—yes, *he*; doctors had confirmed I was having a boy—were taking a special journey together, as his birth was not only going to represent a new beginning for him but for me as well.

I took particular delight in the fact that my baby's estimated due date fell on February 14, which was Frederick Douglass' birthday and fell right in the middle of Black History Month. Franklin, Izaiah, and Esther were all present at his birth. Esther actually held up my left leg as I pushed the baby out. Unlike Franklin's ninety-four-hour labor and delivery, this one only took ten hours. My baby was born naturally and full-term, arriving two days after the estimated due date.

I'd made a short list of boys' names but only one felt right: Langston Attickus. The middle name was an homage to Crispus Attucks, a Black man from Boston who was the first casualty of the American Revolutionary War and crossed the color line after he died by being buried in a whites-only cemetery, and to Atticus Finch, the protagonist's father in *To Kill a Mockingbird* who, as a lawyer, agreed to defend a Black man who had been accused of raping a white woman. The first name was a tribute to the celebrated Black poet, writer, and leader of the Harlem Renaissance Langston Hughes, who was also born in February. In particular, I was inspired by Hughes' "Mother to Son," a hopeful poem that acknowledges life's many hardships and celebrates perseverance. I'd always admired Hughes' poetry, which to me felt like a form of activism and revolution during an era when white supremacy was widespread and in many places openly supported. Hughes was known as "the people's poet." His words were like food to the Black community, and they continue to nourish those who read them today.

As beautiful as Langston's birth was, it also required me to revisit one of the great fallacies of our society, which had plagued me my entire life: our government's demand for us to check boxes on legal forms categorizing ourselves in certain ways. Hardly a minute passes after we're born before we're assigned a name, a sex and therefore a gender, and a race. Our identities are assumed to be accurate based on the testimony of others. As we grow, more boxes are added to the forms we're constantly filling out: religion, sexual orientation, age, language. Many of us come to understand that these boxes hold very little meaning compared to the way we actually feel about ourselves. Time and time again, these narrow categories have proven to cause more harm than good. At the end of the day, we're all part of the same group: human.

After how much attention the way I'd checked the race category on the application for the police ombudsman position had gotten, I knew that how I chose to racially categorize Langston on his birth certificate application was likely to attract scrutiny. Langston's father was Black, but in Washington State, the way the mother identified was by default the way her child was identified. I selected WHITE *and* BLACK for Langston because, while I acknowledged that I had some visibly European phenotypes, I also remained unapologetically Black and I refused to allow a form to whitewash my son's identity.

Several weeks later, while taking Langston to see a pediatric urologist, I was asked to fill out an intake form and saw that, unlike some medical forms that state "Check all that apply" or include an "Other" category, this one required me to choose a single race. No matter how I chose to fill out the form, I felt like it would have contained a degree of inaccuracy, because I believed that the premise of race was flawed and that using one parent's racial identity to determine a child's racial identity was flawed as well. That these forms and the racial categories on them differed from office to office and state to state was indicative of how weak a foundation the idea of race rested upon and, as a consequence, how prone definitions based on that idea were to falling apart.

Langston's birth also succeeded in reigniting the animosity that had been directed at me for nearly a decade and that had become especially virulent after the previous summer. On Twitter, some hateful person hiding behind the handle @7YearOlds responded to a photo I'd posted of Langston wearing Mickey Mouse pajamas and sleeping in an infant swing by writing, "I hope someone puts a gun in his mouth and blows his dirty little nigger brains all over your stupid white ass!" Commenting on a photo of Langston's feet, the same vile person wrote, "Why do I see pictures of your stupid nigger sons [sic] bare ass feet? Those should be work boots I see!"

What kind of world were we living in that someone could direct this kind of hatred toward a mother and her newborn baby? As young Black men in America, Franklin and Izaiah had already faced such hostility many times in their short lives. I wished I could have made the world a better place for Langston to grow up in, but with my voice largely silenced by the fabricated scandal involving me, I was going to have to live with shielding him from the pain and teaching him how to redirect the fear and anger he was inevitably going to experience.

During my pregnancy, I painted some inspirational art for Langston's nursery and wrote letters to him as a way of preparing him for the world he was about to enter. As the mother of two Black sons, I knew how hard life could be for them, and unless a great change came over our society, I feared it would be much the same for Langston. My hope was that if for some reason I weren't around to advise him in the future, he could look at these paintings and read these letters and find comfort in the images I'd created and the words I'd written. In my letters, I warned him about the scorn and hate that came from being Black and living in a predominately white environment. From my own experience, I knew how incredibly painful it was to have your body constantly being appraised according to someone else's calculus while your true essence was ignored. I advised him to shut out the noise as best he could and stay focused on his own truth. Who you know yourself to be, I reminded him, was far more important than how you appear to others.

I also told Langston how important it was to be clear about right and wrong and to own up to any mistakes he might make. I recalled some of the mistakes I'd made in my own life: making decisions based on fear, spending too many years trying to be what other people wanted me to be, and not having the courage to talk about my past out of fear of rejection. I've always been a very straightforward and honest person who has strived to balance the ethics of what is true to say with compassion regarding what is kind to say and wisdom in knowing what is necessary to say. Yes, there have been many times when I've failed to strike this balance and made mistakes. I wish there could have been a way for me to be 100 percent truthful about my identity while being 100 percent understood and accepted by others, but I always felt like I had to trade one for the other. I had the joy of living and being seen as who I truly am for five years, but to do that I had to gloss over or hide much of my complex past in favor of simpler stories that I felt would make more sense to other people. I am by no means perfect, but I've finally matured enough to accept imperfections as being an integral part of growing.

At the same time, I told Langston, it's just as important to be able to separate the harm you've caused from the harm created by other people. I'd spent too much of my life beating myself up for "mistakes" that weren't actually my fault and punishing myself with shame and guilt forced on me by other people. As part of my healing process from sexual and psychological traumas in my past, I'd come to understand the importance of not holding myself accountable for the perpetrators' actions. Now, after getting skewered by the press and the general public, I refused to take on more than my fair share of the blame, and if Langston were ever put in a similar position, I hoped he would do the same.

The most important piece of advice I gave him involved finding ways to get through the hard times he was sure to experience in his life. Sometimes these moments only last five minutes, I told him, other times five days, or even five years, but they will always come to an end eventually. Take care of yourself and focus on getting through the day. As much as the passing of time brings us one step closer to death, it can also be a gift. The sun will always set in the evening, bringing even the worst day to an end, and it will always rise again the next morning, offering the possibility of a better one.

If you feel like you're stuck in a dark tunnel that has no end, I reminded him, take it moment by moment, and soon those moments will turn into minutes and the minutes will become hours and the hours days and the days weeks, and you'll eventually make it to the other side, where a new beginning lies. When you experience a series of hardships, you can get overwhelmed by a cumulative sense of sadness. Don't succumb to it. Even when your feet feel like open wounds and your legs have turned to jelly, keep moving forward. Endurance, perseverance, and willpower will be your greatest allies. If someone's not there to hold you up and guide you, you'll have to dig deep and force yourself to keep putting one foot in front of the other. If you do that, you'll eventually reach the end of the tunnel, no matter how long and cold and desolate it is. If you give in to the pain and take a break, it will only make the journey longer and harder. If you stop and sit down, you may never stand up again.

Keep moving forward and don't ever give up.

Epilogue

WHEN I TELL PEOPLE I STILL IDENTIFY AS BLACK, they want to know why. I explain that Black is the closest descriptive category that represents the essential essence of who I am. For me, Blackness is more than a set of racialized physical features. It involves acknowledging our common human ancestry with roots in Africa. It means fighting for freedom, equality, and justice for people of African heritage around the world. And it requires understanding the legacy and context of Blackness beyond the physical into the realms of the spiritual, psychological, historical, and emotional. I know from personal experience that our true selves consist of much more than the color of our skin or the texture of our hair. It's the culture we choose to inhabit, the lives we choose to live, and the way we're perceived and treated by others. From these experiences, our identities are formed. When my friend Nikki in college, multiple boyfriends and girlfriends, and a professor at Whitworth all made statements to the effect of "Rachel is Blacker than most Black people"—something that still happens to this day— they clearly weren't talking about my complexion or my hair. They were pointing to my commitment to the cause of racial and social justice, my work on behalf of the Black community, and the sense of self it took me multiple decades to fully embrace.

For me, being Black isn't playing dress-up. It's not something I change in and out of or do only when it's convenient. This is who I am. It's the culmination of a lifelong journey during which I've experienced as much heartbreak as I have joy. I doubt I'll ever speak to Larry, Ruthanne, or Uncle Dan ever again, although I recently reconnected with "Uncle" Vern, who confirmed what I'd suspected: that Larry and Ruthanne had intentionally discredited me in an attempt to get Josh's sexual assault charges removed. "I'm not them," he assured me.

My relationships with Ezra and Zach continue to be strained. I haven't spoken to Ezra since I unfriended him on Facebook in 2013 and Zach since March 2015, when he asked me if I could cosign a loan with him so he could buy a new truck. Despite our differences, I remain hopeful that we'll reach an understanding one day and their wounds will heal. They are still the same little babies I once bathed, fed, and rocked to sleep. Out of love, I have already forgiven them.

As hard as it was to sever ties with some members of my biological family, it's been even harder to lose members of my chosen one, so my heart was warmed when my dad reached out to me to offer his love and support after he saw me on television in April 2016. "I just watched the *Today* show," Albert texted me. "I think you did great and I love the way you answered the questions! I have always known you would do good for the human race. No one is perfect and your story will add an important part to history. I wish you the best and will do anything for you if I can. Love to the boys and you." The tears rolling down my cheeks were quickly replaced by one of the biggest smiles I'd had in a very long time.

My sons and my sister continue to be great pillars of support for me. After the public backlash against me, I had Franklin transferred to a new middle school, where he could get a fresh start. Now in high school, he's getting good grades and plays on the football team. Still hoping to pursue a career in film or television, he'd like to study acting at UCLA.

Taking full advantage of the University of Idaho's study abroad program, Izaiah is currently taking classes in South Africa after spending a semester in Spain. Majoring in international studies, sociology, and Spanish, he's been on the dean's list every semester and hopes to go to law school when he's done with his undergraduate work.

Before he'd even turned one, Langston had already racked up an impressive amount of frequent flier miles, having accompanied me on trips to New York for my second appearance on *Today*, Dallas for a festival, London for a BBC interview, and Antigua for the launch of a nonprofit for which I remain a board member at-large. Ahead of schedule for all the important baby milestones, he even tries to count to ten in French along with Franklin. He is the sunshine that brightens all our days.

Even though Esther never got her time in court, she refuses to let it hold her back. Like me, she's a survivor. She continues to live in Spokane, where she works on a hemp farm and teaches piano lessons. I still do her hair every other month, and she stops by regularly to play with her nephew.

As for myself, what can I say? It's been hard. I used to hate going to the grocery store out of fear that some uneducated white person might say something stupid about my hair. Now I hate it because I'm *that woman*, the one who people still laugh at or despise for "pretending to be Black." Ever since my outing, I've been unemployed and have been rejected for every single job I've applied for, many of which I was overqualified for. My name is such poison in the professional world that on October 7, 2016, I legally changed it, adopting a name given to me by a man from the Igbo tribe in Nigeria. He'd reached out to me the year before to say that I was a "twin soul," born with a white veneer but living as a true Nubian in order to fight for justice for the Black family and culture. I can't tell you how liberating it felt to shed my old name and the connotation with victimhood, misrepresentation, and tabloid journalism it had come to embody.

Just as vital to my rebirth has been the support I've received from total strangers. During a layover while flying home from the UN's International Day of the Girl forum in Louisville, I noticed a Black woman with a fair complexion and green eyes glancing over at me from time to time as I ate in a restaurant. When I finished eating and asked for the check, my server informed me that the woman had paid for my meal and left a note behind, telling me to keep my chin up and stay strong. A month later, the owner of a celebrity Black hair store in Dallas, Texas, told me she wanted to sponsor my "next curly look" and put a photo of me wearing her store's brand of hair on a wall next to photos of Sanaa Lathan, the cast of *Empire*, and other Black celebrities. (Unfortunately, her gesture wasn't well received by her clientele, who forced her to remove the picture from the wall as well as from her Instagram account.)

I've also received thousands of letters, emails, and messages online from people telling me how, just like me, they feel trapped somewhere in the confusing gray zone between the Black and white worlds. Some of these people are biracial. Others have said they simply don't appear or feel entirely Black or white. This marginalized group of people grows larger every day. The United States is experiencing a demographic shift that's rapidly turning the white population into a minority—U.S. Census Bureau projections predict that by 2045, the majority of U.S. citizens will be from groups that are now classified as "minorities." Every year families are becoming more culturally mixed and identities of individuals across the spectrum more nuanced.

The number of children born into interracial relationships is also rapidly increasing. According to a Pew Research Center study, 12 percent of all new marriages in the United States in 2013 were between people of different races, up from a mere .4 percent in 1960, a number that will only keep rising. Yet our society's level of acceptance of individuals with plural racial identities remains almost unchanged. Unlike most countries in the world, when it comes to the Black–white divide, the United States requires its citizens to choose one or the other. Racial categories in between those two poles aren't legally or socially recognized, forcing the children of mixed-race couples, caught in the middle, to experience an existential crisis from birth onward. These people are constantly reaching out to me, confirming that I'm not the only one who doesn't fit neatly into society's archaic racial categories. They relate to my struggle because they don't fit into a single box on a census form, but rather somewhere on the spectrum of racial identification. The gray area between Black and white is a very lonely place, and living there can be stressful and exhausting.

I credit these people for inspiring me to write this book. By sharing my experiences with identity, race, culture, religion, class, trauma, and poverty, I hope to provide comfort to those who are struggling with their identities and assure them that they're not alone, that they're not freaks, and that they don't deserve to be ridiculed or shunned by their friends, families, and communities. It's for these people, and for everyone impacted by the belief that humans should be divided into racial categories, that I refuse to be quiet about the racial injustice that pervades our culture. I will consider this book a success if it helps even a single person feel better about where they are on their own journey and makes it easier for them to gain acceptance in the world.

I also wrote this book to set the record straight. I was introduced to the world in the worst possible way, and the story that was told about me wasn't correct or complete. The public's view of my character has been based almost entirely on hearsay and lies, and all my attempts to correct them have been forced through the filter of a writer's pen or a TV host's microphone. In the process, my precise viewpoint has never been fully articulated, creating even more confusion about who I am and what my intentions are.

Having experienced the things I have, I feel like my life has become the perfect metaphor for race as a social construction. Because people observe me through the same distorted lens they use to look at the notion of race in general, they're unable to see my true essence, just like they're unable to grasp that race is a myth, a charade. Understanding how we have been categorized and why humans feel the need to do so is the first step in dismantling a system that was designed to oppress certain people. The "racial score" still needs to be settled in America. Hopefully once the scales are balanced, the next step on the path to justice will be to do away with racial categories altogether, because without race, racism loses its power.

Education is another essential component to solving our country's racial problem. The day after Martin Luther King Jr. was assassinated, Jane Elliot, a third-grade teacher from Riceville, Illinois, conducted an exercise with her class in which she designated the brown-eyed students as being superior to the blue-eyed ones. She gave those with brown eyes more food at lunch and more time on the playground, invited them to sit in the front of the classroom, and encouraged them to play only with each other. Meanwhile, she forced the blue-eyed students to sit in the rear of the classroom, didn't allow them to drink from the same water fountain used by their brown-eyed peers, and reprimanded them for making even the smallest mistakes. By the end of the day, the brown-eyed children were acting as if they truly were superior to their blue-eyed classmates, many of whom had grown noticeably timid and forlorn. The following Monday, Elliott repeated the exercise, but flipped the script, telling the blue-eyed children they were now the superior group. Afterward, some of the children hugged, while others cried. Elliot's point had been made. In most school districts in the country, it's mandatory that students be taught state history, but classes about race, how and why the concept was created, and what sort of ramifications that's had are rarely offered. Imagine what could be achieved if they were. If all students had to take such classes, the racial injustice that exists in our society could be eradicated within a generation or two.

Race, culture, and gender classes exist in the curricula of some universities but are rarely required for most degrees. These courses introduce students to the root of race and gender constructs and the inequities perpetrated by sexism and racism around the globe. But as our world constantly shifts, new paradigms and vocabulary are needed. As we grow and evolve, we should keep in mind that a single person's identity, or even the identity of a group of people, isn't the root problem when it comes to race. How people identify themselves along the racial spectrum and how they are treated based on that identification are only symptomatic of the real problem: racism.

When it came to sexism, the way people were forced to adopt either a masculine or feminine identity, with no tolerance for those who fell in between those two poles, was one of the root problems. Allowing fluidity in gender identity—including transgender as a legitimate identity category—did not make sexism worse; instead, it improved understanding both between people and within individuals. Likewise, if people are permitted to adopt "transracial," biracial, triracial, and even nonracial identities, racism will be weakened, not reinforced. If we are to truly achieve equal access, opportunity, and equity for each individual, regardless of gender, class, sexual orientation, religion, language, nationality, disability, or cultural identity, we must accept *all* identities within the human spectrum.

The only significant regret I have in life is that it took me almost thirty years to give myself permission to name and own the real me. That society has tried to strip me of my identity saddens me, and I look forward to the day when I no longer have to emphasize or suppress different parts of myself to move safely and confidently through the world, a day when I can live as a whole person. Until then, I'm embracing the opportunity to demystify the concept of race and inspire more activism in social justice. After more than three centuries of awkwardness, oppression, and scorn, we're now living in an age when we finally have the opportunity to solve the many problems emanating from racism and the racial divide. If my story can advance that dialogue and provide some measure of comfort to those who find themselves drifting somewhere between Black and white, or with no category at all, I'll consider the struggle I've endured simply for living as my true self to be entirely worth it.

Acknowledgments

THIS BOOK HAS NOT BEEN EASY TO WRITE, nor has the task come at the best time for me, so my heart is filled with immense gratitude for the extraordinary team of people who have contributed their time and energy to support the writing process.

Special appreciation goes to Ambassador Attallah Shabazz for grounding me and helping me remember who I was amid so much external chaos. Her encouragement to tell my story with confidence and conviction always remained at the forefront of my mind.

I'm equally grateful to Jackie, Regina, Siobhan, Gavin, Charles, Anna, Morgan, Bob, Shari, and Bianca, whose friendships have uplifted me and given me hope on days when I wasn't sure if I had anything more to offer the world. Thank you for believing in me and pushing me when I needed it most.

Thanks also to Albert Wilkerson for embracing me and my sons as part of his family, for contributing such a thoughtful foreword to this book, and for sharing so many valuable life lessons and golden nuggets of wisdom over the years. I will never forget his many acts of kindness, which often spring from his motto: "It's nice to be nice."

Without my agent, Michael Wright, this project might never have come to be. After it seemed like it was never going to get off the ground, he kept the vision for it alive for more than a year with his unwavering optimism, and when it came time to finally begin, he did an excellent job assembling a first-rate team.

One of the principal members of that team was Storms Reback, who helped mold the giant lump of clay we started with into a sculpture worthy of a museum. Despite the ambitious schedule we were given, he managed to keep pace with me without losing his mind in the process. I couldn't have met those deadlines or gotten the manuscript into such great shape without him.

I'm also indebted to everyone at BenBella Books who assisted on this project. Publisher Glenn Yeffeth, deputy publisher Adrienne Lang, senior publishing associate Alicia Kania, senior production editor Jessika Rieck, and art director Sarah Dombrowsky were extremely helpful and encouraging, but I'm particularly grateful to editor-in-chief Leah Wilson, who exhibited a rare form of patience and kindness throughout the process. Her comments and suggestions were always spot-on and invaluable.

I'd also like to thank Tatsha Robertson for contributing her own special insight to the book. Her style of direct reflection, whether as encouragement or criticism, ultimately made the book much better.

Finally, I simply couldn't have written this book without the support of my sons, Franklin, Izaiah, and Langston, and my sister Esther. They were always there to give me hugs, love, and support when I needed it most. They lifted me up whenever I struggled to get words on the page and helped me remember some aspects of my life I had tried hard to forget. I can't thank them enough for their bravery and encouragement. They are gifts to me, to each other, and to the world. The four of their lives are intertwined, but each of them has their own unique path as well. I promise to always be there for them and to support and assist them whenever they're ready to write their own stories.

About the Authors

RACHEL DOLEŽAL holds an MFA from Howard University. Her scholarly research focus is the intersection of race, gender, and class in the contemporary Black diaspora, with a specific emphasis on Black women in visual culture. She is a licensed intercultural competence and diversity trainer, dedicated to racial and social justice activism. She has worked as an instructor at North Idaho College and Eastern Washington University, where she also served as advisor for the schools' Black Student Unions, and has guest lectured at Spokane Community College, the University of Idaho, Gonzaga University, and Washington State University.

Doležal began her activism in Mississippi, where she advocated for equal rights and partnered with community developers, tutoring grade-school children in Black history and art and pioneering African American history courses at a predominantly white university. She is the former director of education at the Human Rights Education Institute in Idaho and has served as a consultant for human rights education and inclusivity in regional public schools. She recently led the Office of Police Ombudsman Commission to promote police accountability and justice in law enforcement in Spokane, Washington, and was the president of the Spokane chapter of the NAACP. She is the devoted mother of three sons.

STORMS REBACK is the author of four books, including *The Contractor: How I Landed in a Pakistani Prison and Ignited a Diplomatic Crisis.* He lives in Austin, Texas.